WARREN, FESS, REEVE 18
W9-CFA-233

ACCOUNTING

STUDY GUIDE, VOLUME 1, CHAPTERS 1 - 13

Prepared by

CARL S. WARREN
Professor of Accounting
University of Georgia, Athens

JAMES A. HEINTZ
Professor of Accounting
University of Connecticut, Storrs

SOUTH-WESTERN College Publishing

An International Thomson Publishing Company

AB70SD3

Copyright © 1996
by South-Western Publishing Co.
Cincinnati, Ohio

I(T)P
International Thomson Publishing
South-Western College Publishing is an ITP Company.
The ITP trademark is used under license.

ALL RIGHTS RESERVED

The text of this publication, or any part therof, may not be reproduced or transmitted in any form or by any means, electronic or mechanical, including photocopying, recording, storage in an information retrieval system, or otherwise, without prior written permission of the publisher.

Sponsoring Editor: David L. Shaut
Senior Developmental Editor: Ken Martin
Production Editor: Mark Sears
Marketing Manager: Sharon Oblinger
Cover Design: Craig LaGesse Ramsdell
Cover Illustration © 1995 Glenn Mitsui
Cover illustration acknowledgments:
 Microsoft logo is reprinted with permission of Microsoft Corporation.
 L.L. Bean catalog cover reprinted with permission of L.L. Bean, Inc. 1-800-809-7057.
 Dodge Caravan reproduced courtesy of Chrysler Corporation.
 McDonald's golden arches reproduced with permission of McDonald's Corporation.
 Southwest aircraft reproduced courtesy of Southwest Airlines Co.
 Sony portable CD player reproduced courtesy of Sony Electronics, Inc.
 HERSHEY'S® is a registered trademark and used with permission by Hershey Foods Corporation.
 Coca-Cola boxes are reproduced courtesy of Coca-Cola. "Coca Cola" is a trademark of The Coca-Cola Company
 Wal-Mart storefront is reproduced courtesy of Wal-Mart Stores, Inc.

ISBN: 0-538-83936-8

1 2 3 4 5 6 7 DH 1 0 9 8 7 6 5

Printed in the United States of America

Contents

1   Introduction to Accounting Concepts and Practice

The following hints may be helpful to you in preparing for a quiz or a test over the material covered in Chapter 1.

1. Terminology is important in this chapter. Review the Key Terms. Expect multiple-choice or true-false questions to include the terms introduced on pages 9 -15 of the text. For example, you should recognize accounting as an information system (often called the language of business) and distinguish between CPA and CMA. Pay special attention to the three accounting concepts and principles—business entity concept, cost principle, and business transactions—discussed on pages 14 -15.

2. Know the accounting equation: Assets = Liabilities + Owner's Equity. Be able to compute one amount when given the other two. For example, if assets equal $100,000 and liabilities equal $60,000, owner's equity must equal $40,000. Be able to determine the effect of change in the basic elements on one another. For example, if assets increase by $10,000 and liabilities decrease by $5,000, owner's equity must increase by $15,000.

3. Be able to record business transactions within the framework of the accounting equation. Use the illustration on pages 16 -19 as a basis for review and study. Pay particular attention to items that are increased and decreased by transactions a through h. Note the introduction of new terms such as account payable, account receivable, revenue, and expense. These new terms are highlighted in color in the text.

4. Be able to describe each of the financial statements listed on page 20. You may be required to prepare a short income statement, statement of owner's equity, and balance sheet. You will probably not be required to prepare a statement of cash flows.

5. Review the summary data for Computer King on page 19. Trace the numbers into the statements shown in Exhibit 4 on page 21. Know the format of each statement such as the number of columns and placement of dollar signs. Some of the numbers in Exhibit 4 appear on more than one statement. Sometimes a quiz or a test question will provide partially completed statements, and you will be required to complete the statements. Recognizing amounts that appear on more than one statement will aid you in answering this type of question.

CHAPTER OUTLINE

I. Accounting as an Information System.

A. Accounting is an information system that provides reports to various individuals or groups about economic activities of an organization or other entity.

B. You may think of accounting as the "language of business" because it is the means by which most business information is communicated.

C. The process of using accounting to provide information to users involves (1) identifying user groups and their information needs, (2) recording economic data and activities by the accounting system, and (3) preparing reports to summarize this information for users.

D. Because individuals make decisions based upon the data in accounting reports, accounting has a major impact upon our economic and social system.

II. Profession of Accounting.

A. The demand for accounting services has increased with the increase in the number, size, and complexity of businesses. In addition, new laws and regulations have also created a demand for accounting.

B. Accountants are engaged in either (1) private accounting or (2) public accounting.

1. Accountants employed by a business firm or not-for-profit organization are said to be engaged in private accounting.

a. Private accountants are frequently called management accountants. If they are employed by a manufacturing concern, they may be called industrial or cost accountants. The chief accountant in a business may be called the controller.

b. The certificate in management accounting (CMA) and the certificate in internal auditing (CIA) recognize the professional competency of private accountants.

2. Accountants who render accounting services on a fee basis are said to be engaged in public accounting.

a. In public accounting, an accountant may practice as an individual or as a member of a public accounting firm.

b. Public accountants who meet state laws may become certified public accountants (CPAs).

C. Accountants in both private and public practice have developed ethical standards to guide them.

D. The specialized fields of accounting include financial accounting, managerial accounting, cost accounting, environmental accounting, tax accounting, systems, international accounting, not-for-profit accounting, and social accounting.

III. Generally Accepted Accounting Principles.

A. Generally accepted accounting principles (GAAP) are principles and concepts that are used by accountants in preparing financial reports.

B. Accounting principles and concepts develop from research, accepted accounting practices, and pronouncements of authoritative bodies.

C. The Financial Accounting Standards Board (FASB) has the primary responsibility for developing accounting principles.

D. The business entity concept is based on identifying the individual economic units for which economic data are needed.

    1. The business entity could be an individual, a not-for-profit organization such as a church, or a profit enterprise such as a real estate agency.

    2. Businesses are customarily organized as sole proprietorships, partnerships, or corporations.

E. The cost principle determines the amount entered into the accounting records for purchases of properties and services. The exchange price, or cost, is the amount used in the accounting records for recording purchases of properties or services.

IV. Business Transactions.

A. Not all economic events affecting a business entity are recorded in an accounting system. Only business transactions are recorded in the accounting records.

B. A business transaction is an economic event or condition that directly changes the entity's financial position or directly affects its results of operations.

V. Assets, Liabilities, and Owner's Equity.

A. The properties owned by a business are called assets.

B. The rights or claims to the properties are normally divided into two principal types: (1) the rights of creditors and (2) the rights of owners.

C. The rights of creditors represent debts of the business and are called liabilities.

D. The rights of the owners are called owner's equity.

E. The accounting equation may be expressed as: assets = liabilities + owner's equity.

F. The claim of the owners is sometimes given greater emphasis in the accounting equation by transposing liabilities to the other side of the equation, yielding: assets - liabilities = owner's equity.

VI. Transactions and the Accounting Equation.

A. All business transactions can be expressed in terms of changes in the three elements (assets, liabilities, and owner's equity) of the accounting equation.

B. A purchase on account is a type of transaction that creates a liability, account payable, in which the buyer agrees to pay the seller in the near future.

C. Items such as supplies that will be used in the business in the future are called prepaid expenses, which are assets.

D. The amount charged to customers for goods or services sold to them is called revenue.

E. A sale on account allows the customer to pay later and the selling firm acquires an account receivable.

F. The amount of assets or services used in the process of earning revenue is called expense.

G. In recording the effect of transactions on the accounting equation, the following observations should be noted:

  1. The effect of every transaction is an increase or a decrease in one or more of the accounting equation elements.

  2. The two sides of the accounting equation are always equal.

  3. The owner's equity is increased by amounts invested by the owner and is decreased by withdrawals by the owner. In addition, the owner's equity is increased by revenues and is decreased by expenses.

VII. Financial Statements.

A. The income statement is the summary of the revenue and expenses for a specific period of time.

  1. The excess of revenue over expenses incurred in earning the revenue is called net income or net profit.

  2. If the expenses of the business exceed the revenue, the excess is a net loss.

  3. In determining net income, the expenses incurred in generating revenues must be properly matched against the revenues generated.

B. The statement of owner's equity summarizes the changes in owner's equity that have occurred during a specific period of time.

  1. Three types of transactions may affect owner's equity during the period: (1) investments by the owner, (2) revenues and expenses that result in a net income or a net loss for the period, and (3) withdrawals by the owner.

  2. The statement of owner's equity serves as a connecting link between the balance sheet and the income statement.

C. The balance sheet lists the assets, liabilities, and owner's equity of a business as of a specific date.

  1. The form of balance sheet that resembles the accounting equation, with assets on the left side and the liabilities and owner's equity sections on the right side, is called the report form.

2. The assets section of the balance sheet normally presents assets in the order in which they will be converted into cash or used in operations. The more permanent assets such as land and buildings are presented last.

D. The statement of cash flows is the summary of the cash receipts and cash payments for a specific period of time.

1. The statement of cash flows consists of three sections: (1) operating activities, (2) investing activities, and (3) financing activities.

2. The cash flow from operating activities section reports a summary of cash receipts and cash payments from operations.

    a. The net cash flow from operating activities normally differs from the amount of net income for the period.

    b. The net cash flow from operating activities and net income normally differ because revenues and expenses may not be recorded at the same time that cash is received from customers and cash is paid to creditors.

3. The cash flow from investing activities section reports the cash transactions for the acquisition and sale of relatively long-term or permanent-type assets.

4. The cash flow from financing activities section reports the cash transactions related to cash investments by the owner, borrowings, and cash withdrawals by the owner.

ILLUSTRATIVE PROBLEM

On October 1 of the current year, the assets and liabilities of E. F. Nelson, Attorney-at-Law, are as follows: Cash, $1,000; Accounts Receivable, $2,200; Supplies, $850; Land, $11,450; Accounts Payable, $2,030. E. F. Nelson, Attorney-at-Law, is a sole proprietorship owned and operated by E. F. Nelson. Currently, office space and office equipment are being rented, pending the construction of an office complex on land purchased last year. Business transactions during October are summarized as follows:

a. Received cash from clients for services, $4,928.

b. Paid creditors on account, $1,755.

c. Received cash from E. F. Nelson as an additional investment, $3,700.

d. Paid office rent for the month, $1,200.

e. Charged clients for legal services on account, $1,025.

f. Purchased office supplies on account, $245.

g. Received cash from clients on account, $2,000.

h. Received invoice for paralegal services from Legal Aid Inc. for October (to be paid on November 10), $1,635.

i. Paid the following: wages expense, $850; answering service expense, $250; utilities expense, $325; miscellaneous expense, $75.

j. Determined that the cost of office supplies used during the month was $115.

Instructions

1. Determine the amount of owner's equity (E. F. Nelson's capital) as of October 1 of the current year.

2. State the assets, liabilities, and owner's equity as of October 1 in equation form similar to that shown in this chapter. In tabular form below the equation, indicate the increases and decreases resulting from each transaction and the new balances after each transaction. Explain the nature of each increase and decrease in owner's equity by an appropriate notation at the right of the amount.

3. Prepare (a) an income statement for October, (b) a statement of owner's equity for October, and (c) a balance sheet as of October 31.

Solution

1.

Assets - Liabilities	=	Owner's Equity (E. F. Nelson, capital)
$15,500 - $2,030	=	Owner's Equity (E. F. Nelson, capital)
$13,470	=	Owner's Equity (E. F. Nelson, capital)

2.

	Cash	+	Accounts Receivable	+	Supplies	+	Land	=	Accounts Payable	+	E. F. Nelson, Capital	
Bal.	1,000		2,200		850		11,450		2,030		13,470	
a.	+4,928										+4,928	Fees earned
Bal.	5,928		2,200		850		11,450		2,030		18,398	
b.	-1,755								-1,755			
Bal.	4,173		2,200		850		11,450		275		18,398	
c.	+3,700										+3,700	Investment
Bal.	7,873		2,200		850		11,450		275		22,098	
d.	-1,200										-1,200	Rent expense
Bal.	6,673		2,200		850		11,450		275		20,898	
e.			+1,025								+1,025	Fees earned
Bal.	6,673		3,225		850		11,450		275		21,923	
f.					+245				+245			
Bal.	6,673		3,225		1,095		11,450		520		21,923	
g.	+2,000		-2,000									
Bal.	8,673		1,225		1,095		11,450		520		21,923	
h.									+1,635		-1,635	Paralegal exp.
Bal.	8,673		1,225		1,095		11,450		2,155		20,288	
i.	-1,500										- 850	Wages exp.
											- 250	Ans. svc. exp.
											- 325	Utilities exp.
											- 75	Misc. exp.
Bal.	7,173		1,225		1,095		11,450		2,155		18,788	
j.					-115						-115	Supplies exp.
Bal.	7,173		1,225		980		11,450		2,155		18,673	

Assets = *Liabilities* + *Owner's Equity*

3. a.

E. F. Nelson, Attorney-at-Law
Income Statement
For Month Ended October 31, 19--

Fees earned		5 9 5 3 00
Operating expenses:		
Paralegal expense	1 6 3 5 00	
Rent expense	1 2 0 0 00	
Wages expense	8 5 0 00	
Utilities expense	3 2 5 00	
Answering service expense	2 5 0 00	
Supplies expense	1 1 5 00	
Miscellaneous expense	7 5 00	
Total operating expenses		4 4 5 0 00
Net income		1 5 0 3 00

b.

E. F. Nelson, Attorney-at-Law
Statement of Owner's Equity
For Month Ended October 31, 19--

E. F. Nelson, capital, October 1, 19--		1 3 4 7 0 00
Additional investment by owner	3 7 0 0 00	
Net income for the month	1 5 0 3 00	
Increase in owner's equity		5 2 0 3 00
E. F. Nelson, capital, October 31, 19--		1 8 6 7 3 00

c.

E. F. Nelson, Attorney-at-Law
Balance Sheet
October 31, 19--

Assets		Liabilities	
Cash	7 1 7 3 00	Accounts payable	2 1 5 5 00
Accounts receivable	1 2 2 5 00	Owner's Equity	
Supplies	9 8 0 00	E. F. Nelson, capital	1 8 6 7 3 00
Land	1 1 4 5 0 00	Total liabilities	
Total assets	2 0 8 2 8 00	and owner's equity	2 0 8 2 8 00

MATCHING

Instructions: A list of terms and related statements appear below. From the list of terms, select the one that relates to each statement. Print its identifying letter in the space provided.

A. Account payable
B. Account receivable
C. Accounting equation
D. Assets
E. Balance sheet
F. Corporation
G. Cost principle
H. Expense

I. Income statement
J. Liabilities
K. Net income
L. Partnership
M. Prepaid expenses
N. Revenue
O. Statement of cash flows
P. Statement of owner's equity

_____ 1. The most objective measurement used in recording the purchase of properties and services is in accordance with the (?).

_____ 2. The properties owned by a business.

_____ 3. A separate legal entity in which ownership is divided into shares of stock.

_____ 4. The rights of creditors represent debts of the business and are called (?).

_____ 5. A summary of the cash receipts and cash payments of a business entity for a specific period of time.

_____ 6. Assets = Liabilities + Owner's Equity

_____ 7. The liability created by a purchase on account.

_____ 8. Consumable goods purchased, such as supplies, are considered to be assets, or (?).

_____ 9. The amount charged to customers for goods or services sold to them.

_____ 10. When sales are made on account, allowing the customer to pay later, the business acquires a(n) (?).

_____ 11. The amount of assets consumed or services used in the process of earning revenue.

_____ 12. A list of the assets, liabilities, and owner's equity of a business entity as of a specific date, usually at the close of the last day of a month or a year.

_____ 13. A summary of the revenues and expenses of a business entity for a specific period of time, such as a month or a year.

_____ 14. A summary of the changes in the owner's equity of a business entity that have occurred during a specific period of time, such as a month or a year.

_____ 15. The excess of the revenue over the expenses incurred in earning the revenue is called (?).

TRUE / FALSE

Instructions: Indicate whether each of the following statements is true or false by placing a check mark in the appropriate column.

		True	False
1.	Accounting is often characterized as the "language of business."	___	___
2.	Accountants who render accounting services on a fee basis and staff accountants employed by them, are said to be engaged in private accounting.	___	___
3.	Standards of conduct which have been established to guide CPAs in the conduct of their practices are called codes of professional responsibility.	___	___
4.	The concept that expenses incurred in generating revenue should be matched against the revenue in determining net income or net loss is called the cost concept.	___	___
5.	The financing activities section of the statement of cash flows includes cash transactions that enter into the determination of net income.	___	___
6.	The debts of a business are called its accounts receivable.	___	___
7.	A partnership is owned by not less than four individuals. .	___	___
8.	A business transaction is the occurrence of an event or of a condition that must be recorded.	___	___
9.	A summary of the changes in the owner's equity of a business entity that have occurred during a specific period of time, such as a month or a year, is called a statement of cash flows.	___	___
10.	A claim against a customer for sales made on credit is an account payable.	___	___

MULTIPLE CHOICE

Instructions: Circle the best answer for each of the following questions.

1. Accountants employed by a particular business firm or not-for-profit organization, perhaps as chief accountant, controller, or financial vice-president, are said to be engaged in:
   a. general accounting
   b. public accounting
   c. independent accounting
   d. private accounting

2. Authoritative accounting pronouncements on accounting principles are issued by the:
   a. Accounting Principles Commission
   b. Accounting Procedures Committee
   c. Financial Accounting Standards Board
   d. General Accounting Principles Board

3. The records of properties and services purchased by a business are maintained in accordance with the:
   a. business entity concept
   b. cost principle
   c. matching principle
   d. proprietorship principle

4. Another way of writing the accounting equation is:
   a. Assets + Liabilities = Owner's Equity
   b. Owner's Equity + Assets = Liabilities
   c. Assets = Owner's Equity - Liabilities
   d. Assets - Liabilities = Owner's Equity

5. The form of balance sheet that resembles the accounting equation is called the:
   a. report form
   b. balancing form
   c. account form
   d. systematic form

EXERCISE 1-1

Instructions: Some typical transactions of Clem's Laundry Service are presented below. For each transaction, indicate the increase (+), the decrease (-), or no change (o) in the assets (A), liabilities (L), and owner's equity (OE) by placing the appropriate sign(s) in the appropriate column(s). More than one sign may have to be placed in the A, L, or OE column for a given transaction.

	A	L	OE
1. Received cash from owner as an additional investment	___	___	___
2. Purchased supplies on account	___	___	___
3. Charged customers for services sold on account . . .	___	___	___
4. Received cash from cash customers	___	___	___
5. Paid cash for rent on building	___	___	___
6. Collected an account receivable in full	___	___	___
7. Paid cash for supplies	___	___	___
8. Returned supplies purchased on account and not yet paid for	___	___	___
9. Paid cash to creditors on account	___	___	___
10. Paid cash to owner for personal use	___	___	___

PROBLEM 1-1

Instructions: The assets, liabilities, and owner's equity of Ed Casey, who operates a small repair shop, are expressed in equation form below. Following the equation are ten transactions completed by Casey. On each of the numbered lines, show by addition or subtraction the effect of each of the transactions on the equation. For each transaction, identify the changes in owner's equity by placing the letter R (revenue), E (expense), D (drawing), or I (investment) at the right of each increase or decrease in owner's equity. On the lines labeled "Bal.," show the new equation resulting from the transaction.

	Assets	=	Liabilities	=	Owner's Equity
	Cash + Supplies + Land	=	Accounts Payable	=	Ed Casey, Capital

1. Casey started a repair shop and deposited $40,000 cash in the bank for use by the business. . . . . (1) _____

2. Casey purchased $2,000 of supplies on account. . . . (2) _____
Bal. _____

3. Casey purchased land for a future building site for $14,000 cash. . . . . (3) _____
Bal. _____

4. Casey paid creditors $1,800 on account. . . . . (4) _____
Bal. _____

5. Casey withdrew $2,000 for personal use. . . . . (5) _____
Bal. _____

6. Casey paid $2,800 for building and equipment rent for the month. . . . . (6) _____
Bal. _____

7. During the month, another $900 of expenses were incurred on account by the business. . . . . (7) _____
Bal. _____

8. During the month, Casey deposited another $10,000 of personal funds in the business bank account. . . (8) _____
Bal. _____

9. Casey received $500 for a cash service call. . . . . . (9) _____
Bal. _____

10. Casey used $600 worth of supplies. . . . . (10) _____
Bal. _____

PROBLEM 1-2

The amounts of the assets and liabilities of Tom's Painting Service at December 31 of the current year, and the revenues and expenses for the year are as follows:

Cash	$10,050
Accounts receivable	8,950
Supplies	4,000
Accounts payable	4,450
Sales	27,450
Supplies expense	5,450
Advertising expense	4,825
Truck rental expense	1,525
Utilities expense	700
Miscellaneous expense	1,400

The capital of Tom Wallace, owner, was $4,000 at the beginning of the current year. During the year, Wallace withdrew $1,000, and made an additional investment of $2,000.

Instructions: Using the forms provided, prepare the following:

(1) An income statement for the year ended December 31, 19--.

(2) A statement of owner's equity for the year ended December 31, 19--.

(3) A balance sheet as of December 31, 19--.

(1)

Tom's Painting Service

Income Statement

For Year Ended December 31, 19--

(2)

Tom's Painting Service

Statement of Owner's Equity

For Year Ended December 31, 19--

(3)

Tom's Painting Service

Balance Sheet

December 31, 19--

2

Analyzing Transactions

QUIZ AND TEST HINTS

The following hints may be helpful to you in preparing for a quiz or a test over the material covered in Chapter 2.

1. Terminology is important in this chapter. Review the Key Terms. Pay special attention to major account classifications discussed on page 43 of the text.

2. Memorize the "Rules of Debit and Credit" and the "Normal Balances of Accounts." All instructors will ask questions to test your knowledge of these items.

3. Be able to prepare general journal entries for the types of transactions presented in this chapter. Review the illustration beginning on page 46, and be sure you understand each entry. Be especially careful not to confuse debits and credits. Remember that a credit is indented slightly to the right when preparing a general journal entry. A good review is to rework the Illustrative Problem in the Chapter Review.

4. You should be familiar with the process of posting accounts for working assigned problems. However, you will probably not be required to post accounts on an examination.

5. You may be required to prepare a trial balance from a list of accounts with normal balances.

6. You might expect one or two questions on how to correct errors. These types of questions may require you to prepare a correcting journal entry. Review the section of the chapter and illustration containing this information.

CHAPTER OUTLINE

I. **Usefulness of an Account.**

   A. The record of the increases and decreases in individual financial statement items is called an account.

   B. A group of accounts for a business entity is a ledger.

   C. A list of accounts in the ledger is called a chart of accounts. A chart of accounts normally lists the accounts in the order in which they appear in the financial statements.

   D. Assets are physical items (tangible) or rights (intangible) that have value and that are owned by the business entity.

   E. Liabilities are debts owed to outsiders (creditors) and are often identified by account titles that include the word "payable." Revenue received in advance is also classified as a liability and is often called unearned revenue.

F. Owner's equity is the owner's right to assets of the business.

   1. Owner's equity on the balance sheet is represented by the owner's capital account.

   2. A drawing account represents the amount of withdrawals made by the owner.

G. Revenues are increases in the owner's equity as a result of the rendering of services or the selling of products to customers.

H. Assets used up or services consumed in the process of generating revenues are expenses.

II. Characteristics of an Account.

A. In simplest form an account has three parts.

   1. A title, which is the name of the item recorded in the account.

   2. A space for recording increases in the amount of the item.

   3. A space for recording decreases in the amount of the item.

B. The simplest form of the account is known as the T account.

C. The left side of an account is called the debit side.

D. The right side of an account is called the credit side.

E. Amounts entered on the left side of the account are called debits to the account.

F. Amounts entered on the right side of the account are called credits to the account.

G. Subtraction of the smaller of the total debits or credits from the larger amount yields the balance of the account.

III. Analyzing and Summarizing Transactions in Accounts.

A. Recording transactions in balance sheet accounts (asset, liability, and owner's equity accounts) includes the following considerations:

   1. Every business transaction affects a minimum of two accounts.

   2. Transaction data are initially entered in a record called a journal.

   3. The process of recording a transaction in the journal is called journalizing and the form of presentation is called a journal entry.

   4. The rules of debit and credit for balance sheet accounts may be stated as follows:

   Debit may signify:

   Increase in asset accounts

   Decrease in liability accounts

   Decrease in owner's equity accounts

Credit may signify:

 Decrease in asset accounts

 Increase in liability accounts

 Increase in owner's equity accounts

5. The rules of debit and credit for balance sheet accounts may also be stated in relationship to the accounting equation as follows:

Asset Accounts

Debit for increases	Credit for decreases

Liability Accounts

Debit for decreases	Credit for increases

Owner's Equity Accounts

Debit for decreases	Credit for inreases

B. Transactions in income statement accounts (revenue and expense accounts) are analyzed and recorded depending upon how each transaction affects owner's equity.

1. Increases in revenue accounts increase owner's equity and thus, are recorded as credits. In contrast, decreases in revenue accounts are recorded as debits.

2. Increases in expense accounts decrease owner's equity and thus, are recorded as debits. In contrast, decreases in expense accounts are recorded as credits.

3. The equality of debits and credits for each transaction is inherent in the accounting equation, and the system is known as double-entry accounting.

4. The rules of debit and credit for income statement accounts are summarized below:

Debit for decreases in owner's equity

Expense Accounts

Debit for increases	Credit for decreases

Credit for increases in owner's equity

Revenue Accounts

Debit for decreases	Credit for increases

C. Withdrawals by an owner are recorded as debits to a drawing account.

D. Normal balances of accounts.

    1. The sum of the increases in an account is usually equal to or greater than the decreases in an account; therefore, an account is said to have a normal balance.

    2. The rules of debit and credit and the normal balances of balance sheet and income statement accounts are summarized as follows:

	Increase (Normal Balance)	Decrease
Balance sheet accounts:		
Asset	Debit	Credit
Liability	Credit	Debit
Owner's equity:		
Capital	Credit	Debit
Drawing	Debit	Credit
Income statement accounts:		
Revenue	Credit	Debit
Expense	Debit	Credit

IV. Illustration of Analyzing and Summarizing Transactions.

A. The process of transferring the debits and credits from the journal entries to the accounts is called posting.

B. The flow of a transaction from its authorization to its posting in the accounts is shown in the diagram below:

Business TRANSACTION authorized	Business TRANSACTION occurs	Business DOCUMENT prepared	Entry recorded in JOURNAL	Entry posted to LEDGER

C. The analysis of transactions using the double-entry accounting system can be summarized as follows:

    1. Determine whether an asset, a liability, owner's equity, revenue, or expense is affected.

    2. Determine whether the affected asset, liability, owner's equity, revenue, or expense increases or decreases.

    3. Determine whether the effect of the transaction should be recorded as a debit or as a credit in an asset, liability, owner's equity, revenue, or expense account.

D. Transactions may be recorded using an all-purpose (two-column) journal.

E. The debits and credits for each journal entry are posted to the accounts in the order that they occur in the journal. In posting to the standard account, the following procedures are used:

1. The date is entered in the account.
2. The amount of the entry is entered in the account.
3. The journal page number is inserted in the Posting Reference column of the account.
4. The account number is inserted in the Posting Reference column of the journal.

F. The journalizing and posting process for a month's transactions is illustrated on pages 51-61 of the text. To reduce repetition, some of the transactions are stated in summary form.

V. Trial Balance.

A. The equality of debits and credits in the ledger should be verified at the end of each accounting period through the preparation of a trial balance.

B. The trial balance does not provide complete proof of the accuracy of the ledger. It indicates only that the debits and credits are equal.

VI. Discovery and Correction of Errors.

A. If the two totals of a trial balance are not equal, it is probably due to one or more of the following types of errors:

1. Error in preparing the trial balance, such as:
   a. One of the columns of the trial balance was incorrectly added.
   b. The amount of an account balance was incorrectly recorded on the trial balance.
   c. A debit balance was recorded on the trial balance as a credit, or vice versa, or a balance was omitted entirely.
2. Error in determining the account balances, such as:
   a. A balance was incorrectly computed.
   b. A balance was entered in the wrong balance column.
3. Error in recording a transaction in the ledger, such as:
   a. An erroneous amount was posted to the account.
   b. A debit entry was posted as a credit, or vice versa.
   c. A debit or a credit posting was omitted.

B. Among the types of errors that will not cause an inequality in the trial balance totals are the following:

1. Failure to record a transaction or to post a transaction.
2. Recording the same erroneous amount for both the debit and the credit parts of a transaction.
3. Recording the same transaction more than once.
4. Posting a part of a transaction correctly as a debit or credit but to the wrong account.

C. Two common types of errors are known as transpositions (an erroneous arrangement of digits) and slides (the movement of an entire number erroneously one or more spaces to the right or left).

D. The discovery of an error usually involves the retracing of the various steps in the accounting process.

E. Occasional errors in journalizing and posting transactions are unavoidable. Procedures used to correct errors in the journal and ledger vary according to the nature of the error and the phase of the accounting cycle in which it is discovered.

F. The procedures for correction of errors are summarized in the following table:

Error	Correction Procedure
Journal entry incorrect, but not posted.	Draw line through the error and insert correct title or amount.
Journal entry correct, but posted incorrectly.	Draw line through the error and post correctly.
Journal entry incorrect and posted.	Journalize and post a correcting entry.

ILLUSTRATIVE PROBLEM

Judy K. Schmidt, M.D., has been practicing as a pediatrician for three years. During June, she completed the following transactions in her practice of pediatrics:

June 1. Paid office rent for June, $600.

2. Purchased equipment on account, $2,100.

5. Received cash on account from patients, $4,150.

8. Purchased X-ray film and other supplies on account, $145.

9. One of the items of equipment purchased on June 2 was defective. It was returned with the permission of the supplier, who agreed to reduce the account for the amount charged for the item, $125.

12. Paid cash to creditors on account, $1,250.

16. Sold X-ray film to another doctor at cost, receiving cash, $63. (Record the credit in the supplies account.)

17. Paid cash for renewal of a 2-year property insurance policy, $370.

20. Discovered that the balances of the cash account and of the accounts payable account as of June 1 were overstated by $50. A payment of that amount to a creditor in May had not been recorded. Journalize the $50 payment as of June 20.

23. Paid cash for laboratory analyses, $245.

27. Paid cash from business bank account for personal and family expenses, $1,250.

30. Recorded the cash received in payment of services (on a cash basis) to patients during June, $1,720.

30. Paid salaries of receptionist and nurses, $1,725.

30. Paid gas and electricity expense, $157.

30. Paid water expense, $29.

30. Recorded fees charged to patients on account for services performed in June, $4,145.

30. Paid telephone expense, $74.

30. Paid miscellaneous expenses, $132.

Schmidt's account titles, numbers, and balances as of June 1 (all normal balances) are listed as follows: Cash, 11, $3,123; Accounts Receivable, 12, $6,725; Supplies, 13, $290; Prepaid Insurance, 14, $365; Equipment, 18, $19,745; Accounts Payable, 22, $765; Judy K. Schmidt, Capital, 31, $29,483; Judy K. Schmidt, Drawing, 32; Professional Fees, 41; Salary Expense, 51; Rent Expense, 53; Laboratory Expense, 55; Utilities Expense, 56; Miscellaneous Expense, 59.

Instructions

1. Open a ledger of standard four-column accounts for Dr. Schmidt as of June 1 of the current year. Enter the balances in the appropriate balance columns and place a check mark (√) in the posting reference column. (It is ad-

visable to verify the equality of the debit and credit balances in the ledger before proceeding with the next instruction.)

2. Journalize each transaction in a two-column journal.

3. Post the journal to the ledger, extending the month-end balances to the appropriate balance columns after each posting.

4. Prepare a trial balance as of June 30.

Solution

2. and 3.

JOURNAL

PAGE **27**

	DATE		DESCRIPTION	POST. REF.	DEBIT	CREDIT	
1	19-- June	1	Rent Expense	53	6 0 0 00		1
2			Cash	11		6 0 0 00	2
3							3
4		2	Equipment	18	2 1 0 0 00		4
5			Accounts Payable	22		2 1 0 0 00	5
6							6
7		5	Cash	11	4 1 5 0 00		7
8			Accounts Receivable	12		4 1 5 0 00	8
9							9
10		8	Supplies	13	1 4 5 00		10
11			Accounts Payable	22		1 4 5 00	11
12							12
13		9	Accounts Payable	22	1 2 5 00		13
14			Equipment	18		1 2 5 00	14
15							15
16		12	Accounts Payable	22	1 2 5 0 00		16
17			Cash	11		1 2 5 0 00	17
18							18
19		16	Cash	11	6 3 00		19
20			Supplies	13		6 3 00	20
21							21
22		17	Prepaid Insurance	14	3 7 0 00		22
23			Cash	11		3 7 0 00	23
24							24
25		20	Accounts Payable	22	5 0 00		25
26			Cash	11		5 0 00	26

JOURNAL

	DATE		DESCRIPTION	POST. REF.	DEBIT	CREDIT	
1	June	23	Laboratory Expense	55	2 4 5 00		1
2			Cash	11		2 4 5 00	2
3							3
4		27	Judy K. Schmidt, Drawing	32	1 2 5 0 00		4
5			Cash	11		1 2 5 0 00	5
6							6
7		30	Cash	11	1 7 2 0 00		7
8			Professional Fees	41		1 7 2 0 00	8
9							9
10		30	Salary Expense	51	1 7 2 5 00		10
11			Cash	11		1 7 2 5 00	11
12							12
13		30	Utilities Expense	56	1 5 7 00		13
14			Cash	11		1 5 7 00	14
15							15
16		30	Utilities Expense	56	2 9 00		16
17			Cash	11		2 9 00	17
18							18
19		30	Accounts Receivable	12	4 1 4 5 00		19
20			Professional Fees	41		4 1 4 5 00	20
21							21
22		30	Utilities Expense	56	7 4 00		22
23			Cash	11		7 4 00	23
24							24
25		30	Miscellaneous Expense	59	1 3 2 00		25
26			Cash	11		1 3 2 00	26
27							27
28							28
29							29
30							30
31							31
32							32

1. and 3.   **GENERAL LEDGER**

ACCOUNT   *Cash*   ACCOUNT NO.   11

DATE		ITEM	POST. REF.	DEBIT	CREDIT	BALANCE	
						DEBIT	CREDIT
19-- June	1	Balance	✓			3 1 2 3 00	
	1		27		6 0 0 00	2 5 2 3 00	
	5		27	4 1 5 0 00		6 6 7 3 00	
	12		27		1 2 5 0 00	5 4 2 3 00	
	16		27	6 3 00		5 4 8 6 00	
	17		27		3 7 0 00	5 1 1 6 00	
	20		27		5 0 00	5 0 6 6 00	
	23		28		2 4 5 00	4 8 2 1 00	
	27		28		1 2 5 0 00	3 5 7 1 00	
	30		28	1 7 2 0 00		5 2 9 1 00	
	30		28		1 7 2 5 00	3 5 6 6 00	
	30		28		1 5 7 00	3 4 0 9 00	
	30		28		2 9 00	3 3 8 0 00	
	30		28		7 4 00	3 3 0 6 00	
	30		28		1 3 2 00	3 1 7 4 00	

ACCOUNT   *Accounts Receivable*   ACCOUNT NO.   12

DATE		ITEM	POST. REF.	DEBIT	CREDIT	BALANCE	
						DEBIT	CREDIT
19-- June	1	Balance	✓			6 7 2 5 00	
	5		27		4 1 5 0 00	2 5 7 5 00	
	30		28	4 1 4 5 00		6 7 2 0 00	

ACCOUNT   *Supplies*   ACCOUNT NO.   13

DATE		ITEM	POST. REF.	DEBIT	CREDIT	BALANCE	
						DEBIT	CREDIT
19-- June	1	Balance	✓			2 9 0 00	
	8		27	1 4 5 00		4 3 5 00	
	16		27		6 3 00	3 7 2 00	

ACCOUNT *Prepaid Insurance* ACCOUNT NO. 14

DATE		ITEM	POST. REF.	DEBIT	CREDIT	BALANCE DEBIT	BALANCE CREDIT
19-- June	1	Balance	✓			3 6 5 00	
	17		27	3 7 0 00		7 3 5 00	

ACCOUNT *Equipment* ACCOUNT NO. 18

DATE		ITEM	POST. REF.	DEBIT	CREDIT	BALANCE DEBIT	BALANCE CREDIT
19-- June	1	Balance	✓			19 7 4 5 00	
	2		27	2 1 0 0 00		21 8 4 5 00	
	9		27		1 2 5 00	21 7 2 0 00	

ACCOUNT *Accounts Payable* ACCOUNT NO. 22

DATE		ITEM	POST. REF.	DEBIT	CREDIT	BALANCE DEBIT	BALANCE CREDIT
19-- June	1	Balance	✓				7 6 5 00
	2		27		2 1 0 0 00		2 8 6 5 00
	8		27		1 4 5 00		3 0 1 0 00
	9		27	1 2 5 00			2 8 8 5 00
	12		27	1 2 5 0 00			1 6 3 5 00
	20		27	5 0 00			1 5 8 5 00

ACCOUNT *Judy K. Schmidt, Capital* ACCOUNT NO. 31

DATE		ITEM	POST. REF.	DEBIT	CREDIT	BALANCE DEBIT	BALANCE CREDIT
19-- June	1	Balance	✓				29 4 8 3 00

ACCOUNT   Judy K. Schmidt, Drawing   ACCOUNT NO.   32

DATE		ITEM	POST. REF.	DEBIT	CREDIT	BALANCE	
						DEBIT	CREDIT
19-- June	27		28	1250 00		1250 00	

ACCOUNT   Professional Fees   ACCOUNT NO.   41

DATE		ITEM	POST. REF.	DEBIT	CREDIT	BALANCE	
						DEBIT	CREDIT
19-- June	30		28		1720 00		1720 00
	30		28		4145 00		5865 00

ACCOUNT   Salary Expense   ACCOUNT NO.   51

DATE		ITEM	POST. REF.	DEBIT	CREDIT	BALANCE	
						DEBIT	CREDIT
19-- June	30		28	1725 00		1725 00	

ACCOUNT   Rent Expense   ACCOUNT NO.   53

DATE		ITEM	POST. REF.	DEBIT	CREDIT	BALANCE	
						DEBIT	CREDIT
19-- June	1		27	600 00		600 00	

ACCOUNT   Laboratory Expense   ACCOUNT NO.   55

DATE		ITEM	POST. REF.	DEBIT	CREDIT	BALANCE	
						DEBIT	CREDIT
19-- June	23		28	245 00		245 00	

ACCOUNT **Utilities Expense** ACCOUNT NO. **56**

DATE		ITEM	POST. REF.	DEBIT	CREDIT	BALANCE	
						DEBIT	CREDIT
19-- June	30		28	1 5 7 00		1 5 7 00	
	30		28	2 9 00		1 8 6 00	
	30		28	7 4 00		2 6 0 00	

ACCOUNT **Miscellaneous Expense** ACCOUNT NO. **59**

DATE		ITEM	POST. REF.	DEBIT	CREDIT	BALANCE	
						DEBIT	CREDIT
19-- June	30		28	1 3 2 00		1 3 2 00	

4.

Judy K. Schmidt, M.D.

Trial Balance

June 30, 19--

	Debit	Credit
Cash	3 1 7 4 00	
Accounts Receivable	6 7 2 0 00	
Supplies	3 7 2 00	
Prepaid Insurance	7 3 5 00	
Equipment	2 1 7 2 0 00	
Accounts Payable		1 5 8 5 00
Judy K. Schmidt, Capital		2 9 4 8 3 00
Judy K. Schmidt, Drawing	1 2 5 0 00	
Professional Fees		5 8 6 5 00
Salary Expense	1 7 2 5 00	
Rent Expense	6 0 0 00	
Laboratory Expense	2 4 5 00	
Utilities Expense	2 6 0 00	
Miscellaneous Expense	1 3 2 00	
	3 6 9 3 3 00	3 6 9 3 3 00

MATCHING

Instructions: A list of terms and related statements appear below. From the list of terms, select the one that relates to each statement. Print its identifying letter in the space provided.

A. Account
B. Assets
C. Chart of accounts
D. Double-entry accounting
E. Drawing
F. Expenses
G. Journalizing

H. Ledger
I. Liabilities
J. Owner's equity
K. Posting
L. Revenues
M. Trial balance

_____ 1. A group of related accounts that comprise a complete unit, such as all of the accounts of a specific business.

_____ 2. The process of recording a transaction in the journal.

_____ 3. The process by which the data in the journal entry is transferred to the appropriate accounts.

_____ 4. The system of accounts that make up the ledger for a business.

_____ 5. Physical items (tangibles) or rights (intangibles) that have value and that are owned by the business entity.

_____ 6. Assets or services consumed in the process of generating revenue.

_____ 7. Debts owed to outsiders.

_____ 8. A system for recording transactions, based on recording increases and decreases in accounts so that debits always equal credits.

_____ 9. The amount of withdrawals made by the owner of a sole proprietorship.

_____ 10. The residual claim against the assets of the business after the total liabilities are deducted.

_____ 11. Increase in owner's equity as a result of providing services or selling products to customers.

_____ 12. The form used to record additions and deductions for each individual asset, liability, owner's equity, revenue, and expense.

TRUE / FALSE

Instructions: Indicate whether each of the following statements is true or false by placing a check mark in the appropriate column.

                                                                    True   False

1. Amounts entered on the left side of an account, regardless of the account title, are called credits or charges to the account. . . . .   _____ _____

True   False

2. The difference between the total debits and the total credits posted to an account yields a figure called the balance of the account. . . . . _____ _____

3. Accounting systems provide information on business transactions for use by management in directing operations and preparing financial statements. . . . . _____ _____

4. Accounts receivable are claims against debtors evidenced by a written promise to pay a certain sum of money at a definite time to the order of a specified person or to bearer. _____ _____

5. The residual claim against the assets of a business after the total liabilities are deducted is called owner's equity. . . _____ _____

6. Every business transaction affects a minimum of one account. . . . . _____ _____

7. The process of recording a transaction in a journal is called posting. . . . . _____ _____

8. A group of accounts for a business entity is called a journal. _____ _____

9. A listing of the accounts in a ledger is called a chart of accounts. . . . . _____ _____

10. A recording error caused by the erroneous rearrangement of digits, such as writing $627 as $672, is called a slide. . _____ _____

MULTIPLE CHOICE

Instructions: Circle the best answer for each of the following questions.

1. A journal entry composed of two or more debits or two or more credits is called a:
   a. multiple journal entry
   b. compound journal entry
   c. complex journal entry
   d. double journal entry

2. The first step in recording a transaction in a two-column journal is to:
   a. write an explanation
   b. record the debit
   c. record the credit
   d. record the date

3. The drawing account of a sole proprietorship is debited when:
   a. the owner invests cash
   b. the owner withdraws cash
   c. a liability is paid
   d. an expense is paid

4. The equality of debits and credits in the ledger should be verified at the end of each accounting period by preparing a(n):

   a. accounting statement

   b. balance report

   c. trial balance

   d. account verification report

5. Of the following errors, the one that will cause an inequality in the trial balance totals is:

   a. incorrectly computing an account balance

   b. failure to record a transaction

   c. recording the same transaction more than once

   d. posting a transaction to the wrong account

6. Credits to cash result in:

   a. an increase in owner's equity

   b. a decrease in assets

   c. an increase in liabilities

   d. an increase in revenue

7. Debits to expense accounts signify:

   a. increases in capital

   b. decreases in capital

   c. increases in assets

   d. increases in liabilities

8. When rent is prepaid for several months in advance, the debit is to:

   a. an expense account

   b. a capital account

   c. a liability account

   d. an asset account

9. When an asset is purchased on account, the credit is to:

   a. a capital account

   b. a revenue account

   c. a liability account

   d. an expense account

10. When a payment is made to a supplier for goods previously purchased on account, the debit is to:

    a. an asset account

    b. a liability account

    c. a capital account

    d. an expense account

EXERCISE 2-1

Eight transactions are recorded in the following T accounts:

Cash			
(1)	20,000	(5)	2,500
(7)	2,000	(8)	3,500

Machinery	
(2)	6,300

Ann Moran, Drawing	
(8)	3,500

Accounts Receivable			
(4)	5,000	(7)	2,000

Accounts Payable			
(5)	2,500	(2)	6,300
		(3)	820
		(6)	1,600

Service Revenue	
(4)	5,000

Supplies	
(3)	820

Alan Moran, Capital	
(1)	20,000

Operating Expenses	
(6)	1,600

Instructions: For each debit and each credit, indicate in the following form the type of account affected (asset, liability, owner's equity, revenue, or expense) and whether the account was increased (+) or decreased (-).

Transaction	Account Debited		Account Credited	
	Type	Effect	Type	Effect
(1)				
(2)				
(3)				
(4)				
(5)				
(6)				
(7)				
(8)				

PROBLEM 2-1

During June of the current year, Joan Star started Star Service Company.

Instructions:

(1) Record the following transactions in the two-column journal given below.

June 1. Invested $5,000 in cash, equipment valued at $14,500, and a van worth $21,000.

16. Purchased additional equipment on account, $5,500.
28. Purchased supplies on account, $500.
30. Paid $2,100 to creditors on account.

(2) Post to the appropriate ledger accounts on the next page.
(3) Prepare a trial balance of the ledger accounts of Star Service Company as of June 30 of the current year, using the form below.

(1) **JOURNAL** PAGE

	DATE	DESCRIPTION	POST. REF.	DEBIT	CREDIT	
1						1
2						2
3						3
4						4
5						5
6						6
7						7
8						8
9						9
10						10
11						11
12						12
13						13
14						14
15						15
16						16
17						17
18						18
19						19
20						20

(2) LEDGER ACCOUNTS

ACCOUNT *Cash*   ACCOUNT NO. *11*

DATE	ITEM	POST. REF.	DEBIT	CREDIT	BALANCE DEBIT	BALANCE CREDIT

ACCOUNT *Supplies*   ACCOUNT NO. *12*

DATE	ITEM	POST. REF.	DEBIT	CREDIT	BALANCE DEBIT	BALANCE CREDIT

ACCOUNT *Equipment*   ACCOUNT NO. *18*

DATE	ITEM	POST. REF.	DEBIT	CREDIT	BALANCE DEBIT	BALANCE CREDIT

ACCOUNT *Vehicles*   ACCOUNT NO. *19*

DATE	ITEM	POST. REF.	DEBIT	CREDIT	BALANCE DEBIT	BALANCE CREDIT

ACCOUNT *Accounts Payable*   ACCOUNT NO. *21*

DATE	ITEM	POST. REF.	DEBIT	CREDIT	BALANCE DEBIT	BALANCE CREDIT

ACCOUNT   *Joan Star, Capital*   ACCOUNT NO.   *31*

DATE		ITEM	POST. REF.	DEBIT	CREDIT	BALANCE	
						DEBIT	CREDIT

(3)

PROBLEM 2-2

On January 2, 19--, Judy Turner, an attorney, opened a law office. The following transactions were completed during the month.

a. Invested $20,000 cash and $13,200 worth of office equipment in the business.
b. Paid a month's rent of $2,500.
c. Paid $1,000 for office supplies.
d. Collected legal fees of $19,600.
e. Paid secretary a salary of $1,100.
f. Purchased $200 worth of office supplies on account.
g. Bought an auto for business use. It cost $13,000. Turner paid $2,600 down and charged the balance.
h. Withdrew $5,000 from the firm for personal use.
i. Paid $800 for auto repairs and maintenance.
j. Received a $240 telephone bill.
k. Paid the $240 telephone bill.
l. Paid premiums of $1,700 on property insurance.
m. Paid $2,000 on accounts payable.
n. Paid $5,000 cash for books for the law library.
o. Paid $500 cash for janitor service.

Instructions:
(1) Record the transactions in the T accounts that follow.
(2) Prepare a trial balance, using the form on the following page.

(1)

Cash	Prepaid Insurance	Auto

	Library	Accounts Payable

Office Supplies	Office Equipment	Judy Turner, Capital

Judy Turner, Drawing	Salary Expense	Janitor Expense

Legal Fees	Telephone Expense

Rent Expense	Auto Repairs & Maintenance Expense

(2)

PROBLEM 2-3

The following errors were made in journalizing and posting transactions:

a. A $1,000 premium paid for insurance was debited to Prepaid Rent and credited to Cash.

b. A $200 purchase of supplies on account was recorded as a debit to Supplies and a credit to Accounts Receivable.

c. A withdrawal by the owner of $1,500 was debited to Cash and credited to the drawing account.

Instructions: Prepare entries in the two-column journal provided below to correct these errors.

JOURNAL
PAGE

	DATE	DESCRIPTION	POST. REF.	DEBIT	CREDIT	
1						1
2						2
3						3
4						4
5						5
6						6
7						7
8						8
9						9
10						10
11						11
12						12
13						13
14						14
15						15
16						16
17						17
18						18
19						19
20						20
21						21
22						22
23						23
24						24
25						25

CONTINUING PROBLEM

The following problem will continue through the next several chapters. The ledger on pages 42-54 of this Study Guide will be used in these chapters.

Egor J. Gribbet is a professional magician who has been performing since the beginning of the current year (1996). He is operating the business as "Egor the Magician."

Egor rents an office from which he secures bookings for his act and in which he stores his props and equipment. He also leases a van for use in the business. Egor sometimes hires or subcontracts other acts, such as George the Mysterious, to perform with him.

The account balances for Egor the Magician at the end of November of the current year are as follows:

Account	Dr.	Cr.
Cash	$ 5,504	
Fees Receivable	2,486	
Supplies & Props	1,083	
Office Supplies	789	
Prepaid Insurance	1,400	
Furniture & Fixtures	6,400	
Equipment--Stage	10,800	
Accounts Payable		$ 1,495
Theater Services Payable		2,005
Subcontractors Payable		750
Notes Payable (long term)		1,500
E. J. Gribbet, Capital		21,852
E. J. Gribbet, Drawing	400	
Fees Earned		15,100
Theater Services Expense	4,000	
Subcontractor Expense	2,010	
Van Expense	2,900	
Cosmetics Expense	230	
Rent Expense	4,400	
Telephone Expense	300	
Total	$ 42,702	$ 42,702

The following transactions were completed by Egor the Magician during December:

Dec. **1.** Paid office rent for December, $400.

1. Paid van lease for December, $200.

2. Paid cash for a one-year property insurance policy, $600.

2. Billed clients for work done for the last two months, $9,800.

4. Received payment for a performance billed in November, $1,000.

8. Received cash for a performance today, $1,200.

11. Paid George the Mysterious for his performance in November, $750.

14. Paid the Chi-Town Theater for its use in November, $2,005.

15. Purchased supplies and props on account, $185.

Dec. 16. Purchased equipment worth $1,200 by paying $200 down and putting the remainder on account.

17. Paid cash to creditors, $1,100.

18. Recorded cash collected from jobs in December, $5,200. These jobs had not yet been recorded.

21. Paid cash for cosmetics, $73.

24. Collected cash from the December 2 billings, $5,200.

29. Paid telephone expense, $95.

30. Paid Jane the Fantastic for her performance, $450.

31. Bought new furniture by paying $2,000 cash and signing a long-term 6% note for $5,000 with the 1st National Bank.

31. Paid cash for cosmetics, $125.

31. Paid for gas used in the van during the month, $150.

Instructions:

(1) Journalize each transaction in a two-column journal.

(2) Post the journal to the ledger. Some accounts (such as Income Summary and Sales Discounts) in the ledger on pages 42-54 will be used in later chapters. In working this portion of the Continuing Problem, ignore these accounts.

(3) Prepare a trial balance as of December 31, 1996.

JOURNAL   PAGE

	DATE		DESCRIPTION	POST. REF.	DEBIT	CREDIT	
1							1
2							2
3							3
4							4
5							5
6							6
7							7
8							8
9							9
10							10
11							11
12							12
13							13
14							14
15							15
16							16

JOURNAL

PAGE

	DATE	DESCRIPTION	POST. REF.	DEBIT	CREDIT	
1						1
2						2
3						3
4						4
5						5
6						6
7						7
8						8
9						9
10						10
11						11
12						12
13						13
14						14
15						15
16						16
17						17
18						18
19						19
20						20
21						21
22						22
23						23
24						24
25						25
26						26
27						27
28						28
29						29
30						30
31						31
32						32
33						33

JOURNAL

	DATE	DESCRIPTION	POST. REF.	DEBIT	CREDIT	
1						1
2						2
3						3
4						4
5						5
6						6
7						7
8						8
9						9
10						10
11						11
12						12
13						13
14						14
15						15
16						16
17						17
18						18
19						19
20						20
21						21
22						22
23						23
24						24
25						25
26						26
27						27
28						28
29						29
30						30
31						31
32						32
33						33

GENERAL LEDGER

ACCOUNT   *Cash*   ACCOUNT NO.   *110*

DATE		ITEM	POST. REF.	DEBIT	CREDIT	BALANCE	
						DEBIT	CREDIT
1996 Nov.	30	Balance	✓			5 5 0 4	

ACCOUNT   *Cash (Continued)*   ACCOUNT NO.   *110*

DATE		ITEM	POST. REF.	DEBIT	CREDIT	BALANCE	
						DEBIT	CREDIT

ACCOUNT   *Accounts Receivable*   ACCOUNT NO.   *111*

DATE		ITEM	POST. REF.	DEBIT	CREDIT	BALANCE	
						DEBIT	CREDIT

ACCOUNT *Fees Receivable*   ACCOUNT NO.   *112*

DATE		ITEM	POST. REF.	DEBIT	CREDIT	BALANCE	
						DEBIT	CREDIT
1996 Nov.	30	Balance	✓			2 4 8 6	

ACCOUNT *Merchandise Inventory*   ACCOUNT NO.   *115*

DATE		ITEM	POST. REF.	DEBIT	CREDIT	BALANCE	
						DEBIT	CREDIT

ACCOUNT *Supplies & Props*   ACCOUNT NO.   *116*

DATE		ITEM	POST. REF.	DEBIT	CREDIT	BALANCE	
						DEBIT	CREDIT
1996 Nov.	30	Balance	✓			1 0 8 3	

ACCOUNT *Office Supplies*   ACCOUNT NO.   *117*

DATE		ITEM	POST. REF.	DEBIT	CREDIT	BALANCE	
						DEBIT	CREDIT
1996 Nov.	30	Balance	✓			7 8 9	

ACCOUNT   *Prepaid Insurance*   ACCOUNT NO.   *118*

DATE		ITEM	POST. REF.	DEBIT	CREDIT	BALANCE	
						DEBIT	CREDIT
1996 Nov.	30	Balance	✓			1 4 0 0	

ACCOUNT   *Furniture & Fixtures*   ACCOUNT NO.   *121*

DATE		ITEM	POST. REF.	DEBIT	CREDIT	BALANCE	
						DEBIT	CREDIT
1996 Nov.	30	Balance	✓			6 4 0 0	

ACCOUNT   *Accumulated Depreciation–Furniture & Fixtures*   ACCOUNT NO.   *122*

DATE	ITEM	POST. REF.	DEBIT	CREDIT	BALANCE	
					DEBIT	CREDIT

ACCOUNT   *Equipment--Stage*   ACCOUNT NO.   *123*

DATE		ITEM	POST. REF.	DEBIT	CREDIT	BALANCE	
						DEBIT	CREDIT
1996 Nov.	30	Balance	✓			10 8 0 0	

ACCOUNT   *Accumulated Depreciation–Equipment–Stage*   ACCOUNT NO.   *124*

DATE	ITEM	POST. REF.	DEBIT	CREDIT	BALANCE	
					DEBIT	CREDIT

ACCOUNT   *Accounts Payable*   ACCOUNT NO.   *211*

DATE		ITEM	POST. REF.	DEBIT	CREDIT	BALANCE	
						DEBIT	CREDIT
1996 Nov.	30	Balance	✓				1 4 9 5

ACCOUNT   *Salaries Payable*   ACCOUNT NO.   *212*

DATE	ITEM	POST. REF.	DEBIT	CREDIT	BALANCE	
					DEBIT	CREDIT

ACCOUNT   *Theater Services Payable*   ACCOUNT NO.   *213*

DATE		ITEM	POST. REF.	DEBIT	CREDIT	BALANCE	
						DEBIT	CREDIT
1996 Nov.	30	Balance	✓				2 0 0 5

ACCOUNT   *Subcontractors Payable*   ACCOUNT NO.   *214*

DATE		ITEM	POST. REF.	DEBIT	CREDIT	BALANCE	
						DEBIT	CREDIT
1996 Nov.	30	Balance	✓				7 5 0

ACCOUNT *Interest Payable*   ACCOUNT NO. *215*

DATE	ITEM	POST. REF.	DEBIT	CREDIT	BALANCE DEBIT	BALANCE CREDIT

ACCOUNT *Notes Payable*   ACCOUNT NO. *220*

DATE	ITEM	POST. REF.	DEBIT	CREDIT	BALANCE DEBIT	BALANCE CREDIT
1996 Nov. 30	Balance	✓				1 5 0 0

ACCOUNT *E. J. Gribbet, Capital*   ACCOUNT NO. *310*

DATE	ITEM	POST. REF.	DEBIT	CREDIT	BALANCE DEBIT	BALANCE CREDIT
1996 Nov. 30	Balance	✓				21 8 5 2

ACCOUNT *E. J. Gribbet, Drawing*   ACCOUNT NO. *311*

DATE	ITEM	POST. REF.	DEBIT	CREDIT	BALANCE DEBIT	BALANCE CREDIT
1996 Nov. 30	Balance	✓			4 0 0	

ACCOUNT   *Income Summary*   ACCOUNT NO.   *312*

DATE		ITEM	POST. REF.	DEBIT	CREDIT	BALANCE	
						DEBIT	CREDIT

ACCOUNT   *Fees Earned*   ACCOUNT NO.   *410*

DATE		ITEM	POST. REF.	DEBIT	CREDIT	BALANCE	
						DEBIT	CREDIT
1996 Nov.	30	Balance	✓				15 1 0 0

ACCOUNT   *Sales*   ACCOUNT NO.   *411*

DATE		ITEM	POST. REF.	DEBIT	CREDIT	BALANCE	
						DEBIT	CREDIT

ACCOUNT   *Sales Returns and Allowances*   ACCOUNT NO.   *412*

DATE	ITEM	POST. REF.	DEBIT	CREDIT	BALANCE DEBIT	BALANCE CREDIT

ACCOUNT   *Sales Discounts*   ACCOUNT NO.   *413*

DATE	ITEM	POST. REF.	DEBIT	CREDIT	BALANCE DEBIT	BALANCE CREDIT

ACCOUNT   *Salary Expense*   ACCOUNT NO.   *520*

DATE	ITEM	POST. REF.	DEBIT	CREDIT	BALANCE DEBIT	BALANCE CREDIT

ACCOUNT   *Theater Services Expense*   ACCOUNT NO.   *521*

DATE		ITEM	POST. REF.	DEBIT	CREDIT	BALANCE	
						DEBIT	CREDIT
1996 Nov.	30	Balance	✓			4 0 0 0	

ACCOUNT   *Subcontractor Expense*   ACCOUNT NO.   *522*

DATE		ITEM	POST. REF.	DEBIT	CREDIT	BALANCE	
						DEBIT	CREDIT
1996 Nov.	30	Balance	✓			2 0 1 0	

ACCOUNT   *Van Expense*   ACCOUNT NO.   *524*

DATE		ITEM	POST. REF.	DEBIT	CREDIT	BALANCE	
						DEBIT	CREDIT
1996 Nov.	30	Balance	✓			2 9 0 0	

ACCOUNT   *Cosmetics Expense*   ACCOUNT NO.   *525*

DATE		ITEM	POST. REF.	DEBIT	CREDIT	BALANCE DEBIT	BALANCE CREDIT
1996 Nov.	30	Balance	✓			2 3 0	

ACCOUNT   *Depreciation Expense--Furniture & Fixtures*   ACCOUNT NO.   *527*

DATE	ITEM	POST. REF.	DEBIT	CREDIT	BALANCE DEBIT	BALANCE CREDIT

ACCOUNT   *Depreciation Expense--Equipment*   ACCOUNT NO.   *528*

DATE	ITEM	POST. REF.	DEBIT	CREDIT	BALANCE DEBIT	BALANCE CREDIT

ACCOUNT   *Insurance Expense*   ACCOUNT NO.   *529*

DATE	ITEM	POST. REF.	DEBIT	CREDIT	BALANCE	
					DEBIT	CREDIT

ACCOUNT   *Office Supplies Expense*   ACCOUNT NO.   *531*

DATE	ITEM	POST. REF.	DEBIT	CREDIT	BALANCE	
					DEBIT	CREDIT

ACCOUNT   *Rent Expense*   ACCOUNT NO.   *532*

DATE	ITEM	POST. REF.	DEBIT	CREDIT	BALANCE	
					DEBIT	CREDIT
1996 Nov. 30	Balance	✓			4 4 0 0	

ACCOUNT   *Supplies and Props Expense*   ACCOUNT NO.   533

DATE	ITEM	POST. REF.	DEBIT	CREDIT	BALANCE DEBIT	BALANCE CREDIT

ACCOUNT   *Telephone Expense*   ACCOUNT NO.   534

DATE		ITEM	POST. REF.	DEBIT	CREDIT	BALANCE DEBIT	BALANCE CREDIT
1996 Nov.	30	Balance	√			3 0 0	

ACCOUNT   *Transportation Out*   ACCOUNT NO.   535

DATE	ITEM	POST. REF.	DEBIT	CREDIT	BALANCE DEBIT	BALANCE CREDIT

ACCOUNT   *Interest Expense*   ACCOUNT NO.   *710*

DATE	ITEM	POST. REF.	DEBIT	CREDIT	BALANCE	
					DEBIT	CREDIT

Trial Balance

3

The Matching Concept and the Adjusting Process

QUIZ AND TEST HINTS

The following hints may be helpful to you in preparing for a quiz or a test over the material covered in Chapter 3.

1. Terminology is important in this chapter. Review the Key Terms in the text.

2. The major focus of this chapter is the adjusting process. You should be able to prepare adjusting entries for each of the four types of adjustments: deferred expenses, deferred revenues, accrued expenses, and accrued revenues. You should also be able to prepare the adjusting entry for depreciation. Review the illustrations in the chapter and the adjusting entries required in the Illustrative Problem in the Chapter Review.

3. Most instructors will not require you to prepare a work sheet from scratch. However, some instructors may give you a partially completed work sheet and ask you to complete it. Or, you may be given a work sheet that has a Trial Balance and Adjusted Trial Balance columns completed, but has no data entered in the Adjustments columns. You would then be asked to figure out what the adjusting entries must have been. Practice working this type of problem by covering up the Adjustments columns with a sheet of paper and attempting to figure out the adjusting entries using Exhibit 7 on page 103 of the text or the Illustrative Problem in the Chapter Review.

CHAPTER OUTLINE

I. The Matching Concept.

A. The accounting period concept assumes that the economic life of the business can be divided into time periods. As a result, accountants must determine in which period the revenues and expenses of the business should be reported.

B. Accountants normally use either (1) the cash basis of accounting or (2) the accrual basis of accounting.

1. Under the cash basis, revenues and expenses are reported in the income statement in the period in which cash is received or paid.

2. Under the accrual basis, the revenue recognition principle leads to reporting revenues in the income statement in the period in which they are earned. Using the matching concept, expenses are reported in the same period as the revenues to which they relate.

C. Generally accepted accounting principles require the use of the accrual basis. However, small service businesses may use the cash basis when the financial statements are similar to those that would have been reported using the accrual basis.

D. The accrual basis and its related matching concept require an analysis and updating of some accounts when financial statements are prepared. This process is called the adjusting process.

II. Nature of the Adjusting Process.

A. The entries required at the end of the accounting period to bring the accounts up to date and to ensure the proper matching of revenues and expenses are called adjusting entries.

B. Two basic classifications of items give rise to adjusting entries: deferrals and accruals.

C. Deferrals are created by recording a transaction in a way that delays or defers the recognition of an expense or revenue.

    1. Deferred expenses are items that have been initially recorded as assets, but which are expected to become expenses over time or through the normal operations of the business. Examples include supplies and prepaid insurance. Deferred expenses are often called prepaid expenses.

    2. Deferred revenues are items that have been initially recorded as liabilities, but which are expected to become revenues over time or through the normal operations of the business. Examples include tuition and subscriptions received in advance. Deferred revenues are often called unearned revenues.

D. Accruals are created by the failure to record an expense that has been incurred or a revenue that has been earned.

    1. Accrued expenses are expenses that have been incurred, but which have not been recorded in the accounts. Examples include wages and interest.

    2. Accrued revenues are revenues that have been earned, but which have not been recorded in the accounts. Examples include unrecorded fees earned by an attorney or real estate agent.

E. How do you tell the difference between deferrals and accruals?

    1. Deferrals normally arise when cash is received or paid in the current period, but the related revenue or expense is to be recorded in a future period.

    2. Accruals normally arise when a revenue or expense is recorded in the current period, but the related cash is received or paid in a future period.

III. Recording Adjusting Entries.

A. An adjusting entry always affects a balance sheet account and an income statement account.

B. If an adjusting entry is omitted or erroneously recorded, both the balance sheet and the income statement will be affected.

C. The adjusting entry for deferred (prepaid) expenses debits an expense account and credits the deferred (prepaid) expense account.

D. The adjusting entry for deferred (unearned) revenue debits a deferred (unearned) revenue account and credits a revenue account.

E. The adjusting entry for accrued expenses (liabilities) debits an expense account and credits a liability account.

F. The adjusting entry for accrued revenues (assets) debits an asset account and credits a revenue account.

G. Tangible assets that are permanent or have a long life and are used in the business are called plant assets or fixed assets. The decrease in usefulness of a plant asset is generally referred to as depreciation.

    1. Depreciation, in an accounting sense, refers to the systematic allocation of the cost of a plant asset to expense.

    2. The adjusting entry to record depreciation debits a depreciation expense account and credits a contra asset account, accumulated depreciation.

    3. An accumulated depreciation account is normally maintained for each plant asset except land, which does not depreciate.

    4. The difference between the balance of a plant asset and its related accumulated depreciation (contra asset) account is called the book value of the asset.

IV. Work Sheet.

A. At the end of an accounting period, a work sheet may be prepared by the accountant to facilitate the preparation of the financial statements and the necessary adjusting journal entries.

B. The Trial Balance columns of the work sheet are taken directly from the balances of the various ledger accounts at the end of the accounting period.

C. The necessary debit and credit portions of the adjusting entries are entered on the work sheet in the Adjustments columns.

D. After the adjusting entries have been entered on the work sheet, the account balances are extended to the Adjusted Trial Balance columns. The debit and credit columns are then totaled and compared to prove that no arithmetical errors have been made up to this point.

E. The completion of the work sheet, including the preparation of financial statements, is discussed in the next chapter.

ILLUSTRATIVE PROBLEM

Two years ago, K. L. Waters organized Star Realty as a sole proprietorship. At March 31, 1997, the end of the current year, the trial balance of Star Realty is as follows:

Cash	$ 2,425	
Accounts Receivable	5,000	
Supplies	1,870	
Prepaid Insurance	620	
Office Equipment	32,650	
Accumulated Depreciation		$9,700
Accounts Payable		925
Unearned Fees		1,250
K. L. Waters, Capital		20,930
K. L. Waters, Drawing	10,200	
Fees Earned		39,125
Wages Expense	12,415	
Rent Expense	3,600	
Utilities Expense	2,715	
Miscellaneous Expense	435	
	$71,930	$71,930

The data needed to determine year-end adjustments are as follows:

a. Supplies on hand at March 31, 1997	$ 480
b. Insurance premiums expired during the year	315
c. Depreciation on equipment during the year	1,950
d. Wages accrued but not paid at March 31, 1997	140
e. Accrued fees earned but not recorded at March 31, 1997	1,000
f. Unearned fees on March 31, 1997	750

Instructions

1. Enter the March 31, 1997 trial balance on a work sheet.

2. Using the adjustment data, enter the necessary adjustments on the work sheet.

3. Extend the adjustment data on the work sheet to the adjusted trial balance columns.

Solution
1., 2., and 3.

Star Realty
Work Sheet
For Year Ended March 31, 1997

ACCOUNT TITLE	TRIAL BALANCE DEBIT	TRIAL BALANCE CREDIT	ADJUSTMENTS DEBIT	ADJUSTMENTS CREDIT	ADJUSTED TRIAL BALANCE DEBIT	ADJUSTED TRIAL BALANCE CREDIT
Cash	2 4 2 5 00				2 4 2 5 00	
Accounts Receivable	5 0 0 0 00		(e) 1 0 0 0 00		6 0 0 0 00	
Supplies	1 8 7 0 00			(a) 1 3 9 0 00	4 8 0 00	
Prepaid Insurance	6 2 0 00			(b) 3 1 5 00	3 0 5 00	
Office Equipment	3 6 5 0 00				3 6 5 0 00	
Accumulated Depreciation		9 7 0 0 00		(c) 1 9 5 0 00		1 1 6 5 0 00
Accounts Payable		9 2 5 00				9 2 5 00
Unearned Fees		1 2 5 0 00	(f) 5 0 0 00			7 5 0 00
K.L. Waters, Capital		2 0 9 3 0 00				2 0 9 3 0 00
K.L. Waters, Drawing	1 0 2 0 0 00				1 0 2 0 0 00	
Fees Earned		3 9 1 2 5 00		(e) 1 0 0 0 00 (f) 5 0 0 00		4 0 6 2 5 00
Wages Expense	1 2 4 1 5 00		(d) 1 4 0 00		1 2 5 5 5 00	
Rent Expense	3 6 0 0 00				3 6 0 0 00	
Utilities Expense	2 7 1 5 00				2 7 1 5 00	
Miscellaneous Expense	4 3 5 00				4 3 5 00	
	7 1 9 3 0 00	7 1 9 3 0 00				
Supplies Expense			(a) 1 3 9 0 00		1 3 9 0 00	
Insurance Expense			(b) 3 1 5 00		3 1 5 00	
Depreciation Expense			(c) 1 9 5 0 00		1 9 5 0 00	
Wages Payable				(d) 1 4 0 00		1 4 0 00
			5 2 9 5 00	5 2 9 5 00	7 5 0 2 0 00	7 5 0 2 0 00

MATCHING

Instructions: A list of terms and related statements appear below. From the list of terms, select the one that relates to each statement. Print its identifying letter in the space provided.

A. Accrual basis
B. Accrued expense
C. Adjusting entries
D. Book value of the asset
E. Cash basis
F. Closing entries
G. Contra account

H. Deferral
I. Depreciation
J. General ledger
K. Matching principle
L. Plant assets
M. Work sheet

_____   1. A basis of accounting in which revenues are reported in the period in which they are earned, and expenses are reported in the period in which they are incurred in an attempt to produce revenues.

_____   2. The entries required at the end of an accounting period to bring the accounts up to date and to assure the proper matching of revenues and expenses.

_____   3. The allocation of the cost of a plant asset to expense over the accounting periods making up its useful life.

_____   4. An account which is "offset against" another account.

_____   5. An accumulated expense that is unpaid and unrecorded.

_____   6. A delay of the recognition of an expense already paid, or of a revenue already received.

_____   7. Tangible assets that are permanent or have a long life and are used in the business.

_____   8. A working paper often used by accountants to summarize adjusting entries.

_____   9. The process of matching revenues and expenses.

_____   10. The difference between the accumulated depreciation account and the related plant asset account.

TRUE / FALSE

Instructions: Indicate whether each of the following statements is true or false by placing a check mark in the appropriate column.

	True	False

1. Most businesses use the accrual basis of accounting. . . . _____ _____

2. When the reduction in prepaid expenses is not properly recorded, this causes the asset accounts and expense accounts to be overstated. . . . . _____ _____

3. Accumulated depreciation accounts may be referred to as contra asset accounts. . . . . _____ _____

4. When the Adjustments columns of the work sheet are totaled, if the debit column total is greater than the credit column total, the excess is the net income. . . . . _____ _____

5. After all necessary adjustments are entered on the work sheet, the two Adjustments columns are totaled to prove the equality of debits and credits. . . . . _____ _____

6. The adjusting entry to record depreciation of plant assets consists of a debit to a depreciation expense account and a credit to an accumulated depreciation account. . . . . . . _____ _____

7. When services are not paid for until after they have been performed, the accrued expense is recorded in the accounts by an adjusting entry at the end of the accounting period. . . . . _____ _____

8. A deferral is an expense that has not been paid or a revenue that has not been received. . . . . _____ _____

9. Accrued expenses may be described on the balance sheet as accrued liabilities. . . . . _____ _____

10. The amount of accrued revenue is recorded by debiting a liability account and crediting a revenue account. . . . . . _____ _____

MULTIPLE CHOICE

Instructions: Circle the best answer for each of the following questions.

1. Entries required at the end of an accounting period to bring the accounts up to date and to assure the proper matching of revenues and expenses are called:
   a. matching entries
   b. adjusting entries
   c. contra entries
   d. correcting entries

2. The decrease in usefulness of plant assets as time passes is called:
   a. consumption
   b. deterioration
   c. depreciation
   d. contra asset

3. The difference between the plant asset account and the related accumulated depreciation account is called the:
   a. book value of the asset
   b. fair market value of the asset
   c. net cost of the asset
   d. contra account balance of the asset

4. If a $250 adjustment for depreciation is not recorded, which of the following financial statement errors will occur?
   a. expenses will be overstated
   b. net income will be understated
   c. assets will be understated
   d. owner's equity will be overstated

5. The amount of accrued but unpaid expenses at the end of the fiscal period is both an expense and a(n):
   a. liability
   b. asset
   c. deferral
   d. revenue

EXERCISE 3-1

Don Taylor closes his books at the end of each year (December 31). On May 1 of the current year, Don insured the business assets for three years at a premium of $5,400.

Instructions:

(1) Using the T accounts below, enter the adjusting entry that should be made by Taylor as of December 31 to record the amount of insurance expired as of that date. The May 1 premium payment is recorded in the T accounts.

Cash		Prepaid Insurance		Insurance Expense	
May 1 5,400		May 1 5,400			

(2) Taylor's balance sheet as of December 31 should show the asset value of the unexpired insurance as . . . . $ _____

(3) Taylor's income statement for the year ended December 31 should show insurance expense of . . . . $ _____

EXERCISE 3-2

Jan Olin closes her books at the end of each month. Olin has only one employee, who is paid at the rate of $50 per day. The employee is paid every Friday at the end of the day. Each workweek is composed of five days, starting on Monday. Assume that the Fridays of this month (October) fall on the 7th, 14th, 21st, and 28th.

Instructions:

(1) Using the T accounts below, enter the four weekly wage payments for October. Then enter the adjusting entry that should be made by Olin as of October 31, to record the salary owed the employee but unpaid as of that date.

Cash	Salary Expense	Salaries Payable

(2) Olin's income statement for October should show total
salary expense of . . . . $ _____

(3) Olin's balance sheet as of October 31 should show a
liability for salaries payable of . . . . $ _____

EXERCISE 3-3

Keller Co.'s unearned rent account has a balance of $6,000 as of December 31 of the current year. This amount represents the rental of an apartment for a period of one year. The lease began on December 1 of the current year.

Instructions: Using the T accounts below, record the adjusting entry as of December 31 to recognize the rent income for the appropriate portion of the year. Then journalize the entry.

```
        Unearned Rent                          Rent Income
        Dec. 1    6,000
```

JOURNAL   PAGE

	DATE	DESCRIPTION	POST. REF.	DEBIT	CREDIT	
1						1
2						2
3						3
4						4
5						5
6						6
7						7
8						8
9						9
10						10
11						11
12						12
13						13
14						14
15						15
16						16
17						17
18						18
19						19
20						20
21						21
22						22
23						23

EXERCISE 3-4

Garret Co. has accrued but uncollected interest of $320 as of December 31 on a note receivable.

Instructions: Using the T accounts below, record the adjusting entry for accrued interest income as of December 31. Then journalize the entry.

Interest Receivable	Interest Income

JOURNAL

PAGE

	DATE	DESCRIPTION	POST. REF.	DEBIT	CREDIT	
1						1
2						2
3						3
4						4
5						5
6						6
7						7
8						8
9						9
10						10
11						11
12						12
13						13
14						14
15						15
16						16
17						17
18						18
19						19
20						20
21						21
22						22
23						23
24						24
25						25

PROBLEM 3-1

A partial work sheet with the trial balance portion completed is shown on the next page for Bob's Service Company for July.

Instructions:

(1) Record the following adjustments in the Adjustments columns:

   (a) Salaries accrued but not paid at the end of the month amount to $2,000.

   (b) The $8,712 debit in the prepaid rent account is the payment of one year's rent on July 1.

   (c) The supplies on hand as of July 31 cost $1,000.

   (d) Depreciation of the tools and equipment for July is estimated at $400.

   (e) Fees for service rendered in July but collected in August amount to $2,100.

(2) Complete the Adjusted Trial Balance columns of the work sheet.

Omit "00" in the cents columns.

Bob's Service Company
Partial Work Sheet
For Month Ended July 31, 19—

ACCOUNT TITLE	TRIAL BALANCE		ADJUSTMENTS		ADJUSTED TRIAL BALANCE	
	DEBIT	CREDIT	DEBIT	CREDIT	DEBIT	CREDIT
Cash	9218					
Accounts Receivable	7277					
Supplies	2750					
Prepaid Rent	8712					
Tools & Equipment	21829					
Accumulated Depreciation		1535				
Accounts Payable		7117				
Bob Jones, Capital		37417				
Bob Jones, Drawing	3234					
Service Fees		28699				
Salary Expense	15929					
Miscellaneous Expense	5819					
	74768	74768				

CONTINUING PROBLEM

The trial balance for Egor the Magician at the end of 1996 is shown in the partial work sheet on the next page.

Instructions:

(4) Enter the following adjustments in the Adjustments columns:

    (a) Office supplies on hand as of December 31, $210.

    (b) Supplies and props on hand as of December 31, $365.

    (c) The November 30 balance of prepaid insurance was used up as of December 31. The new policy purchased on December 2 must be adjusted for the amount used as of December 31.

    (d) The notes payable account contains two notes. The first note is for $1,500 at 7% and was issued January 2. Interest accrued on this note is $105. The second note is for $5,000 at 6% and was issued December 31, and therefore no interest has accrued on this note.

    (e) Mr. Gribbet owes the theater $850 for its services, which have not been recorded.

    (f) Mr. Gribbet owes J. P. Magic $600 for a performance in November.

    (g) Depreciation on the furniture and fixtures for the year, $2,680.

    (h) Depreciation on the equipment, $2,400.

(5) Complete the Adjusted Trial Balance columns of the work sheet.

(4) and (5) *Omit "00" in the cents columns.*

Egor the Magician
Partial Work Sheet
For the Year Ended Decemember 31, 1996

ACCOUNT TITLE	TRIAL BALANCE		ADJUSTMENTS		ADJUSTED TRIAL BALANCE	
	DEBIT	CREDIT	DEBIT	CREDIT	DEBIT	CREDIT
Cash	9956					
Fees Receivable	6086					
Supplies & Props	1268					
Office Supplies	789					
Prepaid Insurance	2000					
Furniture & Fixtures	13400					
Equipment--Stage	12000					
Accounts Payable		1580				
Theater Services Payable						
Subcontractors Payable						
Notes Payable		6500				
E.J. Gribbet, Capital		21852				
E.J. Gribbet, Drawing	400					
Fees Earned		31300				
Theater Services Expense	4000					
Subcontractor Expense	2460					
Auto Expense	3250					
Cosmetics Expense	428					
Rent Expense	4800					
Telephone Expense	395					
	61232	61232				

4 Completing the Accounting Cycle

QUIZ AND TEST HINTS

The following hints may be helpful to you in preparing for a quiz or a test over the material covered in Chapter 4.

1. The completion of the work sheet is an important part of this chapter. Although most instructors will not require you to prepare a work sheet from scratch, a test question might include a partially completed work sheet that you would be asked to complete.

2. Be thoroughly familiar with the financial statements presented in Exhibit 5 in the text. Know the financial statement captions and how the statements tie together. In a test situation, you may be provided with partially completed financial statements that you would be asked to complete.

3. You should be able to prepare the formal adjusting entries and closing entries in general journal form. You may have to prepare these entries from a completed work sheet.

4. The accounting cycle is an essential part of accounting. Expect multiple-choice or other types of short answer questions related to the accounting cycle.

5. Your instructor may or may not have discussed the material in the end-of-chapter appendix on reversing entries. If your instructor covered the appendix, you should know what adjusting entries normally require reversing entries, and be able to prepare reversing entries.

CHAPTER OUTLINE

I. Work Sheet.

A. At the end of an accounting period, a work sheet may be prepared by the accountant to facilitate the preparation of the financial statements and the necessary adjusting journal entries.

B. The Trial Balance columns of the work sheet are taken directly from the balances of the various ledger accounts at the end of the accounting period.

C. The necessary debit and credit portions of the adjusting entries are entered on the work sheet in the Adjustments columns.

D. After the adjusting entries have been entered on the work sheet, the account balances are extended to the Adjusted Trial Balance columns.

The debit and credit columns are then totaled and compared to prove that no arithmetical errors have been made up to this point.

E. The data in the Adjusted Trial Balance columns are extended to the Income Statement and Balance Sheet columns of the work sheet. After all of the balances have been extended, each of the four columns is totaled. The net income or the net loss for the period is the amount of the difference between the totals of the two Income Statement columns. This net income or net loss is entered on the work sheet so that the Income Statement debit and credit columns and the Balance Sheet debit and credit columns balance.

II. Financial Statements.

A. The Income Statement columns of the work sheet are the source for all of the data reported on the income statement.

B. The work sheet is the source for all the data reported on the statement of owner's equity, with the exception of any increases in the capital of a sole proprietorship which have occurred during the period. It is necessary to refer to the capital account in the ledger to determine the beginning balance and any such additional investments.

C. The work sheet is the source of all the data reported on the balance sheet, with the exception of the amount of a sole proprietor's capital, which can be obtained from the statement of owner's equity.

D. The balance sheet may be expanded to include additional subsections for current assets, plant assets, and current liabilities. Such a balance sheet is sometimes called a classified balance sheet.

1. Cash and other assets that are expected to be converted to cash or sold or used up within one year or less, through the normal operations of the business, are called current assets.

2. Plant assets include equipment, machinery, buildings, and land. The cost, accumulated depreciation, and book value of each major category of plant asset is normally reported on the balance sheet.

3. Liabilities that will be due within a short time (usually one year or less) and that are to be paid out of current assets are called current liabilities. Examples of current liabilities include short-term notes payable and accounts payable.

4. Liabilities that will not be due for a long time (usually more than one year) are called long-term liabilities or fixed liabilities. As they come due within one year and are to be paid, such liabilities become current. Examples include long-term notes payable and mortgage notes payable.

5. Owner's equity is the owner's claim against the assets of the business entity after the total liabilities have been deducted. The total liabilities of the business plus the owner's equity must equal total assets.

III. Journalizing and Posting Adjusting Entries.

A. At the end of the accounting period, the adjusting entries appearing in the work sheet are recorded in the journal and posted to the ledger.

B. The process of journalizing and posting adjusting journal entries at the end of the accounting period brings the ledger into agreement with the data reported on the financial statements.

IV. Nature of the Closing Process.

A. The balances of all revenue and expense accounts should be zero at the beginning of each period.

B. Because the balances of revenue and expense accounts are not carried forward, they are sometimes called temporary accounts or nominal accounts.

C. Because the balances of balance sheet accounts are carried forward from year to year, they are sometimes called real accounts.

D. To zero out the balances of the revenue and expense accounts at the end of the period, the balances of these accounts are transferred to an account called Income Summary.

    1. Income Summary is only used at the end of the period.

    2. Income Summary has no beginning or ending balance, but is used to clear the revenue and expense accounts. For this reason, Income Summary is sometimes called a clearing account.

F. The balance of the owner's drawing account is transferred at the end of the period to the owner's capital account.

G. Revenue, expense, and drawing account balances are transferred to the owner's capital account by a series of entries called closing entries. The process of transferring these balances to the owner's capital account is called the closing process.

H. The following four entries are required in order to close the temporary accounts of a sole proprietorship at the end of the period.

    1. Each revenue account is debited for the amount of its balance, and Income Summary is credited for the total revenue.

    2. Each expense account is credited for the amount of its balance, and Income Summary is debited for the total expense.

    3. Income Summary is debited for the amount of its balance (net income), and the capital account is credited for the same amount. (Debit and credit are reversed if there is a net loss.)

    4. The drawing account is credited for the amount of its balance, and the capital account is debited for the same amount.

I. After the closing entries have been journalized, the balance in the capital account will correspond to the amounts reported on the statement of owner's equity and the balance sheet. In addition, the revenue, expense, and drawing accounts will have zero balances.

J. The last procedure for a period is the preparation of a post-closing trial balance after all of the temporary accounts have been closed.

K. The purpose of the post-closing trial balance is to make sure the ledger is in balance at the beginning of the new accounting period. The accounts and amounts should agree exactly with the accounts and amounts listed on the balance sheet at the end of the period.

V. Fiscal Year.

A. The maximum length of an accounting period is usually one year, which includes a complete cycle of business activities.

B. The annual accounting period adopted by a business is known as its fiscal year.

C. An accounting period ending when a business's activities have reached the lowest point in its annual operating cycle is termed the natural business year.

D. The long-term financial history of a business may be shown by a succession of balance sheets, prepared every year. The history of operations for the intervening periods is represented in a series of income statements.

VI. Accounting Cycle.

A. The sequence of accounting procedures of a fiscal period is called the accounting cycle.

B. The basic steps of the accounting cycle are as follows:

1. Transactions analyzed and recorded in journal.
2. Transactions posted to ledger.
3. Trial balance prepared, adjustment data assembled, and work sheet completed.
4. Financial statements prepared.
5. Adjusting entries journalized and posted to ledger.
6. Closing entries journalized and posted to ledger.
7. Post-closing trial balance prepared.

C. The most important output of the accounting cycle is the financial statements.

ILLUSTRATIVE PROBLEM

Two years ago, K. L. Waters organized Star Realty as a sole proprietorship. At March 31, 1997, the end of the current fiscal year, the trial balance of Star Realty is as follows:

Star Realty
Trial Balance
March 31, 1997

Cash	$ 2,425	
Accounts Receivable	5,000	
Supplies	1,870	
Prepaid Insurance	620	
Office Equipment	32,650	
Accumulated Depreciation		$ 9,700
Accounts Payable		925
Unearned Fees		1,250
K.L. Waters, Capital		20,930
K.L. Waters, Drawing	10,200	
Fees Earned		39,125
Wages Expense	12,415	
Rent Expense	3,600	
Utilities Expense	2,715	
Miscellaneous Expense	435	
	$71,930	$71,930

The following adjustment data have been entered on the 10-column work sheet:

a. Supplies on hand at March 31, 1997, are $480.
b. Insurance premiums expired during the year are $315.
c. Depreciation of equipment during the year is $1,950.
d. Wages accrued but not paid at March 31, 1997, are $140.
e. Accrued fees earned but not recorded at March 31, 1997, are $1,000.
f. Unearned fees on March 31, 1997, are $750.

Instructions

1. Complete the 10-column work sheet.
2. Prepare an income statement, a statement of owner's equity (no additional investments were made during the year), and a balance sheet.
3. On the basis of the adjustment data in the work sheet, journalize the adjusting entries.
4. On the basis of the data in the work sheet, journalize the closing entries.

Solution

1.

	ACCOUNT TITLE	TRIAL BALANCE DEBIT	TRIAL BALANCE CREDIT	ADJUSTMENTS DEBIT	ADJUSTMENTS CREDIT	
1	Cash	2425				1
2	Accounts Receivable	5000		e) 1000		2
3	Supplies	1870			a) 1390	3
4	Prepaid Insurance	620			b) 315	4
5	Office Equipment	32650				5
6	Accumulated Depreciation		9700		c) 1950	6
7	Accounts Payable		925			7
8	Unearned Fees		1250	f) 500		8
9	K.L. Waters, Capital		20930			9
10	K.L. Waters, Drawing	10200				10
11	Fees Earned		39125		e) 1000	11
12					f) 500	12
13	Wages Expense	12415		d) 140		13
14	Rent Expense	3600				14
15	Utilities Expense	2715				15
16	Miscellaneous Expense	435				16
17		71930	71930			17
18	Supplies Expense			a) 1390		18
19	Insurance Expense			b) 315		19
20	Depreciation Expense			c) 1950		20
21	Wages Payable				d) 140	21
22				5295	5295	22
23	Net Income					23
24						24
25						25
26						26
27						27
28						28
29						29
30						30

Realty

Sheet

Ended March 31, 1997

	ADJUSTED TRIAL BALANCE		INCOME STATEMENT		BALANCE SHEET		
	DEBIT	CREDIT	DEBIT	CREDIT	DEBIT	CREDIT	
1	2425				2425		1
2	6000				6000		2
3	480				480		3
4	305				305		4
5	32650				32650		5
6		11650				11650	6
7		925				925	7
8		750				750	8
9		20930				20930	9
10	10200				10200		10
11		40625		40625			11
12							12
13	12555		12555				13
14	3600		3600				14
15	2715		2715				15
16	435		435				16
17							17
18	1390		1390				18
19	315		315				19
20	1950		1950				20
21		140				140	21
22	75020	75020	22960	40625	52060	34395	22
23			17665			17665	23
24			40625	40625	52060	52060	24
25							25
26							26
27							27
28							28
29							29
30							30

2.

Star Realty

Income Statement

For Year Ended March 31, 1997

Fees earned				4 0 6 2 5
Operating expenses:				
Wages expense	1 2 5 5 5			
Rent expense	3 6 0 0			
Utilities expense	2 7 1 5			
Depreciation expense	1 9 5 0			
Supplies expense	1 3 9 0			
Insurance expense	3 1 5			
Miscellaneous expense	4 3 5			
Total operating expenses			2 2 9 6 0	
Net income			1 7 6 6 5	

Star Realty

Statement of Owner's Equity

For Year Ended March 31, 1997

K.L. Waters, capital, April 1, 1996				2 0 9 3 0
Net income for the year	1 7 6 6 5			
Less withdrawals	1 0 2 0 0			
Increase in owner's equity				7 4 6 5
K.L. Waters, capital, March 31, 1997				2 8 3 9 5

Star Realty

Balance Sheet

March 31, 1997

Assets			
Current assets:			
Cash		2 4 2 5	
Accounts receivable		6 0 0 0	
Supplies		4 8 0	
Prepaid insurance		3 0 5	
Total current assets			9 2 1 0
Plant assets:			
Office equipment		3 2 6 5 0	
Less accumulated depreciation		1 1 6 5 0	2 1 0 0 0
Total assets			3 0 2 1 0

Liabilities			
Current liabilities:			
Accounts payable		9 2 5	
Unearned fees		7 5 0	
Wages payable		1 4 0	
Total liabilities			1 8 1 5
Owner's Equity			
K. L. Waters, capital			2 8 3 9 5
Total liabilities and			
owner's equity			3 0 2 1 0

JOURNAL

PAGE

	DATE		DESCRIPTION	POST. REF.	DEBIT	CREDIT	
1			*Adjusting Entries*				1
2	1997 Mar.	31	Supplies Expense		1 3 9 0		2
3			Supplies			1 3 9 0	3
4		31	Insurance Expense		3 1 5		4
5			Prepaid Insurance			3 1 5	5
6		31	Depreciation Expense		1 9 5 0		6
7			Accumulated Depreciation			1 9 5 0	7
8		31	Wages Expense		1 4 0		8
9			Wages Payable			1 4 0	9
10		31	Accounts Receivable		1 0 0 0		10
11			Fees Earned			1 0 0 0	11
12		31	Unearned Fees		5 0 0		12
13			Fees Earned			5 0 0	13
14							14
15			*Closing Entries*				15
16		31	Fees Earned		4 0 6 2 5		16
17			Income Summary			4 0 6 2 5	17
18		31	Income Summary		2 2 9 6 0		18
19			Wages Expense			1 2 5 5 5	19
20			Rent Expense			3 6 0 0	20
21			Utilities Expense			2 7 1 5	21
22			Miscellaneous Expense			4 3 5	22
23			Supplies Expense			1 3 9 0	23
24			Insurance Expense			3 1 5	24
25			Depreciation Expense			1 9 5 0	25
26		31	Income Summary		1 7 6 6 5		26
27			K.L. Waters, Capital			1 7 6 6 5	27
28		31	K.L. Waters, Capital		1 0 2 0 0		28
29			K.L. Waters, Drawing			1 0 2 0 0	29
30							30
31							31
32							32

MATCHING

Instructions: A list of terms and related statements appear below. From the list of terms, select the one that relates to each statement. Print its identifying letter in the space provided.

A. Accounting cycle
B. Accounts receivable
C. Adjusting entries
D. Adjusting process
E. Capital account
F. Closing entries
G. Closing process
H. Current asset

I. Fiscal year
J. Income summary
K. Long-term liability
L. Natural business year
M. Notes receivable
N. Post-closing trial balance
O. Unadjusted trial balance

_____   1. A liability that is not due within one year.

_____   2. The sequence of accounting procedures for processing transactions during a fiscal period.

_____   3. Cash or another asset that is expected to be converted to cash or sold or consumed within one year or less, through the normal operation of a business.

_____   4. Written claims against debtors who promise to pay the amount and possibly interest, at an agreed date, to a specified person or bearer.

_____   5. The process of transferring revenue, expenses, and drawing account balances to the owner's capital account by a series of entries.

_____   6. The balances are removed from the temporary accounts so that they will be ready for use in accumulating data for the following accounting period by means of (?).

_____   7. An account that is used for summarizing the data in the revenue and expense accounts at the end of the accounting period.

_____   8. A listing prepared in order to make sure that the ledger is in balance at the beginning of the new accounting period.

_____   9. The annual accounting period adopted by a business.

_____ 10. A period ending when a business's activities have reached the lowest point in its annual operating cycle.

TRUE / FALSE

Instructions: Indicate whether each of the following statements is true or false by placing a check mark in the appropriate column.

                                                               True   False

1. The balance of Accumulated Depreciation--Equipment is extended to the Income Statement columns of the work sheet. . . . . ____ ____

2. The difference between the debit and credit columns of the Income Statement section of the work sheet is normally larger than the difference between the debit and credit columns of the Balance Sheet section. . . . . ____ ____

3. The first item normally presented in the statement of owner's equity is the balance of the proprietor's capital account at the beginning of the period. . . . . ____ ____

4. The balance that is transferred from the income summary account to the capital account is the net income or net loss for the period. . . . . ____ ____

5. The balances of the accounts reported in the balance sheet are carried from year to year and are called temporary accounts. . . . . ____ ____

6. An account titled Income Summary is normally used for transferring the revenue and expense account balances to the owner's capital account at the end of the period. . . . ____ ____

7. If the Income Statement debit column is greater than the Income Statement credit column, the difference is net income. . . . . ____ ____

8. A type of working paper frequently used by accountants prior to the preparation of financial statements is called a post-closing trial balance. . . . . ____ ____

9. At the end of the period, the balances are removed from the temporary accounts and the net effect is recorded in the permanent account by means of closing entries. . . . . ____ ____

10. The annual accounting period adopted by a business is known as its fiscal year. . . . . ____ ____

MULTIPLE CHOICE

Instructions: Circle the best answer for each of the following questions.

1. A work sheet is completed by:
   a. extending the adjusted trial balance amounts to the Income Statement and Balance Sheet columns
   b. totaling the Adjustment columns
   c. extending the work sheet adjustments to the Adjusted Trial Balance columns
   d. footing the trial balance

2. If the Income Statement credit column is greater than the Income Statement debit column:
   a. a net income exists
   b. a net loss exists
   c. an asset account is debited
   d. a liability account is credited

3. Notes receivable are written claims against:
   a. creditors
   b. owner's equity
   c. debtors
   d. assets

4. The maximum length of an accounting period is normally:
   a. 6 months
   b. 1 year
   c. 2 years
   d. 3 years

5. The complete sequence of accounting procedures for a fiscal period is frequently called the:
   a. work sheet process
   b. opening and closing cycle
   c. accounting cycle
   d. fiscal cycle

EXERCISE 4-1

The account titles and Adjustments columns of the work sheet for Sally's Small Engine Repair are listed below.

Sally's Small Engine Repair
Work Sheet
For Month Ended August 31, 19--

	Adjustments			
	Debit		Credit	
Cash				
Accounts Receivable	(e)	3,200		
Supplies			(c)	700
Prepaid Rent			(b)	560
Tools/Equipment				
Accumulated Depreciation			(d)	1,000
Accounts Payable				
Sally Sand, Capital				
Sally Sand, Drawing				
Repair Fees			(e)	3,200
Salary Expense	(a)	1,500		
Miscellaneous Expense				
Salaries Payable			(a)	1,500
Rent Expense	(b)	560		
Supplies Expense	(c)	700		
Depreciation Expense	(d)	1,000		

Instructions: Prepare journal entries for the adjustments indicated for Sally's Small Engine Repair.

JOURNAL   PAGE

	DATE		DESCRIPTION	POST. REF.	DEBIT	CREDIT	
1							1
2							2
3							3
4							4
5							5
6							6
7							7
8							8
9							9
10							10
11							11
12							12
13							13
14							14

Name: _____

EXERCISE 4-2

Instructions: The journal, the income summary account, the service fees account, the salary expense account, and the supplies expense account of Tony Brown as of March 31, the first month of the current fiscal year, follow. In the journal, prepare the entries to close Brown's revenue and expense accounts into the income summary account. Then post to the ledger.

JOURNAL

PAGE _____

	DATE		DESCRIPTION	POST. REF.	DEBIT	CREDIT	
1							1
2							2
3							3
4							4
5							5
6							6
7							7
8							8
9							9
10							10
11							11
12							12
13							13
14							14
15							15
16							16
17							17
18							18
19							19
20							20
21							21
22							22
23							23
24							24
25							25
26							26
27							27
28							28

ACCOUNT   *Income Summary*   ACCOUNT NO.   45

DATE		ITEM	POST. REF.	DEBIT	CREDIT	BALANCE	
						DEBIT	CREDIT

ACCOUNT   *Service Fees*   ACCOUNT NO.   50

DATE		ITEM	POST. REF.	DEBIT	CREDIT	BALANCE	
						DEBIT	CREDIT
19-- Mar.	15		5		4 8 5 0		4 8 5 0
	31		6		14 3 7 5		19 2 2 5

ACCOUNT   *Salary Expense*   ACCOUNT NO.   58

DATE		ITEM	POST. REF.	DEBIT	CREDIT	BALANCE	
						DEBIT	CREDIT
19-- Mar.	31		5	8 5 5 0		8 5 5 0	

ACCOUNT   *Supplies Expense*   ACCOUNT NO.   67

DATE		ITEM	POST. REF.	DEBIT	CREDIT	BALANCE	
						DEBIT	CREDIT
19-- Mar.	15		5	2 4 3 0		2 4 3 0	
	25		6	1 7 2 0		4 1 5 0	
	31		6	1 2 8 0		5 4 3 0	

PROBLEM 4-1

The partially completed ten-column work sheet of Castle Shop for the fiscal year ended April 30, 19--, appears on the following page. The following adjustment data have been entered in the Adjustments columns of the work sheet:

(a) Supplies on hand as of April 30, 19--, 1,800.
(b) Rent prepaid for 12 months on April 1, $9,504.
(c) Depreciation on tools and equipment during the year, $1,000.
(d) Wages accrued but not paid as of April 30, 19--, $2,000.
(e) Accrued fees earned but not recorded as of April 30, 19--, $3,000.
(f) Unearned fees as of April 30, 19--, $1,500.

Instructions:

(1) Complete the ten-column work sheet.
(2) Prepare an income statement, statement of owner's equity, and a balance sheet.

Castle

Work

For the Year

	ACCOUNT TITLE	TRIAL BALANCE DEBIT	TRIAL BALANCE CREDIT	ADJUSTMENTS DEBIT	ADJUSTMENTS CREDIT	
1	Cash	1 0 0 5 6				1
2	Accounts Receivable	7 9 3 8		(e) 3 0 0 0		2
3	Supplies	3 0 0 0			(a) 1 2 0 0	3
4	Prepaid Rent	9 5 0 4			(b) 7 9 2	4
5	Tools & Equipment	2 3 8 1 4				5
6	Accumulated Depreciation		1 6 7 4		(c) 1 0 0 0	6
7	Accounts Payable		7 7 6 4			7
8	Unearned Fees		2 0 0 0	(f) 5 0 0		8
9	Castle, Capital		3 8 8 1 8			9
10	Castle, Drawing	3 5 2 8				10
11	Service Fees		3 1 3 0 8		(e) 3 0 0 0	11
12					(f) 5 0 0	12
13	Wages Expense	1 7 3 7 6		(d) 2 0 0 0		13
14	Miscellaneous Expense	6 3 4 8				14
15		8 1 5 6 4	8 1 5 6 4			15
16						16
17	Wages Payable				(d) 2 0 0 0	17
18	Rent Expense			(b) 7 9 2		18
19	Supplies Expense			(a) 1 2 0 0		19
20	Depreciation Expense			(c) 1 0 0 0		20
21				8 4 9 2	8 4 9 2	21

Shop

Sheet

Ended April 30, 19--

	ADJUSTED TRIAL BALANCE		INCOME STATEMENT		BALANCE SHEET		
	DEBIT	CREDIT	DEBIT	CREDIT	DEBIT	CREDIT	
1							1
2							2
3							3
4							4
5							5
6							6
7							7
8							8
9							9
10							10
11							11
12							12
13							13
14							14
15							15
16							16
17							17
18							18
19							19
20							20
21							21
22							22
23							23
24							24
25							25
26							26
27							27
28							28
29							29
30							30
31							31

PROBLEM 4-2

Instructions:

(1) On the basis of the data in the Adjustments columns of the work sheet in Problem 4 -1, journalize the adjusting entries.

(2) On the basis of the data in the Income Statement and Balance Sheet columns of the work sheet in Problem 4-1, journalize the closing entries.

JOURNAL

PAGE

	DATE	DESCRIPTION	POST. REF.	DEBIT	CREDIT	
1						1
2						2
3						3
4						4
5						5
6						6
7						7
8						8
9						9
10						10
11						11
12						12
13						13
14						14
15						15
16						16
17						17
18						18
19						19
20						20
21						21
22						22
23						23
24						24
25						25
26						26
27						27
28						28

CONTINUING PROBLEM

The work sheet for Egor the Magician at the end of 1996, on the next two pages, shows the trial balance, adjustments, and adjusted trial balance.

Instructions:

(6) Complete the work sheet.

(7) Prepare an income statement, a statement of owner's equity, and a balance sheet.

(8) Journalize the adjusting entries and post them to the ledger on pages 42-54.

(9) Journalize the closing entries and post them to the ledger on pages 42-54.

| | ACCOUNT TITLE | TRIAL BALANCE | | ADJUSTMENTS | |
		DEBIT	CREDIT	DEBIT	CREDIT
1	Cash	9 9 5 6			
2	Fees Receivable	6 0 8 6			
3	Supplies & Props	1 2 6 8			(b) 9 0 3
4	Office Supplies	7 8 9			(a) 5 7 9
5	Prepaid Insurance	2 0 0 0			(c) 1 4 5 0
6	Furniture & Fixtures	1 3 4 0 0			
7	Equipment--Stage	1 2 0 0 0			
8	Accounts Payable		1 5 8 0		
9	Theater Services Payable				(e) 8 5 0
10	Subcontractors Payable				(f) 6 0 0
11	Notes Payable		6 5 0 0		
12	E. J. Gribbet, Capital		2 1 8 5 2		
13	E. J. Gribbet, Drawing	4 0 0			
14	Fees Earned		3 1 3 0 0		
15	Theater Services Expense	4 0 0 0		(e) 8 5 0	
16	Subcontractor Expense	2 4 6 0		(f) 6 0 0	
17	Van Expense	3 2 5 0			
18	Cosmetics Expense	4 2 8			
19	Rent Expense	4 8 0 0			
20	Telephone Expense	3 9 5			
21		6 1 2 3 2	6 1 2 3 2		
22	Office Supplies Expense			(a) 5 7 9	
23	Supplies & Props Expense			(b) 9 0 3	
24	Insurance Expense			(c) 1 4 5 0	
25	Interest Expense			(d) 1 0 5	
26	Interest Payable				(d) 1 0 5
27	Depr. Exp.--Furniture & Fixtures			(g) 2 6 8 0	
28	Accum. Depr.--Furniture & Fix.				(g) 2 6 8 0
29	Depr. Exp.--Equipment			(h) 2 4 0 0	
30	Accum. Depr.--Equipment				(h) 2 4 0 0
31				9 5 6 7	9 5 6 7
32					
33					

Magician
Sheet
December 31, 1996

	ADJUSTED TRIAL BALANCE		INCOME STATEMENT		BALANCE SHEET		
	DEBIT	CREDIT	DEBIT	CREDIT	DEBIT	CREDIT	
1	9 9 5 6						1
2	6 0 8 6						2
3	3 6 5						3
4	2 1 0						4
5	5 5 0						5
6	1 3 4 0 0						6
7	1 2 0 0 0						7
8		1 5 8 0					8
9		8 5 0					9
10		6 0 0					10
11		6 5 0 0					11
12		2 1 8 5 2					12
13	4 0 0						13
14		3 1 3 0 0					14
15	4 8 5 0						15
16	3 0 6 0						16
17	3 2 5 0						17
18	4 2 8						18
19	4 8 0 0						19
20	3 9 5						20
21							21
22	5 7 9						22
23	9 0 3						23
24	1 4 5 0						24
25	1 0 5						25
26		1 0 5					26
27	2 6 8 0						27
28		2 6 8 0					28
29	2 4 0 0						29
30		2 4 0 0					30
31	6 7 8 6 7	6 7 8 6 7					31
32							32
33							33

JOURNAL

PAGE _____

	DATE		DESCRIPTION	POST. REF.	DEBIT	CREDIT	
1							1
2							2
3							3
4							4
5							5
6							6
7							7
8							8
9							9
10							10
11							11
12							12
13							13
14							14
15							15
16							16
17							17
18							18
19							19
20							20
21							21
22							22
23							23
24							24
25							25
26							26
27							27
28							28
29							29
30							30
31							31
32							32

JOURNAL

PAGE

	DATE		DESCRIPTION	POST. REF.	DEBIT	CREDIT	
1							1
2							2
3							3
4							4
5							5
6							6
7							7
8							8
9							9
10							10
11							11
12							12
13							13
14							14
15							15
16							16
17							17
18							18
19							19
20							20
21							21
22							22
23							23
24							24
25							25
26							26
27							27
28							28
29							29
30							30
31							31
32							32

5 Accounting Systems, Internal Controls, and Special Journals

QUIZ AND TEST HINTS

The following hints may be helpful to you in preparing for a quiz or a test over the material covered in Chapter 5.

1. You should be familiar with the terminology related to accounting systems and internal controls. Pay close attention to the terms related to a business' internal control structure. Carefully review the Key Terms before any quiz or test.

2. Chapter 5 focuses on the recording of transactions using subsidiary ledgers and special journals. Carefully review the content and format of the various special journals illustrated throughout the chapter.

3. Your instructor may provide a list of transactions and ask you to identify the journal in which each transaction would be recorded. Remember, if a transaction does not fit into any of the special journals, it would be recorded in the general journal. In addition, any time the accounts receivable or accounts payable accounts are debited or credited, their related subsidiary ledgers must also be posted. The diagram at the top of page 174 is helpful in indicating the types of transactions recorded in each special journal. In addition, the Illustrative Problem in the Chapter Review is typical of the problems that commonly appear on quizzes and tests.

CHAPTER OUTLINE

I. Principles of Accounting Systems.

A. The methods and procedures for recording and reporting financial information make up a business's accounting system.

1. Each accounting system is uniquely designed for a business because of differences in management's information needs, the type and number of transactions to be recorded, and the information needs of external users of financial statements.

2. Although accounting systems vary from business to business, this chapter discusses a number of broad principles that apply to all systems.

B. A major consideration in designing an accounting system is balancing the benefits against the cost of the information. In general, the benefits should be at least equal to the cost of producing the information.

C. To be effective, the reports generated by an accounting system must be prepared in a timely, clear, and concise manner.

D. As the environment in which a business operates changes, an accounting system must be able to adapt to the changing needs for information for all levels of management.

E. The detailed policies and procedures used to direct operations toward desired goals, ensure accurate financial reports, and ensure compliance with applicable laws and regulations are called internal controls. An accounting system should be designed with adequate internal controls.

II. Accounting Systems Installation and Revision.

A. The job of installing or changing an accounting system is made up of three phases: (1) analysis, (2) design, and (3) implementation.

B. The goal of systems analysis is to determine information needs, the sources of such information, any weaknesses in the procedures, and data processing methods being used.

   1. The source of much of the information for systems analysis is found in a firm's <u>Systems Manual</u>.

   2. The data needed by a business to satisfy its information needs is called its database.

C. Systems design requires creativity, imagination, and the ability to evaluate alternative data processing methods.

D. The final phase of systems installation is to carry out, or implement, the systems design.

   1. All personnel responsible for operating the system must be carefully trained and supervised until the system is fully operational.

   2. Many companies implement new or revised systems in stages over a period of time.

   3. Some companies conduct parallel tests in which the old and new systems are run at the same time.

III. Internal Control.

A. The objectives of internal control are to provide reasonable assurance that:

   1. Operations are managed to achieve desired goals.

   2. Financial reports are accurate.

   3. Laws and regulations are complied with.

B. An internal control framework consists of five major elements:

   1. Control environment

   2. Risk assessment

   3. Control procedures

   4. Monitoring

   5. Information and communication.

C. A business's control environment is the overall attitude of management and employees about the importance of controls. Some of the factors that influence a business's control environment include management's philosophy and operating style, the business's organizational structure, and personnel policies and procedures.

D. Risk assessment involves identifying significant risks to the business, analyzing such risks, and taking actions to minimize the affect of risks on the business.

E. Control procedures provide reasonable assurance that business goals will be achieved and fraud will be prevented. Some control procedures that can be integrated throughout the accounting system include:

   1. The successful operation of an accounting system requires competent personnel who are able to perform the duties to which they are assigned. It is also advisable to rotate clerical personnel periodically from job to job and require mandatory vacations.

   2. If employees are to work efficiently, their responsibilities must be clearly defined.

   3. To decrease the possibility of errors, inefficiency, and fraud, responsibility for a sequence of related operations should be divided among two or more persons.

   4. To reduce the possibility of errors and fraud, the following functions should be separated:

      a. Accounting for the business's transactions.

      b. Custody of the firm's assets.

      c. Engaging in the firm's operating activities.

   5. Proofs and security measures, such as the use of cash registers and fidelity bonds, safeguard business assets and ensure reliable accounting data.

F. Monitoring the internal control system locates deficiencies and improves control effectiveness.

G. Information and communication are an essential element of an organization's internal control. Information and communication are needed by management to guide operations and ensure compliance with reporting, legal, and regulatory requirements.

IV. Subsidiary Ledgers and Special Journals.

A. When a business has a large number of similar transactions, subsidiary ledgers and special journals may be used to more efficiently record transactions.

B. When there are a large number of accounts with a common characteristic, it is common to place them in a separate ledger called a subsidiary ledger. The primary ledger, which contains all the balance sheet and income statement accounts, is then called the general ledger.

C. Each subsidiary ledger is represented by a summarizing account in the general ledger called a controlling account. The sum of the balances of the accounts in a subsidiary ledger must agree with the balance of the related controlling account.

D. The subsidiary ledger containing the individual accounts for credit customers is called the accounts receivable subsidiary ledger or customers ledger. The related controlling account in the general ledger is Accounts Receivable.

E. The individual accounts with creditors are arranged in alphabetical order in a subsidiary ledger called the accounts payable subsidiary ledger or creditors ledger. The related controlling account in the general ledger is Accounts Payable.

F. One method of processing data more efficiently is to expand the two-column journal to a multicolumn journal. Each amount column included in a multicolumn journal is used only for recording transactions that affect a certain account. Such journals are known as special journals. The two-column journal form used in previous chapters is known as the general journal or simply the journal.

G. The special journals most commonly found in business are as follows:

  1. The revenue (sales) journal is used only for recording fees earned on account. The revenue journal normally has one column for debiting Accounts Receivable and crediting Fees Earned.

   a. As services are rendered on account they are entered in the revenue journal, the debits to Accounts Receivable are posted to the subsidiary ledger.

   b. Periodically the column of the revenue journal is totaled and posted to the general ledger accounts for Accounts Receivable and Fees Earned.

  2. All transactions involving cash receipts are recorded in a cash receipts journal. The special columns of the cash receipts journal normally include an Other (or Miscellaneous) Accounts Credit column, a Fees Earned Credit column, an Accounts Receivable Credit column, and a Cash Debit column.

   a. Amounts in the Other Accounts Credit column are posted to the appropriate general ledger accounts at regular intervals during the month.

   b. Individual credits in the Accounts Receivable Credit column are posted to the accounts receivable subsidiary ledger at regular intervals.

   c. The totals of the special columns are posted to the general ledger accounts on a periodic basis, usually at the end of each month.

   d. After all posting has been completed for the month, the sum of the accounts receivable subsidiary ledger balances and the general ledger accounts receivable balance should be compared and any errors should be corrected.

      e. Internal control is enhanced by separating the function of recording credit sales in the revenue journal from recording cash collections in the cash receipts journal.

   3. The purchases journal is designed to record all purchases on account. The purchases journal has an Accounts Payable Credit column and various debit columns such as a Store Supplies Debit column, and an Other (or Miscellaneous) Accounts Debit column.

      a. The individual credits to accounts payable in the purchases journal are posted to the accounts payable subsidiary ledger as the transactions occur.

      b. The individual amounts in the Other Accounts Debit column are posted to the appropriate general ledger accounts at regular intervals during the month.

      c. The totals of the special columns are posted to the general ledger accounts on a periodic basis, usually at the end of each month.

   4. The cash payments journal is designed to record all cash payments. The special columns of the cash payments journal normally include an Other (or Miscellaneous) Accounts Debit column, Accounts Payable Debit column, and Cash Credit column.

      a. Individual debits to accounts payable are posted to the accounts payable subsidiary ledger at regular intervals during the month.

      b. Amounts in the Other Accounts Debit column are also posted to appropriate general ledger accounts at regular intervals.

      c. At the end of the month, the special columns are totaled and posted to the accounts in the general ledger.

      d. After all posting has been completed for the month, the sum of the balances in the accounts payable subsidiary ledger should be compared with the balance in the general ledger accounts payable account, and any errors should be corrected.

      e. Internal control is enhanced by separating the function of recording purchases in the purchases journal from recording cash payments in the cash payments journal.

V. Adapting Accounting Systems.

  A. Subsidiary ledgers may be used by a business for other accounts, in addition to Accounts Receivable and Accounts Payable.

   1. Subsidiary ledgers are used for accounts that consist of a large number of individual items, each of which has unique characteristics.

   2. Examples of other subsidiary ledgers include a notes receivable (or payable) subsidiary ledger and an equipment subsidiary ledger.

  B. Businesses may modify special journals by adding one or more columns for recording transactions that occur frequently.

   1. A revenue journal is often modified for the collection of sales tax payable.

2. Regardless of the modifications, the basic principles and procedures discussed in this chapter apply.

VI. Computerized Accounting Systems.

    A. The concepts described in this chapter for a manual system also apply to computerized systems.

    B. Computerized accounting systems have three main advantages.

        1. Computerized accounting systems simplify the record keeping process since transactions are simultaneously recorded in journals and posted electronically to general and subsidiary ledger accounts.

        2. Computerized accounting systems are generally more accurate than manual systems since common mistakes, such as math errors, posting errors, and journal recording errors are less likely to occur.

        3. Computerized systems provide management with more timely, current account balance information for decision making, since account balances are normally posted as the transactions occur.

    C. Computerized accounting systems consist of various subsystems such as accounts receivable and accounts payable subsystems.

    D. A computerized accounts receivable subsystem for Computer King is illustrated in Exhibit 8 of the text.

ILLUSTRATIVE PROBLEM

Selected transactions of O'Malley Co. for the month of May are as follows:

a. May   1   Issued Check No. 1001 in payment of rent for May, $1,200.

b.   2   Purchased store supplies on account from McMillan Co., $1,850.

c.   4   Issued Check No. 1003 in payment of utility expenses, $320.

d.   8   Billed Waller Co. for services rendered, Invoice No. 51, $4,500.

e.   9   Issued Check No. 1005 for office supplies purchased, $450.

f.   10   Received cash for office supplies sold to employees at cost, $120.

g.   11   Purchased office equipment on account from Fender Office Products, $15,000.

h.   12   Issued credit for $400 to Waller Co. to settle a dispute over the services performed.

i.   12   Issued Check No. 1010 in payment of the store supplies purchased from McMillan Co. on May 2.

j.   16   Billed Riese Co. for services rendered, Invoice No. 58, $8,000.

k.   18   Received $4,100 from Waller Co. in payment of May 8 invoice.

l.   20   Invested additional cash in the business, $10,000.

m.   25   Rendered services for cash, $15,900.

n.   30   Issued Check No. 1040 for withdrawal of cash for personal use, $1,000.

o.   30   Issued Check No. 1041 in payment of miscellaneous expenses, $150.

p. May 30 Issued Check No. 1042 in payment of office and sales salaries for May, $15,800.

q. 31 Journalized adjusting entries from the work sheet prepared for the fiscal year ended May 31.

O'Malley Co. maintains a revenue journal, a cash receipts journal, a purchases journal, a cash payments journal, and a general journal. In addition, accounts receivable and accounts payable subsidiary ledgers are used.

Instructions

1. Indicate the journal in which each of the preceding transactions (a) through (q) would be recorded.
2. Indicate whether an account in the accounts receivable or accounts payable subsidiary ledgers would be affected for each of the preceding transactions.
3. Journalize transactions (b), (c), (d), (h), (i), and (k) in the appropriate journals.

Solution

1.	**Journal**	**2. Subsidiary Ledger**
a.	Cash payments journal	
b.	Purchases journal	Accounts payable ledger
c.	Cash payments journal	
d.	Revenue journal	Accounts receivable ledger
e.	Cash payments journal	
f.	Cash receipts journal	
g.	Purchases journal	Accounts payable ledger
h.	General journal	Accounts receivable ledger
i.	Cash payments journal	Accounts payable ledger
j.	Revenue journal	Accounts receivable ledger
k.	Cash receipts journal	Accounts receivable ledger
l.	Cash receipts journal	
m.	Cash receipts journal	
n.	Cash payments journal	
o.	Cash payments journal	
p.	Cash payments journal	
q.	General journal	

3. Transaction (b):

PURCHASES JOURNAL

DATE	ACCOUNT CREDITED	POST. REF.	ACCOUNTS PAYABLE CR.	STORE SUPPLIES DR.	OTHER ACCOUNTS DR.
May 2	McMillan Co.		1 8 5 0 00	1 8 5 0 00	

Transactions (c) and (i):

CASH PAYMENTS JOURNAL

DATE	CK. NO.	ACCOUNT DEBITED	POST. REF.	OTHER ACCOUNTS DR.	ACCOUNTS PAYABLE DR.	CASH CR.
May 4	1003	Utility Expense		320 00		320 00
12	1010	McMillan Co.			1850 00	1850 00

Transaction (d):

REVENUE JOURNAL

DATE	INVOICE NO.	ACCOUNT DEBITED	POST. REF.	ACCTS. REC. DR. FEES EARNED CR.
May 8	51	Waller Co.		4500 00

Transaction (h):

JOURNAL   PAGE

DATE	DESCRIPTION	POST. REF.	DEBIT	CREDIT
May 12	Fees Earned		400 00	
	Accounts Receivable--Waller Co.			400 00
	Credit to settle dispute over			
	services performed.			

Transaction (k):

CASH RECEIPTS JOURNAL

DATE	ACCOUNT CREDITED	POST. REF.	OTHER ACCOUNTS CR.	FEES EARNED CR.	ACCOUNTS REC. CR.	CASH DR.
May 18	Waller Co.				4100 00	4100 00

MATCHING

Instructions: A list of terms and related statements appear below. From the list of terms, select the one that relates to each statement. Print its identifying letter in the space provided.

A. Accounts payable subsidiary ledger	G. General ledger
B. Accounts receivable subsidiary ledger	H. Internal control framework
C. Accounting system	I. Internal controls
D. Cash payments journal	J. Purchases journal
E. Cash receipts journal	K. Revenue journal
F. Controlling account	L. Subsidiary ledger

_____ 1. The detailed policies and procedures used to direct operations toward desired goals, ensure accurate financial reports, and ensure compliance with applicable laws and regulations.

_____ 2. A special journal used for recording all items purchased on account.

_____ 3. A special journal used for recording all cash payments.

_____ 4. A supplementary record used to provide detailed information for a control account in the general ledger.

_____ 5. The primary ledger, containing all of the balance sheet and income statement accounts.

_____ 6. A general ledger account which is supported by information in a subsidiary ledger.

_____ 7. A subsidiary ledger containing an account with each creditor.

_____ 8. A subsidiary ledger containing an account with each credit customer.

_____ 9. A special journal used exclusively for recording fees earned on account.

_____ 10. A special journal used to record all cash receipts.

_____ 11. The methods and procedures for recording and reporting financial information.

_____ 12. Consists of the following five elements: control environment, risk assessment, control procedures, monitoring, and information and communication.

TRUE / FALSE

Instructions: Indicate whether each of the following statements is true or false by placing a check mark in the appropriate column.

                                                                    True   False

1. The goal of systems design is to determine information needs, the sources of such information, and the deficiencies in procedures and data processing methods presently used. . . . .   _____ _____

True   False

2. Responsibility for maintaining the accounting records should be separated from the responsibility for custody of the firm's assets. . . . . _____ _____

3. Transactions involving the payment of cash for any purpose usually are recorded in a cash journal. . . . . _____ _____

4. When there are a large number of individual accounts with a common characteristic, it is common to place them in a separate ledger called a detail ledger. . . . . _____ _____

5. For each transaction recorded in the purchases journal, the credit is entered in the "Accounts Payable Cr." column. . . _____ _____

6. Acquisitions on account which are not provided for in special debit columns are recorded in the purchases journal in the final set of columns called "Misc." . . . . _____ _____

7. Debits to creditors accounts for invoices paid are recorded in the "Accounts Payable Dr." column of the cash payments journal. . . . . _____ _____

8. At the end of each month, the total of the amount column of the revenue journal is posted as a debit to Cash and a credit to Fees Earned. _____ _____

9. Each amount in the "Other Accounts Cr." column of the cash receipts journal must be posted individually to an appropriate general ledger account. . . . . _____ _____

10. Accounting systems must be continually reviewed for possible revisions in order to keep pace with the changing information needs of businesses. . . . . _____ _____

11. Many special journals are modified in practice to adapt them to meet the specific needs of a business. . . . . . . _____ _____

12. The high cost of microcomputers makes computerized processing of accounting data unaffordable to small- and medium-size businesses. . . . . _____ _____

13. After all posting has been completed for the month, if the sum of balances in the accounts receivable subsidiary ledger does not agree with the balance of the accounts receivable account in the general ledger, the errors must be located and corrected. . . . . _____ _____

14. The primary ledger that contains all of the balance sheet and income statement accounts is called the general ledger. _____ _____

15. If a business uses computers to process accounting data, the concepts and methods for a manual system are not relevant. . . . . _____ _____

MULTIPLE CHOICE

Instructions: Circle the best answer for each of the following questions.

1. The job of installing or changing an accounting system is made up of three phases: (1) analysis, (2) design, and (3):
   a. installation
   b. verification
   c. management
   d. implementation

2. Which of the following is not an element of the internal control framework?
   a. risk assessment
   b. control environment
   c. management
   d. monitoring

3. The individual amounts in the "Accounts Payable Cr." column of the purchases journal are posted to the appropriate account in the:
   a. general ledger
   b. general journal
   c. accounts payable subsidiary ledger
   d. accounts payable journal

4. Which of the following transactions should be recorded in the revenue journal?
   a. the purchase of supplies on account
   b. the receipt of cash for services rendered
   c. the billing of fees earned on account
   d. the payment of an account payable

5. The controlling account in the general ledger that summarizes the individual accounts with creditors in a subsidiary ledger is titled:
   a. Accounts Payable
   b. Purchases
   c. Accounts Receivable
   d. Sales Returns and Allowances

6. Internal control policies and procedures provide reasonable assurance that:
   a. all liabilities will be paid
   b. a net income will be earned
   c. they are being effectively applied
   d. business goals will be achieved

7. The controlling account for the customers ledger is:

    a. Cash

    b. Accounts Receivable

    c. Accounts Payable

    d. Fees Earned

8. When are the amounts entered in the Accounts Receivable Cr. column of the revenue journal posted:

    a. at regular intervals

    b. at the end of each month

    c. whenever the accounts receivable control account is posted

    d. whenever adjusting entries are prepared and posted

EXERCISE 5-1

Wilco Co. is a computer consulting business. Wilco Co. maintains a cash receipts journal, cash payments journal, revenue journal, purchases journal, and general journal. Selected transactions of Wilco Co. for the month of February are listed below.

Instructions: Indicate the journal in which each of the transactions would be recorded.

Transaction	Journal
Feb. 1. Purchased supplies on account from Winkler's Wholesale. . . .	_____
6. Wilco Co. rendered services to Phil's Grocery Store for cash. .	_____
8. Received credit from Winkler's Wholesale for supplies returned.	_____
11. Issued check no. 1099 for payment of supplies purchased on February 1, less return on February 8, to Winkler's Wholesale.	_____
18. Billed Sally's Shop-N-Save for services rendered on account. .	_____
28. Received full payment on account from Tony's Grocery Store.	_____

EXERCISE 5-2

The following transactions were completed by Mezza Co. during October of the current year.

Oct.   **3.** Billed Blanders Co. for services rendered on account, Invoice No. 2883, $8,250.

4. Billed Montana Co. for services rendered on account, Invoice No. 2884, $5,000.

8. Issued to Blanders Co. a credit for $1,000 due to a misunderstanding of services performed.

13. Received cash from Blanders Co. in payment of Invoice No. 2883.

14. Received cash from Montana Co. in payment of Invoice No. 2884.

25. Received cash for office supplies returned to the manufacturer, $300.

31. Services rendered for cash in October, $39,600.

Instructions: Record the above transactions in the revenue journal, cash receipts journal, or general journal given below.

REVENUE JOURNAL

DATE	INVOICE NO.	ACCOUNT DEBITED	POST. REF.	ACCTS. REC. DR. FEES EARNED CR.

CASH RECEIPTS JOURNAL

DATE	ACCOUNT CREDITED	POST. REF.	OTHER ACCOUNTS CR.	ACCOUNTS REC. CR.	CASH DR.

JOURNAL

DATE	DESCRIPTION	POST. REF.	DEBIT	CREDIT

EXERCISE 5-3

The following transactions related to purchases and cash payments were completed by Kent Company during March of the current year.

March	2.	Purchased store supplies on account from Eastside Co., $1,250.
	8.	Purchased store supplies on account from Bench Co., $600.
	9.	Received credit from Eastside Co., $300 for supplies returned.
	16.	Issued Check No. 230 to Bench Co. in payment of the balance due.
	20.	Issued Check No. 231 for a cash purchase of office supplies, $250.
	27.	Issued Check No. 232 to Eastside Co. in payment of the balance due.
	28.	Purchased the following on account from James & Co.: store supplies, $800, office supplies, $100.

Instructions: Record the above transactions in the purchases journal, cash payments journal, or the general journal given on the next page.

PURCHASES JOURNAL

DATE	ACCOUNT CREDITED	POST. REF.	ACCOUNTS PAYABLE CR.	STORE SUPPLIES DR.	OFFICE SUPPLIES DR.	OTHER ACCOUNTS DR.

CASH PAYMENTS JOURNAL

DATE	CK. NO.	ACCOUNT DEBITED	POST. REF.	OTHER ACCOUNTS DR.	ACCOUNTS PAYABLE DR.	CASH CR.

JOURNAL   PAGE

DATE	DESCRIPTION	POST. REF.	DEBIT	CREDIT

PROBLEM 5-1

Kleco Co., an architectural services firm, completed the following transactions with customers on account during September of the current year.

Sept.   8.   Invoice No. 210 to Robert Poon, $1,220.
          12.   Invoice No. 225 to Jeff Lucas, $750.
          24.   Invoice No. 260 to Pamela Stark, $860.
          30.   Invoice No. 290 to Steve Kocan, $2,500.

Instructions:

(1) Record the above transactions in the revenue journal below.

(2) Post the individual items from the revenue journal to the T accounts for customers. Indicate that each item has been posted by placing a check mark (√) in the Post. Ref. column of the revenue journal.

(3) Post the total of the revenue journal to the T accounts for Accounts Receivable and Fees Earned. Indicate that the posting is completed by inserting the appropriate account numbers in the journal under the amount posted.

REVENUE JOURNAL

DATE	INVOICE NO.	ACCOUNT DEBITED	POST. REF.	ACCTS. REC. DR. FEES EARNED CR.

GENERAL LEDGER

Accounts Receivable 113

Fees Earned   411

ACCOUNTS RECEIVABLE LEDGER

Steve Kocan

Robert Poon

Jeff Lucas

Pamela Stark

(4) Determine that the sum of the balances of the individual accounts in the accounts receivable subsidiary ledger agrees with the balance of the accounts receivable controlling account in the general ledger by completing the following summary form.

Steve Kocan . . . . $ _____
Jeff Lucas . . . . _____
Robert Poon . . . . _____
Pamela Stark . . . . _____
Total accounts receivable . . . . . . $ _____

PROBLEM 5-2

Willbury's, a retail store, completed the following transactions with creditors on account during April of the current year.

April   **14.**   Purchased store supplies on account from Mills Co., $300.
           16.   Purchased office supplies on account from Quick Co., $175.
           22.   Purchased store equipment on account from Mills Co., $5,250.
           30.   Purchased store supplies on account from Mills Co., $280.

Instructions:

(1) Record the above transactions in the purchases journal below.

(2) Post the individual items from the purchases journal to the T accounts in the general and accounts payable subsidiary ledgers. Indicate that each item has been posted by placing a check mark (/) or an account number in the appropriate Post. Ref. column of the purchases journal.

(3) Post the totals of the purchases journal to the general ledger T accounts. Insert the appropriate account numbers in the journal under the amount posted.

PURCHASES JOURNAL

DATE	ACCOUNT CREDITED	POST. REF.	ACCOUNTS PAYABLE CR.	STORE SUPPLIES DR.	OFFICE SUPPLIES DR.	OTHER ACCOUNTS DR.		
						ACCOUNT	POST. REF.	AMOUNT

GENERAL LEDGER

Store Supplies	115		Office Supplies	116

Store Equipment	121		Accounts Payable	211

ACCTS. PAYABLE LEDGER

Mills Co.

Quick Co.

(4) Determine that the sum of the balances of the individual accounts in the accounts payable subsidiary ledger agrees with the balance of the accounts payable controlling account in the general ledger by completing the following summary form:

Mills Co.	$
Quick Co.	
Total accounts payable	$

PROBLEM 5-3

The "Totals" line and one other line of the purchases journal of Hamilton Co. for the month of October are shown below. Also shown are selected T accounts taken from Hamilton's general ledger.

Instructions:

(1) Verify the equality of the debits and the credits in Hamilton's purchases journal for October by completing the following schedule:

Debit Totals		Credit Totals	
Store Supplies	_____	Accounts Payable . . .	_____
Office Supplies	_____		
Other Accounts	_____		
Total	_____	Total	_____

(2) Post all amounts that require posting to the T accounts provided. Show the appropriate posting references in the purchases journal.

PURCHASES JOURNAL

DATE		POST. REF.	ACCOUNTS PAYABLE CR.	STORE SUPPLIES DR.	OFFICE SUPPLIES DR.	OTHER ACCOUNTS DR.		
						ACCOUNT	POST. REF.	AMOUNT
	29	✓	7,620			Store Equip.		7,620
	31		15,890	3,650	1,250			10,990

GENERAL LEDGER

Store Supplies   115

Office Supplies   116

Store Equipment   121

Accounts Payable 211

6

Accounting for Merchandising Businesses

QUIZ AND TEST HINTS

The following hints may be helpful to you in preparing for a quiz or a test over the material covered in this chapter.

1. This chapter introduces merchandising business terminology that you should know. Review the Key Terms.

2. You should be able to prepare general journal entries for the types of transactions illustrated in the chapter. Be sure you can compute purchases discounts and sales discounts. Review the chapter illustrations. The Illustrative Problem in the Chapter Review is an excellent review of the types of entries you might have to prepare.

3. The accounting for transportation costs can be confusing, but you will probably be required to prepare one or more journal entries, or answer one or more multiple-choice questions, involving such costs. Review the chapter discussion and illustration related to such costs.

4. The illustration of the journal entries for both the buyer and seller of merchandise on pages 215-216 of the chapter provides an excellent review. Often, instructors will require students to prepare journal entries based upon the same data for both the buyer and the seller.

5. Review the chart of accounts for a merchandising business as a basis for distinguishing the types of accounts used by merchandising businesses.

6. A major portion of this chapter describes the preparation of financial statements for a merchandising business. Particular emphasis is placed on preparing the income statement. Practice preparing the financial statements for Computer King using Exhibit 6. Your instructor may provide partially completed financial statements, and you will be required to complete the statements.

7. You should be able to prepare the adjusting and closing entries for a merchandising business. These entries are similar to those you prepared in earlier chapters.

8. If your instructor lectures on preparing a merchandising work sheet from the Appendix to the chapter, you may expect some questions related to the work sheet. Often times instructors provide a partially completed work sheet and require students to complete it. You may find it a helpful exercise to cover up portions of Exhibit 10, and see if you know how to complete the covered sections. Except for the merchandising related accounts, a merchandising business work sheet is similar to others you have prepared.

9. If your instructor lectures on the periodic inventory system using the appendix at the end of the text, you may have to prepare journal entries, work sheet, and financial statements using this system.

CHAPTER OUTLINE

I. **Nature of Merchandising Business.**

   A. The primary difference between service and merchandise businesses relates to the revenue activities of the businesses. The revenue generating activities of a service business involve the rendering of services to clients. The revenue generating activities of a merchandise business involve the purchasing and selling of merchandise to customers.

   B. The income statement of a merchandising business reports sales, cost of merchandise sold, and gross profit.

   C. Merchandise that is not sold at the end of an accounting period is called merchandise inventory, which is reported as a current asset on the balance sheet.

II. **Accounting for Purchases.**

   A. There are two systems for accounting for merchandise purchased for sale: perpetual and periodic.

   1. In a perpetual inventory system, each purchase or sale of merchandise is recorded in an inventory account. In this way, the inventory records always (perpetually) disclose the amount of merchandise on hand at any time and the amount sold.

   2. In the periodic inventory system, no attempt is made to keep detailed inventory records of the amounts on hand throughout the period.

      a. A detailed listing of merchandise inventory on hand (called a physical inventory) is prepared at the end of the accounting period.

      b. The physical inventory listing is used to determine the cost of the inventory on hand at the end of the period and the cost of the merchandise sold during the period.

   3. The use of computers and standard bar codes makes perpetual inventory systems practical for even small merchandise businesses. For this reason, the perpetual inventory system is used throughout this chapter.

   B. Under the perpetual inventory system, purchases of merchandise for sale are recorded in the merchandise account in the ledger by debiting Merchandise Inventory.

   C. The terms agreed upon by the buyer and the seller are normally indicated on the invoice or bill that the seller sends to the buyer. The terms agreed upon as to when payments for merchandise are to be made are called the credit terms.

  1. The credit period, during which the buyer is allowed to pay, begins with the date of the sale as shown by the date of the invoice or bill.

  2. If the payment is due within a stated number of days after the date of invoice, for example, 30 days, the terms may be expressed as n/30. If payment is due at the end of the month, the terms may be expressed as n/eom.

  3. The terms 2/10, n/30 mean that, although the credit period is thirty days, the buyer may deduct 2% of the amount of the invoice if payment is made within ten days of the invoice date.

D. Discounts taken by the buyer for early payment of an invoice are called purchases discounts.

  1. Purchases discounts are viewed as a reduction in the cost of the merchandise purchased.

  2. Since most buyers will take advantage of purchases discounts, buyers using perpetual inventory systems normally record merchandise purchases (debit Merchandise Inventory) at their net cost. Net cost is determined as the invoice price less any discounts.

E. If merchandise is returned or a price adjustment is requested by the buyer, the transaction is recorded as a credit to Merchandise Inventory.

  1. The details of the merchandise returned or the price adjustment requested are set forth by the buyer in a debit memorandum.

  2. When a buyer returns merchandise or has been granted an allowance prior to the payment of the invoice, the amount of the debit memorandum is deducted from the invoice amount before the purchases discount is computed.

III. Accounting for Sales.

A. Merchandise sales are recorded by the seller by a credit to a sales account.

  1. Cash sales are recorded by a debit to Cash and a credit to Sales.

  2. Sales to customers who use bank credit cards are recorded as cash sales.

  3. Sales of merchandise on account are recorded by a debit to Accounts Receivable and a credit to Sales.

  4. Sales made by use of nonbank credit cards are recorded as sales on account.

  5. Any service charges for handling bank or nonbank credit cards are debited to an expense account, Bank (Nonbank) Credit Card Expense.

B. Under the perpetual inventory system, the cost of merchandise sold and the reduction in merchandise inventory are also recorded on the date of sale.

1. The cost of merchandise sold account is debited and the merchandise inventory account is credited.

2. At the end of the period, the balance of the cost of merchandise sold account is reported on the income statement along with the related sales for the period.

C. The seller refers to the discounts taken by the buyer for early payment of an invoice as sales discounts. These discounts are recorded by debiting the sales discount account, which is viewed as a reduction in the amount initially recorded as Sales. In this sense, the sales discounts account can be thought of as a contra (or offsetting) account to Sales.

D. Merchandise sold that is returned by the buyer, or for which a price adjustment is made, is recorded by the seller by debiting Sales Returns and Allowances and crediting Accounts Receivable. In addition, under a perpetual inventory system Merchandise Inventory is debited and Cost of Merchandise Sold is credited for the cost of the merchandise returned.

1. A sales return and allowance is granted by the seller by issuing a credit memorandum.

2. Sales returns and allowances are viewed as a reduction of the amount initially recorded as sales. The sales returns and allowances account is a contra (or offsetting) account to sales.

E. Almost all states and many other taxing units levy a tax on sales of merchandise (referred to as a sales tax) which becomes a liability at the time the sale is made.

1. At the time of a cash sale, the seller collects the sales tax and credits a liability account, Sales Tax Payable.

2. Periodically, the sales tax liability is paid to the taxing unit.

F. Trade discounts are special discounts from prices listed in catalogs or offered to certain classes of buyers, such as government agencies, by sellers. Trade discounts are not normally entered into the accounts, but are recorded at the actual purchase price by the buyer and seller.

IV. Transportation Costs.

A. If the ownership of merchandise passes to the buyer when the seller delivers the merchandise to the shipper, the buyer is to absorb the transportation cost, and the terms are said to be FOB shipping point.

1. Transportation costs paid by the buyer should be debited to Merchandise Inventory and credited to Cash.

2. Sellers may prepay the transportation costs and add them to the invoice, as an accommodation to the buyer. In this case, the buyer should debit Merchandise Inventory for the transportation costs and compute any purchases discounts on the amount of the sale rather than on the invoice total. The seller records the prepayment of transportation costs by adding the amount of the total invoice and debiting Accounts Receivable.

B. If ownership of the merchandise passes to the buyer when the merchandise is received by the buyer, the seller is to assume the costs of transportation, and the terms are said to be FOB destination.

   1. The amounts paid by the seller for delivery of merchandise are debited to Transportation Out, or Delivery Expense, or a similarly titled account.

   2. The total of such costs incurred during a period is reported on the seller's income statement as a selling expense.

C. Shipping terms, the passage of title, and whether the buyer or seller is to pay transportation costs is summarized as follows:

	FOB <u>Shipping Point</u>	FOB <u>Desination</u>
Ownership (title) passes to buyer when merchandise is..	delivered to freight carrier	delivered to buyer
Transportation costs are paid by	buyer	seller

V. Illustration of Accounting for Merchandising Transactions.

A. Each merchandising transaction affects both a buyer and a seller.

B. Review the illustration on pages 215-216 of the text where the entries that both the seller and buyer would record are shown for each transaction.

VI. Chart of Accounts for a Merchandising Business.

A. The chart of accounts for a merchandising business will differ from that of a service business.

B. The chart of accounts for Computer King, which uses three-digit account numbers, is shown on page 217. The accounts related to merchandising transactions are shown in color.

VII. Income Statement for a Merchandising Business.

A. The basic financial statements for a merchandising business are similar to those of a service business, except for the following:

   1. The income statement differs in the reporting of revenue, cost of merchandise sold, and gross profit.

   2. A merchandising business balance sheet includes merchandise inventory as a current asset.

B. The multiple-step income statement contains many sections, subsections, and intermediate balances.

   1. The total of all charges to customers for merchandise sold, both for cash and on account, is reported as revenue from sales. Sales returns and allowances and sales discounts are deducted from the gross sales amount to yield net sales.

2. The amount of cost of merchandise sold appears next.

3. The excess of the net revenue from sales over the cost of merchandise sold is called gross profit.

4. Operating expenses are generally grouped into selling expenses and administrative expenses.

5. The excess of gross profit over total operating expenses is called income from operations, or operating income. If operating expenses are greater than gross profit, the excess is loss from operations.

6. Revenue from sources other than the principal activity of a business is classified as other income. In a merchandising business, this category often includes income from interest, rent, dividends, and gains resulting from the sale of plant assets.

7. Expenses that cannot be associated definitely with operations are identified as other expense, or nonoperating expense. Interest expense and losses incurred in the disposal of plant assets are examples of items that are reported in this section.

8. The final figure on the income statement is labeled net income (or net loss).

C. The single-step form of income statement derives its name from the fact that the total of all expenses is deducted from all revenues.

VIII. The Accounting Cycle for a Merchandising Business.

A. This section focuses primarily on the elements of the accounting cycle for a merchandising business that are likely to differ from those of a service business.

B. Normally, the amount of merchandise that should be on hand as indicated by the balance of the merchandise inventory account is larger than the total amount of merchandise counted during the physical inventory. The difference is often called inventory shrinkage or inventory shortage.

1. The adjusting entry for inventory shrinkage debits Cost of Merchandise Sold and credits Merchandise Inventory.

2. If the amount of the shrinkage is abnormally large, it may be disclosed separately on the income statement. In such cases, the shrinkage may be recorded in a separate account, such as Loss From Merchandise Inventory Shrinkage.

C. Merchandising businesses that use a computerized, perpetual inventory system normally prepare financial statements, including adjusting entries, without using a work sheet. The appendix at the end of the chapter illustrates the work sheet and the adjusting entries for a merchandising business that uses a manual accounting system.

D. The statement of owner's equity for a merchandising business is similar to that for a service business.

E. As illustrated in previous chapters, the balance sheet may be presented in the account form. The balance sheet may also be presented in a downward sequence in three sections. The total of the Assets section equals the combined total of the Liabilities and Owner's Equity sections. This form of balance sheet is called the report form.

F. The closing entries for a merchandising business are similar to those for a service business and in a computerized accounting system may be prepared, recorded, and posted to the accounts automatically.

ILLUSTRATIVE PROBLEM

MacBride Discount Stores entered into the following selected transactions during August of the current year:

Aug.
1. Purchased merchandise on account, terms 2/10, n/30, FOB shipping point, $28,500.

2. Paid transportation charges on purchase of August 1, $1,180.

7. Sold merchandise on account, terms 1/10,n/30, FOB destination, $12,400. The cost of merchandise sold was $7,500.

8. Paid transportation charges on sale of August 7, $550.

11. Paid for merchandise purchased on August 1, less discount.

12. Received merchandise returned from sale of August 7, $3,200. The cost of the merchandise returned was $1,750.

14. Purchased merchandise on account, terms 4/15,n/30, FOB destination, $18,300.

16. Returned merchandise purchased on August 14, $5,200.

17. Received cash on account from sale of August 7, less return and discount.

18. Sold merchandise on account, terms 1/10,n/30, FOB shipping point, $8,800. Prepaid transportation costs for the customer's convenience, $250. The cost of the merchandise sold was $5,000.

26. Sold merchandise on bank credit cards, $3,700. The cost of the merchandise sold was $1,900.

29. Paid for merchandise purchased on August 14, less return and discount.

31. Received cash on account from sale of August 18, $9,050.

Instructions

Journalize the entries to record the August transactions.

Solution

JOURNAL   PAGE

	DATE		DESCRIPTION	POST. REF.	DEBIT	CREDIT	
1	Aug.	1	Merchandise Inventory		2 7 9 3 0		1
2			Accounts Payable			2 7 9 3 0	2
3		2	Merchandise Inventory		1 1 8 0		3
4			Cash			1 1 8 0	4
5		7	Accounts Receivable		1 2 4 0 0		5
6			Sales			1 2 4 0 0	6
7		7	Cost of Merchandise Sold		7 5 0 0		7
8			Merchandise Inventory			7 5 0 0	8
9		8	Transportation Out		5 5 0		9
10			Cash			5 5 0	10
11		11	Accounts Payable		2 7 9 3 0		11
12			Cash			2 7 9 3 0	12
13		12	Sales Returns and Allowances		3 2 0 0		13
14			Accounts Receivable			3 2 0 0	14
15		12	Merchandise Inventory		1 7 5 0		15
16			Cost of Merchandise Sold			1 7 5 0	16
17		14	Merchandise Inventory		1 7 5 6 8		17
18			Accounts Payable			1 7 5 6 8	18
19		16	Accounts Payable		4 9 9 2		19
20			Merchandise Inventory			4 9 9 2	20
21		17	Cash		9 1 0 8		21
22			Sales Discounts		9 2		22
23			Accounts Receivable			9 2 0 0	23
24		18	Accounts Receivable		8 8 0 0		24
25			Sales			8 8 0 0	25
26		18	Cost of Merchandise Sold		5 0 0 0		26
27			Merchandise Inventory			5 0 0 0	27
28		18	Accounts Receivable		2 5 0		28
29			Cash			2 5 0	29
30		26	Cash		3 7 0 0		30
31			Sales			3 7 0 0	31
32							32

JOURNAL

	DATE		DESCRIPTION	POST. REF.	DEBIT	CREDIT	
1	Aug.	26	Cost of Merchandise Sold		1900		1
2			Merchandise Inventory			1900	2
3		29	Accounts Payable		12576		3
4			Cash			12576	4
5		31	Cash		9050		5
6			Accounts Receivable			9050	6
7							7
8							8
9							9
10							10
11							11
12							12
13							13
14							14
15							15
16							16
17							17
18							18
19							19
20							20
21							21
22							22
23							23
24							24
25							25
26							26
27							27
28							28
29							29
30							30
31							31
32							32

MATCHING

Instructions: A list of terms and related statements appear below. From the list of terms, select the one that relates to each statement. Print its identifying letter in the space provided.

A. Account form
B. Administrative expenses
C. Cost of Merchandise Sold
D. Credit memorandum
E. Credit terms
F. Debit memorandum
G. FOB destination
H. FOB shipping point
I. Gross profit
J. Income from operations
K. Invoice
L. Merchandise inventory

M. Multiple-step
N. Other expenses
O. Other income
P. Periodic inventory system
Q. Perpetual inventory system
R. Purchases discount
S. Report form
T. Sales discounts
U. Selling expenses
V. Single-step
W. Trade discounts

_____ 1. The terms agreed upon by the buyer and the seller as to when payments for merchandise are to be made are called (?).

_____ 2. The buyer refers to discounts taken for early payment of an invoice as (?).

_____ 3. When merchandise is returned or a price adjustment is requested, the buyer may inform the seller through the use of a (?).

_____ 4. The document issued by the seller, allowing for returns of merchandise or a price reduction.

_____ 5. The seller refers to the discounts taken by the buyer for early payment of an invoice as (?).

_____ 6. If the ownership of the merchandise passes to the buyer when the seller delivers the merchandise to the shipper, the buyer is to absorb the transportation costs, and the terms are said to be (?).

_____ 7. If ownership passes to the buyer when the merchandise is received by the buyer, the seller is to assume the costs of transportation, and the terms are said to be (?).

_____ 8. Under this inventory system, the revenues from sales are recorded when sales are made, but no attempt is made on the sales date to record the cost of the merchandise sold.

_____ 9. Under this inventory system, both the sales amount and the cost of merchandise sold amount are recorded when each item of merchandise is sold.

_____ 10. The bill provided by the seller to a buyer for items purchased.

_____ 11. Special discounts from published list prices, offered by sellers to certain classes of buyers.

_____ 12. The amount of merchandise inventory shrinkage is normally debited to (?).

_____ 13. The form of income statement that has many sections, subsections, and intermediate balances.

_____ 14. The form of income statement in which the total of all expenses is deducted from the total of all revenues.

_____ 15. The excess of the net revenue from sales over the cost of merchandise sold.

_____ 16. Expenses that are incurred directly and entirely in connection with the sale of merchandise are classified as (?).

_____ 17. Expenses incurred in the general operations of the business are classified as (?).

_____ 18. The excess of gross profit over total operating expenses is called (?).

_____ 19. Expenses that cannot be associated definitely with operations are identified as (?).

_____ 20. The form of balance sheet in which the liabilities and owner's equity sections are listed below rather than to the right of the asset section is refered to as the (?).

TRUE / FALSE

Instructions: Indicate whether each of the following statements is true or false by placing a check mark in the appropriate column.

	True	False
1. The two main sytems for accounting for merchandise held for sale are called periodic and perpetual.	_____	_____
2. In a perpetual inventory system, purchases of merchandise are recorded in the purchases account.	_____	_____
3. In a periodic inventory system, no attempt is made to record the cost of merchandise sold at the date of the sale.	_____	_____
4. A discount offered the purchaser of goods as a means of encouraging payment before the end of the credit period is known as a bank discount.	_____	_____
5. Credit terms of "2/10, n/30" mean that the buyer may deduct 2% of the amount of the invoice if payment is made within 10 days of the invoice date.	_____	_____
6. If the seller is to absorb the cost of delivering the goods, the terms are stated FOB (free on board) shipping point. .	_____	_____
7. The liability for the sales tax is incurred at the time the seller receives payment from the buyer.	_____	_____
8. The purchases returns and allowances are credited to Merchandise Inventory.	_____	_____
9. The chart of accounts for a merchandising business will differ from that of a service business.	_____	_____

10. The work sheet procedures for a merchandising business are significantly different from those of a service business.   _____ _____

11. The physical inventory taken at the end of the period is normally larger than the amount of the balance of the merchandise inventory account. . . . .   _____ _____

12. Any merchandise inventory shrinkage is normally debited to the merchandise inventory account. . . . .   _____ _____

13. Expenses incurred directly and entirely in connection with the sale of merchandise are called administrative expenses.   _____ _____

14. Revenue from sources such as income from interest, rent, dividends, and gains resulting from the sale of plant assets is classified as income from operations. . . . .   _____ _____

15. The single-step form of income statement has the advantage of being simple, and it emphasizes total revenues and total expenses as the factors that determine net income. . . . .   _____ _____

16. Gross profit is not calculated in the single-step form of income statement. . . . .   _____ _____

17. The excess of gross profit over total operating expenses is called income from operations. . . . .   _____ _____

18. The traditional balance sheet arrangement of assets on the left-hand side with the liabilities and owner's equity on the right-hand side is called the report form. . . . .   _____ _____

19. After the adjusting and closing entries have been recorded and posted, the general ledger accounts that appear on the balance sheet have no balances . . . .   _____ _____

20. The closing entries are recorded in the journal immediately following the adjusting entries. . . . .   _____ _____

MULTIPLE CHOICE

Instructions: Circle the best answer for each of the following questions.

1. The basic differences between the financial statements of a merchandising business and a service business include reporting cost of merchandise sold on the income statement and the:
   a. stockholders' equity section of the balance sheet
   b. other income section of the income statement
   c. inclusion of merchandise inventory on the balance sheet as a current asset
   d. inclusion of a retained earnings statement

2. A buyer receives an invoice for $60 dated June 10. If the terms are 2/10, n/30, and the buyer pays the invoice within the discount period, what amount will the seller receive?

   a. $60

   b. $58.80

   c. $48

   d. $1.20

3. When a seller of merchandise allows a customer a reduction from the original price for defective goods, the seller usually issues to the customer a(n):

   a. debit memorandum

   b. credit memorandum

   c. sales invoice

   d. inventory slip

4. When the seller prepays the transportation costs and the terms of sale are FOB shipping point, the seller records the payment of the transportation costs by debiting:

   a. Accounts Receivable

   b. Sales

   c. Transportation In

   d. Accounts Payable

5. If the seller collects sales tax at the time of sale, the seller credits the tax to:

   a. Sales

   b. Accounts Receivable

   c. Sales Tax Payable

   d. Sales Tax Receivable

6. The account that appears in the chart of accounts for a merchandising business but not for a service business is:

   a. Accounts Receivable

   b. Advertising Expense

   c. Sales Returns and Allowances

   d. Accumulated Depreciation

7. The excess of net revenue from sales over the cost of merchandise sold is called:

   a. gross profit

   b. operating profit

   c. net profit from operations

   d. merchandising income

8. Income from operations is computed by subtracting from gross profit the:
   a. selling expenses
   b. general expenses
   c. total administrative expenses
   d. total operating expenses

9. After all adjusting entries are posted, the balances of all asset, liability, revenue, and expense accounts correspond exactly to the amounts in the:
   a. work sheet trial balance
   b. general journal
   c. post-closing trial balance
   d. financial statements

10. In a multiple-step income statement of a merchandising business, which of the following would appear as "other income"?
    a. sales
    b. interest income
    c. sales discount
    d. sales returns and allowances

EXERCISE 6-1

Instructions: Prepare entries for each of the following related transactions of Foley Co. in the journal given below.

(1) Purchased $5,000 of merchandise from Phillips Co. on account, terms 2/10, n/30.

(2) Paid Phillips Co. on account for purchases, less discount.

(3) Purchased $3,500 of merchandise from Farris Co. on account, terms FOB shipping point, n/30, with prepaid shipping costs of $80 added to the invoice.

(4) Returned merchandise from Farris Co., $900.

(5) Paid Farris Co. on account for purchases, less return.

JOURNAL   PAGE

	DATE	DESCRIPTION	POST. REF.	DEBIT	CREDIT	
1						1
2						2
3						3
4						4
5						5
6						6
7						7
8						8
9						9
10						10
11						11
12						12
13						13
14						14
15						15
16						16
17						17
18						18
19						19
20						20
21						21
22						22
23						23
24						24

EXERCISE 6-2

Instructions: Prepare entries for each of the following related transactions of Wilson Co. in the journal given below.

(1) Sold merchandise on nonbank credit cards and reported accounts to the card company, $3,150. The cost of the merchandise sold was $2,000.

(2) Sold merchandise for cash, $2,850. The cost of the merchandise sold was $1,380.

(3) Received cash from card company for nonbank credit card sales, less $100 service fee.

(4) Sold merchandise on account to Rask Co., $4,500, terms 2/10, n/30, FOB shipping point. Prepaid transportation costs of $150 at the customer's request. The cost of the merchandise sold was $3,100.

(5) Received merchandise returned by Rask Co., $400. The cost of the merchandise returned was $275.

(6) Received cash on account from Rask Co. for sale and transportation costs, less returns and discount.

JOURNAL

PAGE

	DATE	DESCRIPTION	POST. REF.	DEBIT	CREDIT	
1						1
2						2
3						3
4						4
5						5
6						6
7						7
8						8
9						9
10						10
11						11
12						12
13						13
14						14
15						15
16						16
17						17
18						18
19						19
20						20
21						21

EXERCISE 6-3

Baker Co. had the following purchases and sales transactions during the month of January.

Jan.	**3.**	Purchased $25,000 of merchandise on account from Zeff Co., terms 2/10, n/30.
	5.	Returned merchandise purchased on account from Zeff Co. on January 3, $5,000.
	12.	Sold merchandise on account to Smith Co., $50,000, terms 1/10, n/30. The cost of the merchandise sold was $35,000.
	13.	Paid Zeff Co. for purchase on January 3, on account, less return and discount.
	15.	Received merchandise return on account from Smith Co., $8,000. The cost of the merchandise returned was $5,600.
	22.	Received payment in full on account from Smith Co., less return and discount.

Instructions: Prepare journal entries for the preceding transactions.

JOURNAL
PAGE _____

	DATE	DESCRIPTION	POST. REF.	DEBIT	CREDIT	
1						1
2						2
3						3
4						4
5						5
6						6
7						7
8						8
9						9
10						10
11						11
12						12
13						13
14						14
15						15
16						16
17						17
18						18
19						19
20						20

PROBLEM 6-1

The following transactions were selected from among those completed by the Bowman Company during September of the current year:

Sept. **3.** Purchased merchandise on account from Axel Co., list price $10,000, trade discount 15%, terms FOB destination, 1/10, n/30.

4. Purchased office supplies for cash, $800.

6. Sold merchandise on account to Hart Co., list price $5,000, trade discount 20%, terms 2/10, n/30. The cost of merchandise sold was $3,000.

7. Returned $2,000 of the merchandise purchased on September 3 from Axel Co.

10. Purchased merchandise for cash, $5,000.

12. Sold merchandise on nonbank credit cards and reported accounts to the card company, $5,500. The cost of merchandise sold was $3,200.

13. Paid Axel Co. on account for purchase of September 3, less return of September 7 and discount.

16. Received cash on account from sale of September 6 to Hart Co., less discount.

20. Received cash from card company for nonbank credit sales of September 12, less $300 service fee.

24. Sold merchandise to Wilcox Co., $3,000, terms 1/10, n/30. The cost of merchandise sold was $1,750.

26. Sold merchandise for cash, $2,200. The cost of merchandise sold was $1,400.

30. Received merchandise returned by Wilcox Co. from sale on September 24, $1,000. The cost of the merchandise returned was $600.

Instructions: Journalize the transactions for the Bowman Co., using the journal provided on the following page.

JOURNAL

PAGE

	DATE	DESCRIPTION	POST. REF.	DEBIT	CREDIT	
1						1
2						2
3						3
4						4
5						5
6						6
7						7
8						8
9						9
10						10
11						11
12						12
13						13
14						14
15						15
16						16
17						17
18						18
19						19
20						20
21						21
22						22
23						23
24						24
25						25
26						26
27						27
28						28
29						29
30						30
31						31
32						32

Problem 6-2

The following accounts and their normal balances were taken from the general ledger of Miller Co. after the adjusting entries have been posted for the fiscal year ending March 31.

Cash	43,100
Notes Receivable	6,000
Accounts Receivable	107,780
Interest Receivable	520
Merchandise Inventory	115,800
Office Supplies	1,250
Prepaid Insurance	8,740
Delivery Equipment	60,150
Accum. Depr.-Delivery Equipment	22,950
Accounts Payable	75,300
Salaries Payable	2,000
R. W. Miller, Capital	193,650
R. W. Miller, Drawing	30,000
Sales	1,016,700
Sales Returns and Allowances	13,010
Cost of Merchandise Sold	681,060
Sales Salaries Expense	78,250
Advertising Expense	13,090
Delivery Expense	42,100
Depreciation Expense--Delivery Equipment	9,050
Misc. Selling Expense	13,950
Office Salaries Expense	55,800
Office Supplies Expense	9,100
Insurance Expense	16,000
Misc. Admin. Exp.	6,870
Interest Income	1,020

Instructions:

(a) Prepare a multiple-step income statement for Miller Co.

(b) Prepare a single-step income statement for Miller Co.

(c) Assume that the inventory shrinkage for Miller Co. for the period ending March 31 was $4,200. Prepare the adjusting entry to record the inventory shrinkage.

Multi-Step Income Statement

Single-Step Income Statement

JOURNAL

PAGE _____

	DATE	DESCRIPTION	POST. REF.	DEBIT	CREDIT	
1						1
2						2
3						3
4						4
5						5
6						6
7						7
8						8
9						9
10						10
11						11
12						12
13						13
14						14
15						15
16						16
17						17
18						18
19						19
20						20
21						21
22						22
23						23
24						24
25						25
26						26
27						27
28						28
29						29
30						30
31						31
32						32

Problem 6-3

Using the information in Problem 6-2, prepare a statement of owner's equity for Miller Co.

Problem 6-4

Using the information in Problem 6-2, prepare a balance sheet in report form for Miller Co. as of March 31, 19--.

CONTINUING PROBLEM

Things have been going very well for Egor J. Gribbet. Egor has invented a line of magic tricks that he will begin selling to toy stores and magic shops. Egor has contracted with a factory, Magical Enterprises, to manufacture the tricks. His performance schedule is heavy, however, so he has hired Sam Delisle to manage the retail part of the business on a part-time basis beginning March 15th. Sam Delisle will spend his first several months establishing contacts with suppliers and ordering merchandise from Magical Enterprises. Egor anticipates actually selling merchandise to customers by June, 1997. Egor has decided to use the perpetual inventory system for his merchandising operations.

The following transactions were completed by Egor the Magician during the second year of operations (1997):

Jan.	**2.**	Paid office rent for January through June, $2,400.
	2.	Paid auto lease for January through December, $2,400.
	2.	Paid off the $1,500 note payable plus the $105 of interest that was accrued and recorded at the end of 1996.
	22.	Received payment for performances billed in November of the previous year, $2,486.
Feb.	**11.**	Paid for theater services recorded at the end of 1996, $850.
	24.	Paid J. P. Magic, $600.
Mar.	**15.**	Paid cash for props, $840.
	15.	Paid Sam Delisle's salary for two months, $800.
	31.	Received cash for performances, $9,400.
Apr.	**11.**	Purchased merchandise on account from Magical Enterprises, $4,800, terms FOB destination, 2/10, n/30.
	20.	Paid Magical Enterprises for merchandise purchased, less discount.
May	**15.**	Paid Sam Delisle's salary for two months, $800.
June	**5.**	Sold merchandise on account to Jerome's Toys, $2,200, terms FOB destination, 2/10, n/30. The cost of the merchandise sold was $1,200.
	5.	Paid transportation costs on the merchandise sold, $45.
	30.	Received check from Jerome's Toys for purchase on June 5.
July	**1.**	Paid office rent for July through December, $2,400.
	1.	Paid six months' interest on $5,000, 6% note, $150.
	2.	Paid telephone expense, $120.
	10.	Paid creditors on account, $500.
	15.	Sold merchandise on account to Evan's Magic, $2,850, terms FOB destination, 2/10, n/30. The cost of the merchandise sold was $1,500.
	15.	Paid Sam Delisle's salary for two months, $800.
	18.	Purchased merchandise from Magical Enterprises, $5,800, terms FOB shipping point, 2/10, n/eom.
	20.	Returned to Magical Enterprises $400 of merchandise purchased.

July	24.	Received check due from Evan's Magic.
	28.	Paid Magical Enterprises (less debit memorandum) for the July 18 purchase, less discount.
	31.	Sold merchandise on account to Toy Depot, $4,600, terms FOB destination, n/30. The cost of the merchandise sold was $2,500.
Aug.	1.	Paid transportation costs for merchandise shipped, $75.
	3.	Billed clients for performances during the last two months, $9,200.
	16.	Issued a credit memorandum for $500 to Toy Depot for merchandise returned from sale of July 31. The cost of the merchandise returned was $325.
	30.	Received check due from Toy Depot less credit memorandum of August 16.
Sep.	1.	Collected cash from August 3 billings, $9,200.
	15.	Paid cash for cosmetics, $100.
	15.	Paid Sam Delisle's salary for two months, $800.
Oct.	8.	Paid Jane the Fantastic for a performance, $400.
Nov.	13.	Paid cash to the Apollo Theater for its use, $600.
	15.	Paid Sam Delisle's salary for two months, $800.
Dec.	2.	Paid cash for renewal of property insurance policy for another year, $600.
	2.	Billed clients for work done for the last two months, $8,100.
	11.	Sold merchandise on account to Mystic Emporium, $3,400, terms FOB shipping point, 2/10, n/30. The cost of merchandise sold was $2,170.
	30.	Paid telephone expense, $135.
	31.	E.J. Gribbet withdrew $1,000 for personal use.

Instructions:

(10)   Journalize the transactions for Egor the Magician using the accounts in the ledger on pages 42-54.

(11)   Post the journal to the ledger on pages 42-54.

(12)   On the work sheet for Egor the Magician shown on pages 154-155, prepare a trial balance as of December 31, 1997. Omit accounts with zero balances.

(13)   Enter the following adjustments in the Adjustments columns:

(a) Office supplies on hand at December 31, $100.

(b) Supplies and props on hand as of December 31, $260.

(c) The physical merchandise inventory taken on December 31, 1997, indicated that $2,366 of inventory was on hand. The perpetual inventory account (#115) should be adjusted for any inventory shrinkage.

(d) The January 1 balance of prepaid insurance was used up as of December 31. The new policy purchased on December 2 must be adjusted for the amount used as of December 31.

(e) Interest accrued on note payable, $300.

(f) Egor owes Sam two months' salary, $800.

(g) Depreciation on the furniture and fixtures, $2,680.

(h) Depreciation on equipment, $2,400.

(14) Complete the work sheet.

(15) Prepare an income statement, a statement of owner's equity, and a balance sheet in report form.

(16) Journalize the adjusting entries and post them to the ledger on pages 42-54.

(17) Journalize the closing entries and post them to the ledger.

JOURNAL

PAGE

	DATE	DESCRIPTION	POST. REF.	DEBIT	CREDIT	
1						1
2						2
3						3
4						4
5						5
6						6
7						7
8						8
9						9
10						10
11						11
12						12
13						13
14						14
15						15
16						16
17						17
18						18
19						19
20						20
21						21
22						22
23						23
24						24
25						25

JOURNAL

PAGE _____

	DATE		DESCRIPTION	POST. REF.	DEBIT	CREDIT	
1							1
2							2
3							3
4							4
5							5
6							6
7							7
8							8
9							9
10							10
11							11
12							12
13							13
14							14
15							15
16							16
17							17
18							18
19							19
20							20
21							21
22							22
23							23
24							24
25							25
26							26
27							27
28							28
29							29
30							30
31							31
32							32
33							33
34							34

JOURNAL

PAGE

	DATE		DESCRIPTION	POST. REF.	DEBIT	CREDIT	
1							1
2							2
3							3
4							4
5							5
6							6
7							7
8							8
9							9
10							10
11							11
12							12
13							13
14							14
15							15
16							16
17							17
18							18
19							19
20							20
21							21
22							22
23							23
24							24
25							25
26							26
27							27
28							28
29							29
30							30
31							31
32							32
33							33
34							34

JOURNAL   PAGE

	DATE	DESCRIPTION	POST. REF.	DEBIT	CREDIT	
1						1
2						2
3						3
4						4
5						5
6						6
7						7
8						8
9						9
10						10
11						11
12						12
13						13
14						14
15						15
16						16
17						17
18						18
19						19
20						20
21						21
22						22
23						23
24						24
25						25
26						26
27						27
28						28
29						29
30						30
31						31
32						32
33						33
34						34

JOURNAL

PAGE _____

	DATE		DESCRIPTION	POST. REF.	DEBIT		CREDIT		
1									1
2									2
3									3
4									4
5									5
6									6
7									7
8									8
9									9
10									10
11									11
12									12
13									13
14									14
15									15
16									16
17									17
18									18
19									19
20									20
21									21
22									22
23									23
24									24
25									25
26									26
27									27
28									28
29									29
30									30
31									31
32									32
33									33
34									34

JOURNAL

PAGE _____

	DATE	DESCRIPTION	POST. REF.	DEBIT	CREDIT	
1						1
2						2
3						3
4						4
5						5
6						6
7						7
8						8
9						9
10						10
11						11
12						12
13						13
14						14
15						15
16						16
17						17
18						18
19						19
20						20
21						21
22						22
23						23
24						24
25						25
26						26
27						27
28						28
29						29
30						30
31						31
32						32
33						33
34						34

	ACCOUNT TITLE	TRIAL BALANCE		ADJUSTMENTS		
		DEBIT	CREDIT	DEBIT	CREDIT	
1						1
2						2
3						3
4						4
5						5
6						6
7						7
8						8
9						9
10						10
11						11
12						12
13						13
14						14
15						15
16						16
17						17
18						18
19						19
20						20
21						21
22						22
23						23
24						24
25						25
26						26
27						27
28						28
29						29
30						30
31						31
32						32
33						33
34						34
35						35
36						36
37						37
38						38

	ADJUSTED TRIAL BALANCE		INCOME STATEMENT		BALANCE SHEET		
	DEBIT	CREDIT	DEBIT	CREDIT	DEBIT	CREDIT	
1							1
2							2
3							3
4							4
5							5
6							6
7							7
8							8
9							9
10							10
11							11
12							12
13							13
14							14
15							15
16							16
17							17
18							18
19							19
20							20
21							21
22							22
23							23
24							24
25							25
26							26
27							27
28							28
29							29
30							30
31							31
32							32
33							33
34							34
35							35
36							36
37							37
38							38

Income Statement

Statement of Owner's Equity

Balance Sheet

7 Cash

QUIZ AND TEST HINTS

The following hints may be helpful to you in preparing for a quiz or a test over the material covered in Chapter 7.

1. You may expect some general terminology questions (usually true/false or multiple-choice) related to internal control over cash receipts and cash payments. You should be generally familiar with the basic components of a voucher system.

2. Many instructors like to include short problems or multiple-choice questions related to the advantage of taking all purchase discounts and the use of the purchases discounts lost account. You may have to compute the net advantage of borrowing to take a purchase discount. Also, you should be able to record general journal entries for recording purchases discounts lost.

3. You should be able to prepare journal entries to establish and replenish cash funds including cash change funds and petty cash. In replenishing such funds, the cash short and over account may need to be debited (short) or credited (over).

4. You should be able to prepare a bank reconciliation of the type illustrated in the chapter. Instructors often include short bank reconciliations of the type shown in the Illustrative Problem in the Chapter Review and in Problem 7-1 of this Study Guide. Attempt to work the Illustrative Problem and the Study Guide Problem 7-1 without looking at the solution.

5. Be able to identify in which section of the bank reconciliation different types of reconciling items would be included. The form of the reconciliation illustrated on page 261 may be a helpful study aid. Have a friend read off the reconciling items from the chapter illustration of the bank reconciliation on page 262, and identify whether the item would appear in the section of the reconciliation beginning with "Cash balance according to bank statement" or the section beginning with "Cash balance according to depositor's records."

   Note that sometimes instructors may refer to the "Cash balance according to bank statement" as the "Balance per bank" and "Cash balance according to depositor's records" as "Balance per books."

6. Finally, you should read over and be generally familiar with the presentation of cash on the balance sheet and the use of electronic funds transfer.

CHAPTER OUTLINE

I. **Nature of Cash and Importance of Controls Over Cash.**

A. Cash includes coins, currency (paper money), checks, money orders, and money on deposit that is available for unrestricted withdrawal from banks and other financial institutions. Normally, you can think of cash as anything that a bank would accept for deposit in your account.

B. As you might expect, because of the ease with which money can be transferred, cash is the asset most likely to be diverted and used improperly by employees. A business must therefore design and use controls that safeguard cash and authorize cash transactions.

II. **Internal Control of Cash Receipts.**

A. Cash should be protected from theft or misuse from the time it is received until it is deposited in the bank.

1. Controls designed to protect cash from theft or misuse are called protective controls.

2. Controls designed to detect theft or misuse of cash are called detective controls.

B. Retail businesses normally receive cash from either over-the-counter sales to customers or mail from credit customers.

1. A cash register provides a record of cash received over the counter from cash customers. The amounts in the cash drawer are compared with the cash register tapes at the end of each business day. The cash is taken to the cashier's office and the tapes are sent to the accounting department for proper recording.

2. The employees who open incoming mail should compare the amount of cash received with the amount shown on the accompanying remittance advice to make sure the two amounts agree. The cash should then be forwarded to the cashier's department and the remittance advices should be delivered to the accounting department for proper recording.

3. After cash is deposited in the bank by an employee of the cashier's department, the duplicate deposit slip or bank receipt form is returned to the accounting department where an employee compares the deposit with the recorded cash receipts for the day. Any cash shortages are thus promptly detected.

C. Retail stores usually maintain cash change funds in order to make change for customers.

1. A cash change fund is established by writing a check for the desired amount and debiting Cash on Hand and crediting Cash in Bank.

2. The cash is divided up among the various cash registers and the amounts in each register are recorded for later use in reconciling cash sales for the day.

3. No additional debits or credits to Cash on Hand are made unless the fund is increased or decreased in amount.

D. When the amount of cash actually received during the day does not agree with the record of cash receipts, the difference should be debited or credited to a cash short and over account.

1. A debit balance in the cash short and over account at the end of the fiscal period is listed as an expense on the income statement. A credit balance is listed as a revenue.

2. If the balance of the cash short and over account becomes larger than may be accounted for by minor errors, management should take corrective measures.

III. Internal Control of Cash Payments.

A. It is common practice for businesses to require that all payments of cash be made by checks signed by an authorized individual. In a small business, an owner-manager may sign all checks based upon personal knowledge of all goods and services purchased.

B. In large businesses, the issuance of purchase orders, inspection of goods received, and verification of invoices is divided among the employees of several departments. One system used for this purpose is the voucher system.

C. A voucher system is a set of methods and procedures for authorizing and recording liabilities and cash payments. It normally uses (1) vouchers, (2) a file for unpaid vouchers, and (3) a file for paid vouchers.

1. A voucher is a special form on which is recorded relevant data about a liability and the details of its payment. Vouchers are customarily prepared by the accounting department on the basis of an invoice or a memorandum that serves as proof of an expenditure. A check may not be issued except in payment of an authorized voucher.

2. In a voucher system, each voucher represents a credit to Accounts Payable (sometimes titled Vouchers Payable) and a debit to the appropriate account or accounts.

3. After a voucher has been recorded, it is filed in an unpaid voucher file where it remains until it is paid. The amount due on each voucher represents the credit balance of an account payable.

4. When a voucher is paid, it is removed from the unpaid voucher file and a check is issued for payment. Paid vouchers and the supporting documents should be canceled to prevent accidental or intentional reuse.

5. After payment, vouchers are usually filed in numerical order in a paid voucher file.

D. The voucher system not only provides effective accounting controls but it also aids management in making the best use of cash resources and in planning cash disbursements.

E. Normally, accounts payable should be paid within the discount period so as to take advantage of all purchases discounts. This is true even if the buyer has to borrow to make a payment within the discount period.

F. Purchase discounts may be missed due to oversight, errors in recording due dates, or other reasons. In this case, the amount of the missed discounts may be debited to an expense account called Discounts Lost. The balance of this account represents the cost of failing to take purchase discounts.

G. A petty cash fund is commonly used by businesses for which there is a frequent need for the payment of relatively small amounts, such as for postage due, etc.

   1. In establishing a petty cash fund, the account Petty Cash is debited. If a voucher system is used, Accounts Payable is credited. When the check is drawn to pay the voucher, Accounts Payable is debited and Cash in Bank is credited.

   2. The petty cash fund is replenished by a general journal entry debiting the various expense and asset accounts and crediting Accounts Payable. The check in payment of the voucher is recorded in the usual manner.

   3. Because disbursements are not recorded in the accounts until the fund is replenished, petty cash funds and other special funds that operate in a like manner should be replenished at the end of an accounting period.

H. Other cash funds may also be established to meet other special needs of a business. These funds are accounted for in a manner similar to that for a petty cash fund.

IV. **Bank Accounts: Their Nature and Use as a Control Over Cash.**

A. Businesses normally maintain one or more bank accounts.

   1. The forms used by business in connection with a bank account are a signature card, deposit ticket, check, and a record of checks drawn.

   2. The three parties to a check are the drawer, the one who signs the check; the drawee, the bank on which the check is drawn; and the payee, the one to whose order the check is drawn.

   3. A remittance advice is a notification which indicates to a creditor which specific invoice is being paid.

B. Banks usually mail to each depositor a statement of account once a month which shows the beginning balance, checks and other debits (deductions by the bank), deposits and other credits (additions by the bank), and the balance at the end of the period.

C. A bank account is one of the primary tools a business can use to control cash.

1. Businesses often require that all cash receipts be initially deposited in a bank account. Likewise, all cash payments are often disbursed from one or more bank accounts.

2. When such a system is used, there is a double record of cash transactions--one by the business and the other by the bank.

3. The balance shown on the depositor's records as cash in bank and the ending balance on the bank statement are not likely to be equal on any specific date because of either or both of the following: (1) delay by either party in recording transactions and (2) errors by either party in recording transactions.

4. The difference between the bank statement and the ledger account for cash in the bank should be reconciled. This reconciliation should be prepared by an employee who does not take part in or record cash transactions.

V. Bank Reconciliation.

A. A bank reconciliation is a listing of items and amounts that cause the cash balance reported in the bank statement to differ from the cash in bank account balance.

B. The bank reconciliation is divided into two sections: one section begins with the balance according to the bank statement and ends with the adjusted balance; the other section begins with the balance according to the depositor's records and also ends with the adjusted balance.

C. The form and the content of the bank reconciliation are outlined as follows:

Cash balance according to bank statement		$ XXX
Add: Additions by depositor not on bank statement . .	$ XX	
Bank errors	XX	XX
		$ XXX
Deduct: Deductions by depositor not on bank		
statement	$ XX	
Bank errors	XX	XX
Adjusted balance		$ XXX
Cash balance according to depositor's records		$ XXX
Add: Additions by bank not recorded by depositor . . .	$ XX	
Depositor errors	XX	XX
		$ XXX
Deduct: Deductions by bank not recorded by depositor	$ XX	
Depositor errors	XX	XX
Adjusted balance		$ XXX

D. The following procedures are used in finding reconciling items and determining the adjusted balance of Cash in Bank:

1. Compare individual deposits listed on the bank statement with unrecorded deposits appearing in the preceding period's reconciliation and with deposit receipts or other records of deposits. Add deposits not recorded by the bank to the balance according to the bank statement.

2. Compare paid checks with outstanding checks appearing on the preceding period's reconciliation and with checks recorded. Deduct checks outstanding that have not been paid by the bank from the balance according to the bank statement.

3. Compare bank credit memorandums to entries in the journal. For example, a bank would issue a credit memorandum for a note receivable and interest that it collected for a customer. Add credit memorandums that have not been recorded to the balance according to the depositor's records.

4. Compare bank debit memorandums to entries recording cash payments. For example, a bank normally issues debit memorandums for service charges and check printing charges. A bank also issues debit memorandums for not-sufficient-funds checks. A not-sufficient-funds (NSF) check is a customer's check that was recorded and deposited but was not paid when it was presented to the customer's bank for payment. NSF checks are normally charged back to the customer's account receivable. Deduct debit memorandums that have not been recorded from the balance according to the depositor's records.

5. Listed separately on the reconciliation are any errors discovered during the preceding steps. For example, if an amount has been recorded incorrectly by the depositor, the amount of the error should be added to or deducted from the Cash in Bank balance. Similarly, errors by the bank should be added to or deducted from the cash balance according to the bank statement.

E. Bank memorandums not recorded by the depositor and the depositor's errors shown by the bank reconciliation require that entries be made in the accounts.

1. The data needed for these adjustments are provided by the section of the bank reconciliation that begins with the balance per depositor's records.

2. After the adjusting entries are posted, the cash in bank account will have a balance which agrees with the adjusted balance shown on the bank reconciliation.

VI. Presentation of Cash on the Balance Sheet.

A. Cash is listed as the first asset in the Current Assets section of the balance sheet. Most companies combine all their cash accounts and present only a single cash amount on the balance sheet.

B. A company may invest in short-term, highly liquid investments in order to earn interest. Such investments, which can be readily converted to cash, are called cash equivalents. In such cases, "cash and cash equivalents" are usually reported as one amount on the balance sheet.

   C. Restrictions on the ability to withdraw cash and any compensating balance requirements should be disclosed in the notes to the financial statements.

VII. Electronic Funds Transfer.

   A. Electronic funds transfer is a payment system which uses computerized electronic impulses rather than paper (money, checks, etc.) to effect cash transactions.

   B. More and more companies are using EFT systems to process cash transactions. For example, a business may pay its employees by means of EFT. In addition, some attempts are also being made to use EFT systems in retailing through the use of point-of-sale (POS) systems.

   C. Although EFT systems generally reduce the cost of processing cash transactions, some difficulties have arisen in the use of EFT. For example, concerns have arisen over protecting privacy of information transferred over public telephone lines, documenting transactions, and controlling access to funds.

ILLUSTRATIVE PROBLEM

The bank statement for Dunlap Company for April 30 indicates a balance of $10,443.11. Dunlap Company uses a voucher system in controlling cash payments. All cash receipts are deposited each evening in a night depository, after banking hours. The accounting records indicate the following summary data for cash receipts and payments for April:

CASH IN BANK ACCOUNT
Balance as of April 1 . . . . $ 5,143.50

CASH RECEIPTS JOURNAL
Total cash receipts for April $28,971.60

CHECK REGISTER
Total amount of checks issued in April $26,060.85

Comparison of the bank statement and the accompanying canceled checks and memorandums with the records reveals the following reconciling items:

a. The bank had collected for Dunlap Company $912 on a note left for collection. The face of the note was $900.

b. A deposit of $1,852.21, representing receipts of April 30, had been made too late to appear on the bank statement.

c. Checks outstanding totaled $3,265.27.

d. A check drawn for $79 had been erroneously charged by the bank as $97.

e. A check for $10 returned with the statement had been recorded in the check register as $100. The check was for the payment of an obligation to Davis Equipment Company for the purchase of office supplies on account.

f. Bank service charges for April amounted to $8.20.

Instructions

1. Prepare a bank reconciliation for April.
2. Journalize the entries that should be made by Dunlap Company.

Solution

1.

Dunlap Company

Bank Reconciliation

April 30, 19--

Cash balance according to bank statement		$10,443.11
Add: Deposit of April 30 not recorded by bank	$1,852.21	
Bank error in charging check for $97 instead of $79	18.00	1,870.21
		$12,313.32
Deduct: Outstanding checks		3,265.27
Adjusted balance		$ 9,048.05
Cash balance according to depositor's records		$ 8,054.25*
Add: Proceeds of note collected by bank, including $12 interest .	$ 912.00	
Error in recording check	90.00	1,002.00
		$ 9,056.25
Deduct: Bank service charges		8.20
Adjusted balance		$ 9,048.05

*$5,143.50 + $28,971.60 - $26,060.85

2.

Cash in Bank	1,002.00	
Notes Receivable		900.00
Interest Income		12.00
Accounts Payable		90.00
Miscellaneous Administrative Expense	8.20	
Cash in Bank		8.20

MATCHING

Instructions: A list of terms and related statements appear below. From the list of terms, select the one that relates to each statement. Print its identifying letter in the space provided.

A. Bank reconciliation
B. Compensating balance
C. Credit memorandum
D. Debit memorandum
E. Electronic funds transfer
F. Not-sufficient funds (NSF) check

G. Payee
H. Petty cash fund
I. Remittance advice
J. Unpaid voucher file
K. Voucher

_____ 1. The party to whom payment is made.

_____ 2. A required minimum cash balance maintained in a bank account, generally imposed by the bank as part of a loan agreement.

_____ 3. A notification which accompanies checks issued to a creditor that indicates the specific invoice that is being paid.

_____ 4. An accounting record in which the bank balance according to the bank statement is reconciled with the bank balance according to the depositor's records.

_____ 5. A special form on which is recorded relevant data about a liability and the details of its payment.

_____ 6. After a voucher has been recorded it is filed in a(n) (?).

_____ 7. A form used by the bank to indicate that a customer's account has been decreased (charged) for an amount.

_____ 8. A customer's check that was recorded and deposited, but was not paid when it was presented to the customer's bank for payment.

_____ 9. A special cash fund set aside for the payment of relatively small amounts for which payment by check is not efficient.

_____ 10. A payment system using computerized information rather than paper to effect a cash transaction.

TRUE / FALSE

Instructions: Indicate whether each of the following statements is true or false by placing a check mark in the appropriate column.

	True	False
1. There are four parties to a check.		
2. The drawer is the one to whose order the check is drawn.		
3. In a bank reconciliation, checks issued that have not been paid by the bank are added to the balance according to the bank statement.		
4. Bank memorandums not recorded by the depositor require entries in the depositor's accounts.		
5. For a greater degree of internal control, the bank reconciliation should be prepared by an employee who does not engage in or record cash transactions with the bank.		
6. If there is a debit balance in the cash short and over account at the end of the fiscal period, this represents income to be included in "Miscellaneous general income" in the income statement.		
7. It is common practice for businesses to require that every payment of cash be evidenced by a check signed by the owner.		
8. After vouchers are paid, it is customary to file them in numerical sequence in the paid voucher file.		
9. If a voucher is used, Vouchers Payable should be debited when the petty cash fund is replenished.		
10. A voucher system is a set of methods and procedures for authorizing and recording liabilities and cash payments.		

MULTIPLE CHOICE

Instructions: Circle the best answer for each of the following questions.

1. The bank on which a check is drawn is known as the:
   a. drawer
   b. drawee
   c. payee
   d. creditor

2. In a bank reconciliation, deposits not recorded by the bank are:
   a. added to the balance according to the bank statement
   b. deducted from the balance according to the bank statement
   c. added to the balance according to the depositor's records
   d. deducted from the balance according to the depositor's records

3. For good internal control over cash receipts, remittance advices should be separated from cash received by mail and sent directly to the:
   a. treasurer
   b. cashier's department
   c. accounting department
   d. voucher clerk

4. An important characteristic of the voucher system is the requirement that:
   a. vouchers be prepared by the treasurer
   b. vouchers be paid immediately after they are prepared
   c. the face of the voucher show the account distribution
   d. a voucher be prepared for each expenditure

5. The entry to record the replenishment of the petty cash fund includes a debit to various expense and asset accounts and a credit to:
   a. Cash in Bank
   b. Petty Cash
   c. Accounts Payable
   d. various liability accounts

EXERCISE 7-1

A comparison of the bank statement and the accompanying canceled checks and memorandums with the records of Pearl Co. for the month of September of the current year revealed the following reconciling items:

(1) A check drawn for $25 had been erroneously charged by the bank for $250.

(2) The bank collected $1,920 on a note left for collection. The face of the note was $1,800.

(3) Bank service charges for September totaled $28.

(4) Check No. 231, written to Stanley Optical Warehouse for $2,500, and Check No. 236, written to Stella's Janitorial Service for $100, were outstanding.

(5) A deposit of $5,250 made on September 30 was not recorded on the bank statement.

(6) A canceled check for $1,100, returned with the bank statement, had been recorded erroneously in the check register as $1,000. The check was a payment on account to Charlie's Optical Supply.

Instructions: In the following general journal, prepare the entries that Pearl Co. should make as a result of these reconciling items. The accounts have not been closed.

JOURNAL   PAGE

	DATE	DESCRIPTION	POST. REF.	DEBIT	CREDIT	
1						1
2						2
3						3
4						4
5						5
6						6
7						7
8						8
9						9
10						10
11						11
12						12
13						13
14						14
15						15
16						16
17						17
18						18

EXERCISE 7-2

Instructions: Record the following transactions in the general journal provided below, assuming that any discounts not taken are recorded as Discounts Lost.

Jan. 8. Voucher No. 2710 is prepared for merchandise purchased from Hanks Co., $5,000, terms 2/10, n/60.

10. Voucher No. 2711 is prepared for merchandise purchased from Murphy Co., $12,000, terms 1/10, n/30.

20. Check No. 3210 is issued, payable to Murphy Co., in payment of Voucher No. 2711.

Feb. 9. Check No. 3217 is issued, payable to Hanks Co., in payment of Voucher No. 2710.

JOURNAL

PAGE ____

	DATE		DESCRIPTION	POST. REF.	DEBIT	CREDIT	
1							1
2							2
3							3
4							4
5							5
6							6
7							7
8							8
9							9
10							10
11							11
12							12
13							13
14							14
15							15
16							16
17							17
18							18
19							19
20							20
21							21
22							22
23							23
24							24

EXERCISE 7-3

Instructions: In the general journal provided below, prepare the entries to record the following transactions:

(1) Voucher No. 312 is prepared to establish a petty cash fund of $400.

(2) Check No. 805 is issued in payment of Voucher No. 312.

(3) The amount of cash in the petty cash fund is now $128.34. Voucher No. 443 is prepared to replenish the fund, based on the following summary of petty cash receipts:

Office supplies, $80.25
Miscellaneous selling expense, $115.33
Miscellaneous administrative expense, $78.05

(4) Check No. 844 is issued by the disbursing officer in payment of Voucher No. 443. The check is cashed and the money is placed in the fund.

JOURNAL

PAGE

	DATE	DESCRIPTION	POST. REF.	DEBIT	CREDIT	
1						1
2						2
3						3
4						4
5						5
6						6
7						7
8						8
9						9
10						10
11						11
12						12
13						13
14						14
15						15
16						16
17						17
18						18
19						19
20						20
21						21
22						22

PROBLEM 7-1

On September 30 of the current year, Dumont Co.'s checkbook showed a balance of $7,540 and the bank statement showed a balance of $8,510. A comparison of the bank statement and Dumont's records as of September 30 revealed the following:

(a) A deposit of $1,900, mailed to the bank by Dumont on September 29, was not included in the bank statement of September 30.

(b) The following checks were outstanding: Check No. 255 for $325, Check No. 280 for $100, Check No. 295 for $700

(c) Check No. 289 in payment of a voucher had been written for $140 and had been recorded at that amount by the bank. However, Dumont had recorded it in the check register as $410.

(d) A check for $910 received from a customer was deposited in the bank. The bank recorded it at the correct amount, but Dumont recorded it at $190.

(e) Included with the bank statement was a credit memorandum for $780, representing the proceeds of a $700 note receivable left at the bank for collection. This had not been recorded on Dumont's books.

(f) Included with the bank statement was a debit memorandum for $25 for service charges which had not been recorded on Dumont's books.

Instructions:

(1) Complete the bank reconciliation below.

(2) In the general journal, prepare the entry or entries that Dumont should make as a result of the bank reconciliation.

Dumont Co.

Bank Reconciliation

September 30, 19--

Balance according to bank statement . . . . $

Add:

Deduct:

Adjusted balance . . . . $ _____

Balance according to depositor's records . . . . $

Add:

Deduct:

Adjusted balance . . . . $ _____

JOURNAL

PAGE

	DATE		DESCRIPTION	POST. REF.	DEBIT	CREDIT	
1							1
2							2
3							3
4							4
5							5
6							6
7							7
8							8
9							9
10							10
11							11
12							12
13							13
14							14
15							15
16							16
17							17
18							18
19							19
20							20
21							21
22							22
23							23
24							24
25							25
26							26
27							27
28							28
29							29
30							30
31							31
32							32

8 Receivables and Temporary Investments

QUIZ AND TEST HINTS

The following hints may be helpful to you in preparing for a quiz or test over the material in Chapter 8.

1. You should be able to determine the amount of the adjusting entry for uncollectible receivables (the allowance method) for both estimation methods presented in the chapter (percentage of sales and aging of receivables). Note that the percentage of sales method is the easiest to use since the amount of the entry is the same as the estimate of the uncollectible sales. The aging method requires the entry to be made for an amount that will result in the estimated balance of the allowance account.

2. You should be able to determine the due date, interest, and maturity value of a note receivable and to compute the proceeds for a note receivable that has been discounted.

3. You may be tested on a problem requiring a series of general journal entries that encompass both uncollectible accounts receivable and notes receivable. The materials presented in this Study Guide and the Illustrative Problem in the Chapter Review provide an excellent review.

4. Finally, study the new terminology introduced in this chapter for possible multiple-choice, matching, or true-false questions. The Key Terms at the end of the chapter are a good study aid for reviewing terminology.

CHAPTER OUTLINE

I. Classification of Receivables.

A. The term receivables includes all money claims against people, organizations, or other debtors.

1. A promissory note is a written promise to pay a sum of money on demand or at a definite time. The business owning a note refers to it as a note receivable.

2. Accounts and notes receivable originating from sales transactions are called trade receivables.

3. Other receivables include interest receivable, loans to officers or employees, and loans to affiliated companies.

B. All receivables that are expected to be realized in cash within a year are presented as current assets on the balance sheet. Those not currently collectible, such as long-term loans, are shown as investments.

II. Internal Control of Receivables.

A. The broad principles of internal control should be used to establish procedures to safeguard receivables.

B. The following controls are commonly used:

1. Separation of the business operations and the accounting for receivables.

2. The maintenance of subsidiary records and ledgers for accounts and notes receivable.

3. Proper approval of all credit sales by an authorized company official.

4. Proper authorization of all sales returns and allowances and sales discounts.

5. Effective collection procedures to ensure timely collection and to minimize losses from uncollectible accounts.

III. Uncollectible Receivables.

A. When merchandise or services are sold on credit, a part of the claims against customers will normally not be collectible.

B. Companies attempt to limit the number and amount of uncollectible accounts by using control procedures.

C. Some companies attempt to shift the risk of uncollectible accounts to other companies by accepting only credit cards or factoring their receivables.

D. The operating expense incurred because of the failure to collect receivables is called uncollectible accounts expense, doubtful accounts expense, or bad debts expense.

E. The two methods of accounting for receivables believed to be uncollectible are the allowance method and the direct write-off method.

IV. Allowance Method of Accounting for Uncollectibles.

A. Under the allowance method of accounting for uncollectibles, advance provision for uncollectibility is made by an adjusting entry at the end of the fiscal period.

1. The adjusting entry to record the allowance for uncollectibles is to debit Uncollectible Accounts Expense and credit Allowance for Doubtful Accounts. The account Allowance for Doubtful Accounts is a contra asset account offsetting Accounts Receivable.

2. The balance of the accounts receivable account less the contra account, Allowance for Doubtful Accounts, determines the expected value of the receivables to be realized in the future, called the net realizable value.

   3. Uncollectible accounts expense is reported on the income statement as an administrative expense.

B. When an account is believed to be uncollectible, it is written off against the allowance account by debiting Allowance for Doubtful Accounts and crediting the customer's account receivable.

C. An account receivable that has been written off against the allowance account may later be collected.

   1. The account should be reinstated by an entry that is the exact reverse of the write-off entry; a debit to the customer's account receivable and a credit to Allowance for Doubtful Accounts.

   2. The cash received in payment would be recorded in the usual manner as a debit to Cash and a credit to Accounts Receivable.

D. The estimate of uncollectibles at the end of the fiscal period is based on past experience and forecasts of future business activity. Two methods of estimating uncollectibles are as follows:

   1. The amount of uncollectibles may be estimated based upon the percentage of sales.

   a. Based upon past experience or industry averages, the percentage of sales which will prove to be uncollectible is estimated.

   b. The estimated percentage of uncollectible sales is then multiplied by the credit sales for the period and the Uncollectible Accounts Expense is debited and Allowance for Doubtful Accounts is credited for this amount.

   c. The estimated percentage should ideally be based upon credit sales, but total sales may be used if the ratio of credit sales to total sales does not change much from year to year.

   2. Uncollectibles may be estimated by analyzing the individual account receivable accounts in terms of length of time past due.

   a. An aging of accounts receivable is prepared which lists accounts by due date.

   b. Percentages are applied to each category of past due accounts to estimate the balance of the allowance for doubtful accounts as of the end of the accounting period.

   c. The amount of the adjusting entry at the end of the fiscal period for uncollectible accounts expense is that amount necessary to bring the allowance account to its estimated balance as of the end of the period.

E. Estimates of uncollectible accounts expense based on analysis of the receivables are less common than estimates based on sales.

V. Direct Write-Off Method of Accounting for Uncollectibles.

A. Under the direct write-off method of accounting for uncollectibles, no entry is made for uncollectibility until an account is determined to be worthless. At that time, an entry is made debiting Uncollectible Accounts Expense and crediting the individual customer's account receivable.

B. If the account that has been written off is later collected, the account should be reinstated by reversing the earlier entry to write off the account.

C. The receipt of cash in payment of a reinstated account is recorded in the usual manner.

VI. Characteristics of Notes Receivable.

A. The one to whose order the note is payable is called the payee, and the one making the promise is called the maker.

B. The date a note is to be paid is called the due date or maturity date.

    1. The period of time between the issuance date and the maturity date of a short-term note may be stated either in days or months.

    2. When the term of a note is stated in days, the due date is a specified number of days after its issuance.

    3. When the term of a note is stated as a certain number of months after the issuance date, the due date is determined by counting the number of months from the issuance date. For example, a three-month note dated July 31 would be due on October 31.

C. Interest rates are usually stated in terms of a period of one year, regardless of the actual period of time involved.

    1. The basic formula for computing interest is as follows: Face Amount (or Principal) x Rate x Time = Interest.

    2. For purposes of computing interest, the commercial practice of using 1/12 of a year for a month and a 360-day year will be used.

D. The amount that is due at the maturity or due date of a note is called the maturity value.

VII. Accounting for Notes Receivable.

A. When a note is received from a customer to apply on account, Notes Receivable is debited and Accounts Receivable is credited for the face amount of the note.

B. At the time a note matures and payment is received, Cash is debited, Notes Receivable is credited for the face amount of the note, and Interest Income is credited for the amount of interest due, if any.

C. At the end of the fiscal year, an adjusting entry is necessary to record the accrued interest on any outstanding interest-bearing notes receivable.

D. Instead of retaining a note until maturity, notes receivable may be transferred to a bank by endorsement, a process known as discounting notes receivable.

    1. The interest (discount) charged by the bank is computed on the maturity value of the note for the period of time the bank must hold the note, namely the time that will pass between the date of the transfer and the due date of the note. This period is called the discount period.

2. The amount of the proceeds paid to the endorser is the excess of the maturity value over the discount.

3. The entry to record the discounting of notes receivable is to debit Cash for the proceeds, credit Notes Receivable for the face value of the note, and either debit Interest Expense or credit Interest Income for the amount to balance the entry.

4. The endorser of a note that has been discounted has a contingent liability to the holder of the note for the face amount of the note plus accrued interest and any protest fee. Any significant contingent liabilities should be disclosed on the balance sheet or in an accompanying note.

E. If the maker of the note fails to pay the debt on the due date, the note is said to be dishonored. The entry for a dishonored note is to debit Accounts Receivable for the maturity amount of the note, credit Notes Receivable for the face value of the note, and credit Interest Income for the amount of interest due on the note at maturity. When a discounted note receivable is dishonored, the holder usually notifies the endorser and asks for payment. If request for payment and notification of dishonor are timely, the endorser is legally obligated to pay the amount due on the note, including any accrued interest and protest fee. The payment of a protest fee is debited to the account receivable of the maker.

VIII. Temporary Investments.

A. A business may invest excess cash that it does not need immediately for operations. Such investments are called temporary investments or marketable securities if they meet the following two conditions:

1. The securities are readily marketable and can be sold for cash at any time.

2. Management intends to sell the securities when the business needs more cash for operations.

B. Temporary investments are either debt securities or equity securities.

1. A debt security represents a creditor relationship between the entity issuing the security and the individuals or entities holding the security.

2. An equity security represents ownership in a business. The most common example of an equity security is stock in a corporation.

C. The accounting for temporary investments in debt and equity securities depends upon whether the particular security is classified as a (1) held-to-maturity security, (2) a trading security, or (3) an available-for-sale security.

1. A held-to-maturity security is a debt security that management intends to hold to its maturity. Such securities that will mature within

one year are recorded at their cost and reported as temporary investments on the balance sheet.

2. A trading security can be either a debt security or an equity security that management intends to actively trade for profit. Businesses holding trading securities are those whose normal operations involve buying and selling securities.

3. An available-for-sale security may be a debt or equity security that is not classified as either a held-to-maturity or trading security. Available-for-sale securities that are expected to be sold within one year are reported as temporary investments on the balance sheet.

   a. Available-for-sale securities should be reported at their total fair market value as of the balance sheet date.

   b. Any difference between the fair market value of the securities and their cost is an unrealized holding gain or loss.

IX. Temporary Investments and Receivables in the Balance Sheet.

A. Temporary investments and all receivables that are expected to be realized in cash within a year are presented in the Current Assets section of the balance sheet.

B. It is customary to list the assets in the order of their liquidity, that is, in the order in which they can be converted to cash in normal operations.

C. Unrealized holding gains or losses are reported on the balance sheet, not on the income statement. When temporary investments are sold, however, the difference between their cost and the proceeds from the sale is reported on the income statement as a realized gain or loss.

D. Other disclosures related to receivables are presented either on the face of the financial statements or in the accompanying notes. Such disclosures include:

1. The market (fair) value of the receivables. Generally, the market value of receivables approximates their carrying value.

2. If unusual credit risks exist within the receivables, the nature of the risks should be disclosed.

ILLUSTRATIVE PROBLEM

Rodriguez Company uses the allowance method of accounting for uncollectible accounts receivable. Selected transactions completed by Rodriguez Company are as follows:

Jan.   28. Sold merchandise on account to Lakeland Co., $10,000.

March 1. Accepted a 60-day, 12% note for $10,000 from Lakeland Co. on account.

April 11. Wrote off a $4,500 account from Exdel Co. as uncollectible.

       16. Loaned $7,500 cash to Thomas Glazer, receiving a 90-day, 14% note.

April 30. Received the interest due from Lakeland Co. and a new 90-day, 14% note as a renewal of the loan. (Record both the debit and the credit to the notes receivable account.)

May   1. Discounted the note from Thomas Glazer at the First National Bank at 10%.

June 13. Reinstated the account of Exdel Co., written off on April 11, and received $4,500 in full payment.

July 15. Received notice from First National Bank that Thomas Glazer dishonored his note. Paid the bank the maturity value of the note plus a $20 protest fee.

       29. Received from Lakeland Co. the amount due on its note of April 30.

Aug. 14. Received from Thomas Glazer the amount owed on the dishonored note, plus interest for 30 days at 15%, computed on the maturity value of the note and the protest fee.

Dec. 16. Accepted a 60-day, 12% note for $6,000 from Harden Company on account.

       31. It is estimated that 2% of the credit sales of $958,600 for the year ended December 31 will be uncollectible.

Instructions

1. Journalize the transactions in general journal form.
2. Journalize the adjusting entry to record the accrued interest on December 31.

Solution

1.

Jan.	28	Accounts Receivable--Lakeland Co.	10,000.00	
		Sales		10,000.00
Mar.	1	Notes Receivable--Lakeland Co.	10,000.00	
		Accounts Receivable--Lakeland Co. . . .		10,000.00
Apr.	11	Allowance for Doubtful Accounts	4,500.00	
		Accounts Receivable--Exdel Co.		4,500.00
	16	Notes Receivable--Thomas Glazer	7,500.00	
		Cash		7,500.00

April	30	Notes Receivable--Lakeland Co.	10,000.00	
		Cash	200.00	
		Notes Receivable--Lakeland Co.		10,000.00
		Interest Income		200.00
May	1	Cash	7,600.78	
		Notes Receivable--Thomas Glazer . . .		7,500.00
		Interest Income		100.78

Face value	$7,500.00
Interest on note (90 days at 14%)	262.50
Maturity value	$7,762.50
Discount on maturity value (75 days at 10%)	161.72
Proceeds	$7,600.78

June	13	Accounts Receivable--Exdel Co.	4,500.00	
		Allowance for Doubtful Accounts . . .		4,500.00
	13	Cash	4,500.00	
		Accounts Receivable--Exdel Co. . . .		4,500.00
July	15	Accounts Receivable--Thomas Glazer . .	7,782.50	
		Cash		7,782.50
	29	Cash	10,350.00	
		Notes Receivable--Lakeland Co. . . .		10,000.00
		Interest Income		350.00
Aug.	14	Cash	7,879.78	
		Accounts Receivable--Thomas Glazer		7,782.50
		Interest Income		97.28
		($7,782.50 x 15% x 30/360)		
Dec.	16	Notes Receivable--Harden Company . . .	6,000.00	
		Accounts Receivable--Harden Company		6,000.00
	31	Uncollectible Accounts Expense	19,172.00	
		Allowance for Doubtful Accounts . . .		19,172.00

2.

Dec.	31	Interest Receivable	30.00	
		Interest Income		30.00
		($6,000 x 12% x 15/360)		

MATCHING

Instructions: A list of terms and related statements appear below. From the list of terms, select the one that relates to each statement. Print its identifying letter in the space provided.

A. Aging the receivables	I. Equity security
B. Allowance method	J. Expected realizable value
C. Carrying amount	K. Maturity value
D. Contingent liabilities	L. Proceeds
E. Debt security	M. Promissory note
F. Direct write-off method	N. Realized gain or loss
G. Discount	O. Temporary investments
H. Dishonored	P. Unrealized holding gain or loss

_____ 1. A method of accounting for receivables which provides in advance for uncollectible receivables through the use of an allowance for doubtful accounts.

_____ 2. A method of accounting for uncollectible receivables in which no expense is recognized until individual accounts are determined to be worthless.

_____ 3. The balance of the accounts receivable following the deduction of the allowance for doubtful accounts.

_____ 4. The process of analyzing the receivable accounts in terms of the length of time past due.

_____ 5. A written promise to pay a certain sum of money on demand or at a definite time.

_____ 6. The interest charged by a bank for discounting a note receivable.

_____ 7. The amount received from selling a note receivable prior to its maturity.

_____ 8. Potential obligations that will become actual liabilities only if certain events occur in the future.

_____ 9. If the maker of a note fails to pay the debt on the due date, the note is said to be (?).

_____ 10. The amount that is due at the due date of a note.

_____ 11. Securities that can be readily sold when cash is needed.

_____ 12. The difference between the cost and the proceeds from the sale of temporary investments.

_____ 13. A security that represents a creditor relationship between the entity issuing the security and the individuals or entities holding the security.

_____ 14. The difference between the fair market value and the cost of securities held as temporary investments.

_____ 15. A security that represents ownership in a business.

TRUE / FALSE

Instructions: Indicate whether each of the following statements is true or false by placing a check mark in the appropriate column.

True   False

1. The method of accounting which provides in advance for receivables deemed uncollectible is called the allowance method. . . . .   _____ _____

2. The process of analyzing the receivable accounts in order to estimate the uncollectibles is sometimes called aging the receivables. . . . .   _____ _____

3. The direct write-off method of accounting for uncollectible receivables provides for uncollectible accounts in the year of sale. . . . .   _____ _____

4. Estimation of uncollectible accounts based on the analysis of receivables emphasizes the current net realizable value of the receivables. . . . .   _____ _____

5. Estimation of uncollectible accounts based on the analysis of receivables emphasizes the matching of uncollectible expense with the related sales. . . . .   _____ _____

6. The term *notes* includes all money claims against people, organizations, or other debtors. . . . .   _____ _____

7. Accounts and notes receivable originating from sales transactions are sometimes called trade receivables. . . .   _____ _____

8. For good internal control, an employee who handles the accounting for notes and accounts receivable should not be involved with credit approvals or collections of receivables.   _____ _____

9. When a note is received from a customer on account, this is recorded by debiting Notes Receivable and crediting Sales. . . . .   _____ _____

10. Jacob Co. issues a 90-day, 12% note on May 13, the due date of the note is August 11. . . . .   _____ _____

11. When the holder transfers a note to a bank by endorsement, the discount (interest) charged is computed on the face value of the note for the period of time the bank must hold the note. . . . .   _____ _____

12. When the proceeds from discounting a note receivable are less than the face value, the difference is recorded as interest income. . . . .   _____ _____

13. The endorser of a note that has been discounted has a contingent liability that is in effect until the due date. . . . .   _____ _____

14. A trading security can be either a debt or equity security. .   _____ _____

15. Available-for-sale securities should be reported at the higher of either total cost or fair market value. . . . .   _____ _____

MULTIPLE CHOICE

Instructions: Circle the best answer for each of the following questions.

1. Assume that the allowance account has a credit balance at the end of the year of $170 before adjustment. If the estimate of uncollectible accounts based on aging the receivables is $3,010, the amount of the adjusting entry for uncollectible accounts would be:

   a. $170

   b. $2,840

   c. $3,010

   d. $3,180

2. Assume that the allowance account has a debit balance at the end of the year of $250 before adjustment. If the estimate of uncollectible accounts based on sales for the period is $2,200, the amount of the adjusting entry for uncollectible accounts would be:

   a. $250

   b. $1,950

   c. $2,200

   d. $2,450

3. On a promissory note, the one making the promise to pay is called the:

   a. payee

   b. creditor

   c. maker

   d. noter

4. The amount that is due on a note at the maturity or due date is called the:

   a. terminal value

   b. face value

   c. book value

   d. maturity value

5. When a note is discounted, the excess of the maturity value over the discount is called the:

   a. gain

   b. proceeds

   c. interest

   d. present value

6. When the allowance method is used in accounting for uncollectible accounts, any uncollectible account is written off against the:

   a. allowance account

   b. sales account

   c. accounts receivable account

   d. uncollectible accounts expense account

EXERCISE 8-1

Star Co. uses the allowance method of accounting for uncollectibles. On March 31, 19--, Star deemed that an amount of $3,150 due from Jane Eades was uncollectible and wrote it off. On May 8, 19--, Eades paid the $3,150.

Instructions:

(1) Prepare the entry to write off the account on March 31.

(2) Prepare the entry to reinstate the account on May 8, and to record the cash received.

JOURNAL   PAGE

	DATE		DESCRIPTION	POST. REF.	DEBIT	CREDIT	
1							1
2							2
3							3
4							4
5							5
6							6
7							7
8							8
9							9
10							10
11							11
12							12
13							13
14							14
15							15
16							16
17							17
18							18
19							19
20							20
21							21
22							22
23							23
24							24
25							25
26							26

EXERCISE 8-2

Coco Co. uses the direct write-off method of accounting for uncollectibles. On August 31, 19--, Coco deemed that an amount of $550 due from Don Shore was uncollectible and wrote it off. On October 8, 19--, Shore paid the $550.

Instructions:

(1) Prepare the entry to write off the account on August 31.

(2) Prepare the entry to reinstate the account on October 8, and to record the cash received.

JOURNAL

PAGE _____

	DATE		DESCRIPTION	POST. REF.	DEBIT	CREDIT	
1							1
2							2
3							3
4							4
5							5
6							6
7							7
8							8
9							9
10							10
11							11
12							12
13							13
14							14
15							15
16							16
17							17
18							18
19							19
20							20
21							21
22							22
23							23
24							24
25							25
26							26

EXERCISE 8-3

Instructions: Using the basic formula for interest and assuming a 360-day year, compute the interest on the following notes.

1. $8,000 at 12% for 30 days . . . . $ _____
2. $3,500 at 6% for 60 days . . . . $ _____
3. $2,000 at 12% for 90 days . . . . $ _____
4. $8,000 at 9% for 30 days . . . . $ _____
5. $7,500 at 6% for 60 days . . . . $ _____
6. $12,000 for 90 days at 9% . . . . $ _____
7. $5,250 for 120 days at 12% . . . . $ _____

EXERCISE 8-4

Instructions: Based on the information given, fill in the blanks below.

(1) A 12%, 90-day note receivable for $12,000 was discounted at 14%, 30 days after receiving the note.

Face value . . . . $ _____

Interest on face value . . . . $ _____

Maturity value . . . . $ _____

Discount on maturity value . . . . $ _____

Proceeds . . . . $ _____

(2) An 8%, 120-day note receivable for $15,000 was discounted at 10%, 50 days after receiving the note.

Face value . . . . $ _____

Interest on face value . . . . $ _____

Maturity value . . . . $ _____

Discount on maturity value . . . . $ _____

Proceeds . . . . $ _____

EXERCISE 8-5

Wallace Co. had a temporary investment in a portfolio of available-for-sale equity securities as of December 31, 19--, as follows:

	Cost	Market
Security A	$11,000	$22,500
Security B	$18,000	$16,600
Security C	$21,000	$26,700
Security D	$18,000	$12,400

Instructions: Indicate how the preceding securities would be reported on Wallace's December 31, 19-- balance sheet.

EXERCISE 8-6

The following data regarding the current assets of Walton Company were selected from the accounting records after adjustment at the end of the current fiscal year:

Accounts Receivable	$35,000
Unrealized Holding Loss on Marketable Equity Securities	2,000
Allowance for Doubtful Accounts	1,200
Cash	37,500
Interest Receivable	9,900
Marketable Equity Securities (Cost)	55,000
Notes Receivable	20,000

Instructions: Prepare the Current Assets section of the balance sheet for Walton Company.

PROBLEM 8-1

Instructions: Prepare the appropriate general journal entries for each of the following situations.

(1) Net sales for the year are $800,000, uncollectible accounts expense is estimated at 3% of net sales, and the allowance account has a $425 credit balance before adjustment. Prepare the adjusting entry at year end for the uncollectibles.

(2) Based on an analysis of accounts in the customers ledger, estimated uncollectible accounts total $6,280, and the allowance account has a $325 credit balance before adjustment. Prepare the adjusting entry at year end for the uncollectibles.

(3) A $3,500 account receivable from Bentley Co. is written off as uncollectible. The allowance method is used.

(4) A $1,235 account receivable from Apple Co., which was written off three months earlier, is collected in full. The allowance method is used.

JOURNAL   PAGE

	DATE	DESCRIPTION	POST. REF.	DEBIT	CREDIT	
1						1
2						2
3						3
4						4
5						5
6						6
7						7
8						8
9						9
10						10
11						11
12						12
13						13
14						14
15						15
16						16
17						17
18						18
19						19
20						20
21						21

II. Determining Actual Quantities in the Inventory.

A. The actual quantities of inventory at the end of an accounting period are determined by the process of taking a physical inventory.

B. All the merchandise owned by the business on the inventory date, and only such merchandise, should be included in the inventory.

C. It may be necessary to examine purchases and sales invoices of the last few days of the current accounting period and the first few days of the following period to determine who has legal title to merchandise in transit on the inventory date.

1. When goods are purchased or sold FOB shipping point, title usually passes to the buyer when the goods are shipped. Therefore, these items should be included in inventory by the purchaser on the shipping date.

2. When goods are purchased or sold FOB destination, title usually does not pass to the buyer until the goods are delivered. Therefore, goods shipped under these terms should be included in inventory by the purchaser only when the goods have been received.

D. Special care should be taken in accounting for merchandise that has been shipped on a consignment basis to a retailer (the consignee). Even though the manufacturer does not have physical possession, consigned merchandise should be included in the manufacturer's (the consignor's) inventory.

E. Any errors in the inventory count will affect both the balance sheet and the income statement.

1. Because the physical inventory is the basis for recording the adjusting entry for inventory shrinkage, an error in taking the physical inventory misstates the cost of goods sold, gross profit, and net income on the income statement.

2. Because net income is closed to the owner's equity at the end of the period, owner's equity will also be misstated on the balance sheet. This misstatement of owner's equity will equal the misstatement of the ending inventory, current assets, and total assets.

III. Inventory Costing Methods Under a Perpetual Inventory System.

A. Under the perpetual inventory system, all merchandise increases and decreases are recorded in a manner similar to the recording of increases and decreases in cash. The merchandise inventory account at any point in time reflects the merchandise on hand at that date.

B. The cost of merchandise inventory is made up of the purchase price and all costs incurred in acquiring such merchandise, including transportation, customs duties, and insurance.

C. Some costs of acquiring merchandise, such as the salaries of the Purchasing Department employees and other administrative costs, are not easily allocated to inventory. Such costs are treated as operating expenses of the period.

D. A major accounting issue arises in the use of the perpetual system when identical units of a commodity are acquired at different unit costs during a period. In such cases, when an item is sold it is necessary to determine its unit cost so that the proper accounting entry can be made.

E. If the unit sold can be identified with a specific purchase, the specific identification method can be used.

F. If the specific identification method is not practical, an assumption must be made as to the flow of costs. The three most common cost flow assumptions are as follows:

1. Cost flow is in the order in which the expenditures were made first-in, first-out.

2. Cost flow is in the reverse order in which the expenditures were made last-in, first-out.

3. Cost flow is an average of the expenditures.

G. The first-in, first-out (fifo) method of costing inventory assumes that costs should be charged against revenue in the order in which they were incurred.

1. The inventory remaining is assumed to be made up of the most recent costs.

2. The fifo method is generally consistent with the physical movement of merchandise in a business. To this extent, the fifo method approximates the results that would be obtained by the specific identification of costs.

H. The last-in, first-out (lifo) method assumes that the most recent costs incurred should be charged against revenue.

1. The inventory remaining is assumed to be composed of the earliest costs.

2. Even though it does not represent the physical flow of the goods, the lifo method is widely used in business today.

I. The average cost method assumes that costs should be charged against revenue according to the average unit costs of the goods sold.

1. An average unit cost for each type of inventory is computed each time a purchase is made. This unit cost is used to determine the cost of each sale and the remaining inventory. This average technique is called a moving average.

2. The average cost method is not often used with a perpetual inventory system.

J. If there is a large number of inventory items and/or transactions, businesses will often computerize the perpetual system for faster and more accurate processing of data. By computerizing a system, additional data may be entered into the inventory records so that inventory may be ordered and maintained at optimal levels.

IV. Inventory Costing Methods Under a Periodic Inventory System.

A. When the periodic inventory system is used, only revenue is recorded each time a sale is made. No entry is made at the time of the sale to record the cost of the merchandise sold. At the end of the accounting period, a physical inventory is taken in order to determine the cost of the inventory on hand and the cost of the merchandise sold.

B. Like the perpetual inventory system, a cost flow assumption must be made when identical units of a commodity are acquired at different unit costs during a period. In such cases, the first-in first-out (fifo), last-in, first-out (lifo), or average cost method is normally used.

C. When the first-in, first-out (fifo) method of costing inventory is used, costs are assumed to be charged against revenue in the order in which they were incurred. Hence the inventory remaining is assumed to be made up of the costs of the most recent purchases during the period.

D. When the last-in, first-out (fifo) method of inventory costing inventory is used, the most recent costs incurred are assumed to be matched against revenue. Hence the inventory remaining is assumed to be composed of the earliest costs.

E. The average cost method is sometimes called the weighted average method.

   1. Under the average cost method, costs are assumed to be matched against revenue according to an average of the unit costs of the period.

   2. The average unit costs for the period are also used in determining the cost of the merchandise inventory at the end of the period.

   3. For businesses in which merchandise sales may be made up of various purchases of identical units, the average method approximates the physical flow of goods.

V. Comparing Inventory Costing Methods.

A. Each of the three alternative inventory costing methods is based on a different assumption as to the flow of costs.

   1. If the cost of units and prices at which they are sold remain stable, all three methods yield the same results.

   2. Prices do change, however, and as a result the three methods will yield different amounts for ending inventory, cost of merchandise sold, and gross profit for the period.

   3. In periods of rising prices, the fifo method yields the lowest cost of merchandise sold, the highest net income, and the highest amount for ending inventory.

   4. In periods of rising prices, the lifo method yields the highest cost of merchandise sold, the lowest net income, and lowest ending inventory.

   5. The average cost method yields results that are in between those of fifo and lifo.

B. During periods of rising prices, many companies prefer to use the last-in, first-out method to reduce the amount of income taxes.

C. Often, businesses apply different inventory costing methods to different types of inventory. The method used by a company for inventory costing purposes should be properly disclosed in the financial statements. Any changes in methods should also be disclosed.

VI. Valuation of Inventory at Other than Cost.

A. Although cost is the primary basis for the valuation of inventories, under certain circumstances inventory may be valued at other than cost.

B. If the market price of an inventory item is lower than its cost, the lower of cost or market method is used.

    1. Market means the cost to replace the merchandise on the inventory date, based on quantities purchased from the usual source of supply.

    2. The use of the lower of cost or market method provides two advantages: the gross profit is reduced for the period in which the decline occurred, and an approximately normal gross profit is realized during the period in which the item is sold.

    3. It is possible to apply the lower of cost or market basis to each item in the inventory, major classes or categories, or the inventory as a whole.

C. Obsolete, spoiled, or damaged merchandise and other merchandise that can only be sold at prices below cost should be valued at net realizable value. Net realizable value is the estimated selling price less any direct cost of disposal, such as sales commissions.

VII. Presentation of Merchandise Inventory on the Balance Sheet.

A. Merchandise inventory is usually presented in the Current Assets section of the balance sheet following receivables.

B. Both the method of determining the cost of the inventory (fifo, lifo, or average) and the method of valuing the inventory (cost, or lower of cost or market) should be shown. The details may be disclosed by a parenthetical note on the balance sheet or by a footnote.

VIII. Estimating Inventory Cost.

A. In practice, it may be necessary to know the amount of inventory when it is impractical to take a physical inventory or to maintain perpetual inventory records. In other cases, a disaster may have destroyed the inventory records. In such cases, the retail or gross profit inventory estimation methods may be used.

B. The retail method of estimating inventory costs is based on the relationship of the cost of merchandise available for sale to the retail price of the same merchandise.

    1. The retail prices of all merchandise acquired are accumulated.

2. The inventory at retail is determined by deducting sales for the period from the retail price of the goods that were available for sale during the period.

3. The inventory at retail is then converted to cost on the basis of the ratio of cost to selling (retail) price for the merchandise available for sale.

4. The retail method assumes that the mix of items in the ending inventory, in terms of percent of cost to selling price, is the same as the entire stock of merchandise available for sale.

5. One of the major advantages of the retail method is that it provides inventory figures for monthly or quarterly statements.

6. The retail method can be used with the periodic system when a physical inventory is taken at the end of the year.

C. The gross profit method of estimating inventory costs uses an estimate of the gross profit realized during the period to estimate the ending inventory.

1. The cost of merchandise available for sale is recorded in the accounting records.

2. An estimate of gross profit percentage is multiplied by the sales for the period to determine the estimated cost of merchandise sold.

3. Estimated ending inventory is then determined by subtracting from the merchandise available for sale the estimated cost of merchandise sold for the period.

4. The estimate of the gross profit rate is usually based on the actual rate for the preceding year, adjusted for any changes in the cost and sales prices during the current period.

5. The gross profit method may be used in estimating the cost of merchandise destroyed by fire or other disaster, or in preparing monthly or quarterly statements.

ILLUSTRATIVE PROBLEM

Stewart Co.s beginning inventory and purchases during the fiscal year ended March 31, 1996, were as follows:

		Units	Unit Cost	Total Cost
April 1, 1995	Inventory	1,000	$50.00	$ 50,000
April 10,1995	Purchase	1,200	52.50	63,000
May 30,1995	Purchase	800	55.00	44,000
August 26, 1995	Purchase	2,000	56.00	112,000
October 15,1995	Purchase	1,500	57.00	85,500
December 31, 1995	Purchase	700	58.00	40,600
January 18, 1996	Purchase	1,350	60.00	81,000
March 21, 1996	Purchase	450	62.00	27,900
Total		9,000		$ 504,000

Stewart Co. uses the periodic inventory system, and there are 3,200 units of inventory on March 31, 1996.

Instructions

1. Determine the cost of inventory on March 31, 1996, using each of the following inventory costing methods:

   a. first-in, first-out

   b. last-in, first-out

   c. average cost

2. Assume that during the fiscal year ended March 31, 1996, sales were $536,000 and the estimated gross profit rate was 40%. Estimate the ending inventory at March 31, 1996, using the gross profit method.

Solution

1. a. First-in, first-out method:

450 units at $62	$ 27,900
1,350 units at $60	81,000
700 units at $58	40,600
700 units at $57	39,900
3,200 units	$ 189,400

b. Last-in, first-out method:

1,000 units at $50.00	$ 50,000
1,200 units at $52.50	63,000
800 units at $55.00	44,000
200 units at $56.00	11,200
3,200 units	$ 168,200

c. Average cost method:

Average cost per unit:	$504,000 / 9,000 units = $56
Inventory, March 31, 1996:	3,200 units at $56 = $179,200

2.

Merchandise inventory, April 1, 1995		$ 50,000
Purchases (net), April 1, 1995--March 31, 1996 . .		454,000
Merchandise available for sale		$ 504,000
Sales (net), April 1, 1995--March 31, 1996	$ 536,000	
Less estimated gross profit ($536,000 x 40%) . . .	214,400	
Estimated cost of merchandise sold		321,600
Estimated merchandise inventory, March 31, 1996		$ 182,400

MATCHING

Instructions: A list of terms and related statements appear below. From the list of terms, select the one that relates to each statement. Print its identifying letter in the space provided.

A. Average cost method
B. Consignment inventory
C. First-in, first-out (FIFO) method
D. Gross profit method
E. Last-in, first-out (LIFO) method

F. Lower of cost or market
G. Merchandise inventory
H. Net realizable value
I. Physical inventory
J. Retail inventory method

_____ 1. The inventory of merchandise purchased for resale is commonly called (?).

_____ 2. The detailed listing of merchandise on hand.

_____ 3. Merchandise that is shipped by a manufacturer to a retailer, who acts as the manufacturer's agent when selling the merchandise.

_____ 4. An inventory method that treats the first merchandise acquired as the first merchandise sold.

_____ 5. An inventory method in which the ending inventory is assumed to be composed of the earliest costs.

_____ 6. An inventory method in which the weighted average unit costs are used in determining both ending inventory and cost of goods sold.

_____ 7. A method of inventory pricing in which goods are valued at original cost or replacement cost, whichever is lower.

_____ 8. The estimated selling price of inventory less any direct cost of disposition.

_____ 9. An inventory method based on the relationship of the cost of merchandise available for sale to the retail price of the same merchandise.

_____ 10. An inventory method which uses an estimate of the gross profit realized during the period to estimate the inventory at the end of the period.

TRUE / FALSE

Instructions: Indicate whether each of the following statements is true or false by placing a check mark in the appropriate column.

	True	False
1. If merchandise inventory at the end of the period is understated, gross profit will be overstated.	_____	_____
2. The two principal systems of inventory accounting are periodic and physical.	_____	_____
3. When terms of a sale are FOB destination, title usually does not pass to the buyer until the commodities are delivered.	_____	_____

4. If merchandise inventory at the end of the period is overstated, owner's equity at the end of the period will be understated. . . . . _____ _____

5. During a period of rising prices, the inventory costing method which will result in the highest amount of net income is lifo. _____ _____

6. If the cost of units purchased and the prices at which they were sold remained stable, all three inventory methods would yield the same results. _____ _____

7. When the rate of inflation is high, the larger gross profits that result are frequently called inventory profits. . . . . _____ _____

8. As used in the phrase lower of cost or market, "market" means selling price. . . . . _____ _____

9. When the retail inventory method is used, inventory at retail is converted to cost on the basis of the ratio of cost to replacement cost of the merchandise available for sale. . . _____ _____

10. Merchandise inventory is usually presented on the balance sheet immediately following receivables. . . . . _____ _____

MULTIPLE CHOICE

Instructions: Circle the best answer for each of the following questions.

1. If merchandise inventory at the end of the period is understated:
   a. gross profit will be overstated
   b. owner's equity will be overstated
   c. net income will be understated
   d. cost of merchandise sold will be understated

2. If merchandise inventory at the end of period 1 is overstated, and at the end of period 2 is correct:
   a. gross profit in period 2 will be understated
   b. assets at the end of period 2 will be overstated
   c. owner's equity at the end of period 2 will be understated
   d. cost of merchandise sold in period 2 will be understated

3. The following units of a particular item were purchased and sold during the period:

   Beginning inventory . . . . 10 units at $5
   First purchase . . . . 15 units at $6
   Sale . . . . 10 units
   Second purchase . . . . 10 units at $7
   Sale . . . . 8 units
   Third purchase . . . . 15 units at $8
   Sale . . . . 17 units

What is the total cost of the 15 units on hand at the end of the period, as determined under the perpetual inventory system by the lifo costing method?

a. $80

b. $90

c. $100

d. $120

4. Assuming the data given in No. 3, determine the total cost of the 15 units on hand at the end of the period assuming a perpetual inventory system and the fifo costing method.

a. $80

b. $90

c. $100

d. $120

5. Assuming the data given in No. 3, determine the total cost of the 15 units on hand at the end of the period assuming a periodic inventory system and the lifo costing method.

a. $80

b. $90

c. $100

d. $120

6. Assuming the data given in No. 3, determine the total cost of the 15 units on hand at the end of the period assuming a periodic inventory system and the fifo costing method.

a. $80

b. $90

c. $99

d. $120

7. Assuming the data given in No. 3, determine the total cost of the 15 units on hand at the end of the period assuming a periodic inventory system and the average costing method.

a. $80

b. $90

c. $99

d. $120

8. During a period of rising prices, the inventory costing method that will result in the lowest amount of the net income is:

a. fifo

b. lifo

c. average cost

d. perpetual

9. If the replacement price of an item of inventory is lower than its cost, the use of the lower of cost or market method:

   a. is not permitted unless a perpetual inventory system is maintained

   b. is recommended in order to maximize the reported net income

   c. tends to overstate the gross profit

   d. reduces gross profit for the period in which the decline occurred

10. When lifo is strictly applied to a perpetual inventory system, the unit cost prices assigned to the ending inventory will not necessarily be those associated with the earliest unit costs of the period if:

    a. a physical inventory is taken at the end of the period

    b. physical inventory records are maintained throughout the period in terms of quantities only

    c. at any time during a period the number of units of a commodity sold exceeds the number previously purchased during the same period

    d. moving average inventory cost is maintained

EXERCISE 9-1

The net income, total assets, and owner's equity of Ruby Co. for the past two fiscal years, ended December 31, are as follows:

	19XB	19XA
Net income	$55,000	$40,000
Total assets	$60,000	$55,000
Owner's equity	$50,000	$40,000

During 19XC, it was discovered that merchandise inventory had been understated by $5,000 at the end of year 19XA. The merchandise inventory was correct at the end of year 19XB.

Instructions: In the spaces provided below, indicate the effect of the error in the December 31, 19XA inventory on the net income, total assets, and owner's equity in 19XA and 19XB. For each item, indicate (1) whether it is <u>understated, overstated,</u> or <u>correct;</u> and (2) the dollar amount of the error, if any.

		Net Income	Total Assets	Owner's Equity
19XA	(1)	_____	_____	_____
	(2)	_____	_____	_____
19XB	(1)	_____	_____	_____
	(2)	_____	_____	_____

EXERCISE 9-2

Instructions: Complete the following summary, which illustrates the application of the lower of cost or market rule to individual inventory items of Unks Co.

	Quantity	Unit Cost Price	Unit Market Price	Total Cost	Lower of Cost or Market
Commodity A	750	$5.00	$4.80	$	$
Commodity B	460	6.00	7.00		
Commodity C	200	7.25	6.00		
Commodity D	300	4.80	4.30		
Total				$	$

PROBLEM 9-1

Hawkins Co. is a small wholesaler of hiking shoes. The accounting records show the following purchases and sales of the Mountain model during the first year of business.

A physical count of the Mountain model at the end of the year reveals that 12 are still on hand.

Purchases				Sales	
Date	Units	Price	Total Cost	Date	Units
Jan. 10	10	$ 48	$ 480	Feb. 10	8
Feb. 15	100	54	5,400	Apr. 1	95
July 3	65	55	3,575	Aug. 10	65
Nov. 1	35	58	2,030	Nov. 15	30
Total	210		$ 11,485		198

Instructions:

(1) Determine the cost of the Mountain model inventory as of December 31 by means of the first-in, first-out (fifo) method with a perpetual inventory system.

INVENTORY (Fifo Perpetual)

Date Purchased	Units	Price	Total Cost

(2) Determine the cost of the Mountain Model inventory as of December 31 by means of the last-in, first-out (lifo) method with a perpetual inventory system.

INVENTORY (Lifo Perpetual)

Date Purchased	Units	Price	Total Cost

(3) Determine the cost of the Mountain model inventory as of December 31 by means of the first-in, first-out (fifo) method with a periodic inventory system.

INVENTORY (Fifo Periodic)

Date Purchased	Units	Price	Total Cost

(4) Determine the cost of the Mountain model inventory as of December 31 by means of the last-in, first-out (lifo) method with a periodic inventory system.

INVENTORY (Lifo Periodic)

Date Purchased	Units	Price	Total Cost

(5) Determine the cost of the Mountain model inventory as of December 31 by means of the average cost method with a periodic system.

INVENTORY (Average Cost)

Average unit cost = $_____ = $_____

_____ units in the inventory @ $_____ = $_____

PROBLEM 9-2

Bartle Co. began operating on January 1 of the current year. During the year, Bartle sold 28,000 units at an average price of $80 each, and made the following purchases:

Date of Purchase	Units	Unit Price	Total Cost
January 1	5,400	$ 50	$ 270,000
March 1	4,100	54	221,400
June 1	4,800	56	268,800
September 1	8,400	61	512,400
November 1	5,400	69	372,600
December 1	1,900	73	138,700
	30,000		$1,783,900

Instructions: Using the periodic inventory system, determine the ending inventory, the cost of merchandise sold, and the gross profit for Bartle, using each of the following methods of inventory costing: **(1)** fifo, **(2)** lifo, and **(3)** average cost. (Round unit cost to two decimal places.)

	(1) Fifo	(2) Lifo	(3) Average Cost
Sales	$	$	$
Purchases	$ 1,783,900	$ 1,783,900	$ 1,783,900
Less ending inventory . . .			
Cost of merchandise sold .	$	$	$
Gross profit	$	$	$

PROBLEM 9-3

Knish Co. operates a department store and takes a physical inventory at the end of each calendar year. However, Knish likes to have a balance sheet and an income statement available at the end of each month in order to study financial position and operating trends. Knish estimates inventory at the end of each month for accounting statement preparation purposes. The following information is available as of August 31 of the current year:

	Cost	Retail
Merchandise inventory, August 1	$ 118,500	$ 170,000
Purchases in August	307,125	481,400
Purchases returns and allowances--August .	8,000	8,900
Sales in August		493,200
Sales returns and allowances--August		14,200

Instructions:

(1) Determine the estimated cost of the inventory on August 31, using the retail method.

	Cost	Retail
Merchandise inventory, August 1	$ _____	$ _____
Purchases in August (net)		
Merchandise available for sale	$ _____	$ _____

Ratio of cost to retail:

$$\frac{\$\rule{2cm}{0.4pt}}{\$\rule{2cm}{0.4pt}} = \rule{2cm}{0.4pt}\%$$

Sales in August (net) . . . . _____

Merchandise inventory, August 31, at retail . . . . $ _____

Merchandise inventory, August 31, at estimated cost
($_____ x _____%) . . . . $ _____

(2) Determine the estimated cost of inventory on August 31, using the gross profit method. On the basis of past experience, Knish estimates a rate of gross profit of 30% of net sales.

Merchandise inventory, August 1 . . . . $ _____

Purchases in August (net) . . . . _____

Merchandise available for sale . . . . $ _____

Sales in August (net) . . . . $ _____

Less estimated gross profit ($_____ x _____%) _____

Estimated cost of merchandise sold . . . . $ _____

Estimated merchandise inventory, August 31 . . . . $ _____

10 Plant Assets and Intangible Assets

QUIZ AND TEST HINTS

The following hints may be helpful to you in preparing for a quiz or a test over the material covered in Chapter 10.

1. The chapter emphasizes the computation of depreciation. You should be able to compute depreciation using each of the three methods: straight-line, units-of-production, and declining-balance. If your instructor lectures on the sum-of-the-years-digits method of depreciation in the appendix to the chapter, you should also be prepared to compute depreciation under this method.

2. A common question on quizzes and tests involves the recording of plant asset disposals. You should be able to prepare general journal entries for disposals, including the exchange of similar assets. Exhibit 7 on page 362 may be useful for reviewing the journal entries of exchanges of similar assets.

3. The chapter introduces a significant amount of new terminology. These terms lend themselves to numerous multiple-choice and matching questions. Review the Key Terms.

4. You should expect some questions related to intangible assets. The computation of amortization is relatively simple, and it is similar to the units-of-production depreciation method. This section of the chapter lends itself to multiple-choice questions.

CHAPTER OUTLINE

I. Nature of Plant Assets.

A. Plant assets are long-term or relatively permanent tangible assets that are used in the normal operations of the business. They are owned by the business and are not held for sale in the ordinary course of the business.

1. Another descriptive title often used is property, plant, and equipment.

2. Plant assets may also be described in specific terms such as equipment, furniture, tools, machinery, buildings, and land.

B. There is no standard rule as to the minimum length of life necessary for an asset to be classified as a plant asset or intangible asset. In addition, an asset, such as standby equipment, need not actually be used on an ongoing basis or even often.

C. Assets acquired for resale in the normal course of business are not classified as plant assets, regardless of their permanent nature or the length of time they are held.

D. The normal costs of using or operating a plant asset are reported as expenses on a company's income statement. The costs of acquiring a plant asset become expenses over a period of time through the recording of depreciation expense.

E. The cost of acquiring a plant asset includes all expenditures necessary to get it in place and ready for use. Exhibit 1 summarizes common costs included (and excluded) from the cost of acquiring plant assets.

   1. The cost of land includes not only the negotiated price but also broker's commissions, title fees, surveying fees, etc. If delinquent real estate taxes are assumed by the buyer, they are also chargeable to the land.

   2. The cost of constructing a building includes the fees paid to architects and engineers for plans and supervision, insurance, etc. Interest incurred during the construction should also be included in the cost of the building.

   3. Costs for improvements that are neither as permanent as land nor directly associated with the building may be set apart in a land improvements account. Such items include trees and shrubs, fences, and paved parking areas.

F. Over time, all plant assets, with the exception of land, lose their ability to provide services. As a result, the cost of such assets should be transferred to expense accounts in a systematic manner during their expected useful life. This periodic cost expiration is called depreciation.

   1. Factors that cause a decline in the ability of a plant asset to provide services include physical depreciation (e.g., wear and tear) and functional depreciation (e.g., obsolescence).

   2. The meaning of the term depreciation as used in accounting may be misunderstood, because depreciation is not necessarily associated with declines in the market value of an asset. In addition, depreciation does not provide cash for the replacement of assets.

II. Accounting for Depreciation.

A. Three factors are considered in determining the amount of depreciation expense to be recognized each period. These include (1) the plant asset's initial cost, (2) its expected useful life, and (3) its estimated value at the end of its useful life (residual value).

B. The straight-line method of determining depreciation provides for equal amounts of periodic expense over the estimated life of the asset.

   1. The depreciable cost of the asset is determined by subtracting the estimated residual value from the initial cost of the asset.

   2. The useful life of the asset is then divided into the depreciable cost.

3. The resulting amount is an annual depreciation charge which remains constant over the life of the asset.

4. Straight-line depreciation is often expressed by a percentage rate. The straight-line depreciation rate is equal to 100 divided by the useful life of the asset.

5. The straight-line method is widely used because of its simplicity.

C. The units-of-production method yields a depreciation expense that varies with the amount of the asset's usage.

1. The depreciable cost of the asset is determined by subtracting the estimated residual value from the initial cost of the asset.

2. The estimated life of the asset, expressed in terms of productive capacity, is then divided into the depreciable cost to arrive at the unit or hourly depreciation charge.

3. The actual amount of production usage is then multiplied by this rate to determine the depreciation charge.

D. The declining-balance method yields a declining periodic depreciation expense over the estimated life of the asset.

1. The double-declining balance method uses a rate of depreciation which is double the straight-line depreciation rate.

2. The declining-balance depreciation rate is then applied to the original cost of the asset for the first year, and thereafter to the book value (cost minus accumulated depreciation).

3. The residual value of the asset is not considered in determining the depreciation rate or the depreciation charge each period, except that the asset should not be depreciated below the estimated residual value.

E. If the asset's first use does not coincide with the beginning of the fiscal year, each full year's depreciation should be allocated between the two years benefited.

F. The depreciation method chosen affects the amounts reported on the financial statements.

1. The straight-line method provides uniform periodic charges to depreciation expense over the life of the asset.

2. The units-of-production method provides for periodic charges to depreciation expense that may vary depending upon the amount of use of the asset.

3. The declining-balance method provided for a higher depreciation charge in the first year of use of the asset and a gradually declining periodic charge thereafter. For this reason, this method is often called an accelerated depreciation method.

G. Each of the three depreciation methods described above can be used to determine the amount of depreciation for federal income tax purposes for plant assets acquired prior to 1981.

H. For plant assets acquired after 1980 and before 1987, either the straight-line method or the Accelerated Cost Recovery System (ACRS) may be used to determine depreciation deductions for federal income tax purposes.

I. For plant assets acquired after 1986, either the straight-line method or Modified ACRS (MACRS) may be used.

J. Changes in the estimated useful lives and residual values of assets are accounted for by using the revised estimates to determine the amount of remaining undepreciated asset cost to be charged as an expense in future periods.

K. Revisions of the estimates used in the determination of depreciation does not affect the amounts of depreciation expense recorded in earlier years.

L. Depreciation may be recorded by an entry at the end of each month, or the adjustment may be delayed until the end of the year.

    1. Depreciation is recorded by using a contra asset account, Accumulated Depreciation, or Allowance for Depreciation, so that the original cost of the asset can be reported along with the accumulated depreciation to date.

    2. An exception to the general procedure of recording depreciation monthly or annually is made when a plant asset is sold, traded in, or scrapped, in which case depreciation must be brought up to date as of the date the asset is disposed of.

M. When depreciation is to be computed on a large number of individual assets, a subsidiary ledger is usually maintained.

    1. Subsidiary ledgers for plant assets are useful to accountants in:

        a. Determining the periodic depreciation expense.

        b. Recording the disposal of individual items.

        c. Preparing tax returns.

        d. Preparing insurance claims in the event of insured losses.

    2. Subsidiary ledger accounts may be expanded for accumulating data on the operating efficiency of the assets.

N. Subsidiary ledgers usually are not maintained for classes of plant assets that are made up of individual items of low unit cost. In such cases, the usual depreciation methods are not practical.

O. One common method of accounting for such assets is to treat them as expenses when they are acquired. Another method is to treat them as assets when acquired. An inventory of the items on hand at the end of the year is then taken and the assets' current value estimated. The difference between this value and the original cost or last year's value is debited to an expense account and credited to the plant asset account.

P. Depreciation may be determined for groups of assets, using a single rate. This method is called the composite-rate method.

III. Capital and Revenue Expenditures.

A. Expenditures for additions to plant assets or expenditures that add to the usefulness of plant assets for more than one accounting period are called capital expenditures.

   1. Expenditures for an addition to a plant asset should be debited to the plant asset account.

   2. Expenditures that increase operating efficiency or capacity for the remaining useful life of a plant asset are called betterments and should be debited to the plant asset account.

   3. Expenditures that increase the useful life of the asset beyond the original estimate are called extraordinary repairs and should be debited to the appropriate accumulated depreciation account.

B. Expenditures that benefit only the current period and that are made in order to maintain normal operating efficiency of plant assets are called revenue expenditures.

   1. Expenditures for ordinary maintenance and repairs of a recurring nature are revenue expenditures and should be debited to expense accounts.

   2. Small expenditures are usually treated as repair expense, even though they may have characteristics of capital expenditures.

IV. Disposal of Plant Assets.

A. A plant asset should not be removed from the accounts only because it has been depreciated for the full period of its estimated life. If the asset is still useful to the business, the cost and accumulated depreciation should remain in the ledger. In this way, accountability for the asset is maintained.

B. When plant assets are no longer useful to the business and have no residual market value, they are discarded.

   1. If the asset has been fully depreciated, then no loss is realized.

   2. The entry to record the disposal of a fully depreciated asset with no market value is to debit Accumulated Depreciation and credit the asset account.

   3. If the asset is not fully depreciated, depreciation should be brought up to date before the accumulated depreciation account is debited. The difference between the cost of the plant asset and its accumulated depreciation (book value) is recognized as a loss.

   4. Losses on discarding of plant assets are nonoperating items and are normally reported in the Other Expense section of the income statement.

C. The entry to record the sale of a plant asset is similar to the entry to record the disposal of a plant asset.

   1. The first entry should be to record the depreciation expense for the period.

2. Cash should be debited for the cash received from the sale of the plant asset.

3. Accumulated Depreciation should be debited for its balance, the plant asset account should be credited for its cost, and any difference in the debits and credits to balance the entry should be reported as a gain (credit) or a loss (debit) on the sale of the plant asset.

D. Plant assets may be traded in (exchanged) for new equipment having a similar use.

1. The trade-in allowance is deducted from the price of the new equipment, and the balance owed is called boot.

2. If the trade-in value of the plant asset is greater than its book value, the gain is not recognized for either financial reporting or tax purposes. The new asset's cost is the amount of boot given plus the book value of the old asset. In effect, the gain is indirectly recognized over the useful life of the asset as a reduction in the periodic depreciation charges which would otherwise be recognized.

3. If the trade-in value of the plant asset is less than its book value, the loss is recognized for financial reporting purposes. For tax purposes, the loss is not recognized. Any loss on the exchange is added to the cost of the new asset.

V. Leasing Plant Assets.

A. Instead of owning a plant asset, a business may acquire the use of a plant asset through a lease.

1. A lease is a contract for the use of an asset for a stated period of time.

2. The two parties to a lease are the lessor (the party who owns the asset) and the lessee (the party that obtains the rights to use the asset).

B. Capital leases are defined as leases that include one or more of the following provisions:

1. The lease transfers ownership of the leased asset to the lessee at the end of the lease term.

2. The lease contains an option for a bargain purchase of the leased asset by the lessee.

3. The lease term extends over most of the economic life of the leased asset.

4. The lease requires rental payments which approximate the fair market value of the leased asset.

C. Leases which do not meet the preceding criteria for capital leases are classified as operating leases.

D. A capital lease is accounted for as if the lessee has, in fact, purchased the asset. The lessee will debit an asset account for the fair market value of a leased asset and credit a long-term lease liability account.

E. In accounting for operating leases, rent expense is recognized as the leased asset is used.

F. Financial reporting disclosures require the presentation of future lease commitments in footnotes to the financial statements.

VI. Internal Control of Plant Assets.

A. Effective internal controls over plant assets begin with authorization and approval for the purchase of plant assets.

B. Once authorization and approval has been granted, procedures should exist to assure that the plant asset is acquired at the lowest possible cost.

C. When the asset is received, it should be inspected and tagged for entry into the plant asset subsidiary ledger.

D. A periodic physical inventory of plant assets should be performed to verify the accuracy of the accounting records. Such an inventory could detect missing, obsolete, or idle plant assets.

E. Precautions should be taken to safeguard plant assets from possible theft, misuse, or other damage.

F. All disposals of plant assets should be properly authorized and approved.

VII. Depletion.

A. The periodic allocation of the cost of metal ores and other minerals removed from the earth is called depletion.

B. The periodic cost allocation is based upon a depletion rate which is computed as the cost of the mineral deposit divided by its estimated size. The amount of periodic depletion is determined by multiplying the depletion rate by the quantity extracted during the period.

C. The adjusting entry for depletion is a debit to Depletion Expense and a credit to Accumulated Depletion. The accumulated depletion account is a contra account to the asset to which the cost of the mineral deposit was initially recorded.

VIII. Intangible Assets.

A. Long-term assets that are without physical attributes and not held for sale but are useful in the operations of a business are classified as intangible assets. Intangible assets include such items as patents, copyrights, and goodwill.

B. The basic principles of accounting for intangible assets are like those described earlier for plant assets. The major accounting issues involve the determination of the initial costs and the recognition of periodic cost expiration, called amortization, due to the passage of time or a decline in usefulness of the intangible asset.

C. Patents provide exclusive rights to produce and sell goods with one or more unique features.

1. A business may purchase patent rights from others or it may obtain patents on new products developed in its own research laboratories.

2. The initial cost of a purchased patent should be debited to an asset account and then written off, or amortized, over the years of its expected usefulness.

3. The straight-line method of amortization should be used unless it can be shown that another method is more appropriate.

4. A separate contra asset account is normally not credited for the write-off of patent amortization; the credit is recorded directly to the patent account.

5. Current accounting principles require that research and development costs incurred in the development of patents should be expensed as incurred.

6. Legal fees related to patent purchase or development should be recognized as part of the cost of the patent and amortized over the useful life of the patent.

D. The exclusive right to publish and sell a literary, artistic, or musical composition is obtained by a copyright.

1. The costs assigned to a copyright include all costs of creating the work plus the cost of obtaining the copyright.

2. A copyright that is purchased from another should be recorded at the price paid for it.

3. Because of the uncertainty regarding the useful life of a copyright, it is usually amortized over a relatively short period of time.

E. Goodwill is an intangible asset that attaches to a business as a result of such favorable factors as location, product superiority, reputation, and managerial skill.

1. Goodwill should be recognized in the accounts only if it can be objectively determined by an event or transaction, such as the purchase or sale of a business.

2. Goodwill should be amortized over the years of its useful life, which should not exceed 40 years.

IX. Financial Reporting for Plant Assets and Intangible Assets.

A. The amount of depreciation expense or amortization should be set forth separately in the income statement or disclosed in some other manner.

B. A general description of the method or methods used in computing depreciation or amortization should also be reported in the financial statements.

C. The balance of each major class of depreciable assets should be disclosed in the balance sheet or in notes thereto, together with the related accumulated depreciation, either by major class or in total.

D. The cost of mineral rights or ore deposits is normally shown as part of the plant assets section of the balance sheet. The related accumulated depletion should also be disclosed.

E. Intangible assets are usually presented in the balance sheet in a separate section immediately following plant assets.

ILLUSTRATIVE PROBLEM

Florence Company acquired new equipment at a cost of $75,000 at the beginning of the fiscal year. The equipment has an estimated life of 5 years and an estimated residual value of $6,000. Patrick Florence, the president, has requested information regarding alternative depreciation methods.

Instructions

1. Determine the annual depreciation for each of the five years of estimated useful life of the equipment, the accumulated depreciation at the end of each year, and the book value of the equipment at the end of each year by (a) the straight-line method, and (b) the declining-balance method (at twice the straight-line rate).

2. Assume that the equipment was depreciated under the declining-balance method. In the first week of the fifth year, the equipment was traded in for similar equipment priced at $90,000. The trade-in allowance on the old equipment was $8,000, and cash was paid for the balance.

   a. Journalize the entry to record the exchange.

   b. What is the cost basis of the new equipment for computing the amount of depreciation allowable for income tax purposes?

Solution

1.

	Year	Depreciation Expense	Accumulated Depreciation, End of Year	Book Value, End of Year
a.	1	$13,800	$13,800	$61,200
	2	13,800	27,600	47,400
	3	13,800	41,400	33,600
	4	13,800	55,200	19,800
	5	13,800	69,000	6,000
b.	1	$30,000	$30,000	$45,000
	2	18,000	48,000	27,000
	3	10,800	58,800	16,200
	4	6,480	65,280	9,720
	5	3,720*	69,000	6,000

*The asset is not depreciated below the estimated residual value of $6,000.

2.

a.
Accumulated Depreciation--Equipment	65,280	
Equipment	90,000	
Loss on Disposial of Plant Assets	1,720	
Equipment		75,000
Cash		82,000

b.
Book value of old equipment	$ 9,720
Boot given (cash)	82,000
Cost basis of new equipment for income tax purposes	$ 91,720

MATCHING

Instructions: A list of terms and related statements appear below. From the list of terms, select the one that relates to each statement. Print its identifying letter in the space provided.

A. Accelerated depreciation method
B. Amortization
C. Betterments
D. Boot
E. Capital expenditures
F. Composite-rate method
G. Depletion
H. Depreciation

I. Extraordinary repairs
J. Goodwill
K. Lease
L. Residual value
M. Revenue expenditures
N. Straight-line method
O. Units-of-production method

_____ 1. The allocation of the cost of a plant asset to expense over its expected useful life.

_____ 2. The estimated value of a plant asset at the time that it is to be retired from service.

_____ 3. A method of depreciation which provides for equal periodic charges to expense over the estimated life of the asset.

_____ 4. An intangible asset that attaches to a business as a result of such favorable factors as location, product superiority, reputation, and managerial skill.

_____ 5. Expenditures that add to the usefulness of the asset for more than one accounting period.

_____ 6. Expenditures that benefit only the current period and that are made in order to maintain normal operating efficiency.

_____ 7. The balance owed after the trade-in allowance is deducted from the price of new equipment acquired in a trade for equipment having similar uses.

_____ 8. A depreciation method that provides for a high depreciation charge in the first year of use of an asset and gradually declining periodic charges thereafter.

_____ 9. The periodic allocation of the cost of natural resources to expense as the units are removed.

_____ 10. The allocation to expense of the cost of an intangible asset over the periods of its economic usefulness.

_____ 11. A method of depreciation which yields a depreciation charge that varies with the amount of asset usage.

_____ 12. A method of depreciation that applies a single depreciation rate to entire groups of assets.

_____ 13. Expenditures that increase operating efficiency or capacity for the remaining useful life of a plant asset.

_____ 14. Expenditures that increase the useful life of an asset beyond the original estimate.

_____ 15. A contractual agreement that conveys the right to use an asset for a stated period of time.

TRUE / FALSE

Instructions: Indicate whether each of the following statements is true or false by placing a check mark in the appropriate column.

		True	False
1.	The declining-balance method provides for a higher depreciation charge in the first year of use of the asset, followed by a gradually declining periodic charge.	____	____
2.	The method of depreciation which yields a depreciation charge that varies with the amount of asset usage is known as the units-of-production method.	____	____
3.	In using the declining-balance method, the asset should not be depreciated below the net book value.	____	____
4.	Accelerated depreciation methods are most appropriate for situations in which the decline in productivity or earning power of the asset is proportionately greater in the early years of its use than in later years.	____	____
5.	ACRS depreciation methods permit the use of asset lives that are often much shorter than the actual useful life. . . .	____	____
6.	When an old plant asset is traded in for a new plant asset having a similar use, proper accounting treatment prohibits recognition of a gain.	____	____
7.	A lease which transfers ownership of the leased asset to the lessee at the end of the lease term should be classified as an operating lease.	____	____
8.	Long-lived assets that are without physical characteristics but useful in the operations of a business are classified as plant assets.	____	____
9.	Fully depreciated assets should be retained in the accounting records until disposal has been authorized and they are removed from service.	____	____
10.	Intangible assets are usually reported in the balance sheet in the current asset section.	____	____

MULTIPLE CHOICE

Instructions: Circle the best answer for each of the following questions.

1. If unwanted buildings are located on land acquired for a plant site, the cost of their removal, less any salvage recovered, should be charged to the:
   a. expense accounts
   b. building account
   c. land account
   d. accumulated depreciation account

2. The depreciation method used most often in the financial statements is the:
   a. straight-line method
   b. declining-balance method
   c. units-of-production method
   d. ACRS method

3. The depreciation method that would provide the highest reported net income in the early years of an asset's life would be:
   a. straight-line
   b. declining-balance
   c. 150% straight-line
   d. accelerated

4. Equipment with an estimated useful life of 5 years and an estimated residual value of $1,000 is acquired at a cost of $15,000. Using the declining-balance method (at twice the straight-line rate), what is the amount of depreciation for the first year of use of the equipment?
   a. $2,600
   b. $3,000
   c. $5,600
   d. $6,000

5. Equipment that cost $20,000 was originally estimated to have a useful life of 5 years and a residual value of $2,000. The equipment has been depreciated for 2 years using straight-line depreciation. During the third year it is estimated that the remaining useful life is 2 years (instead of 3) and that the residual value is $1,000 (instead of $2,000). The depreciation expense on the equipment in year 3 using the straight-line method would be:
   a. $5,500
   b. $5,900
   c. $6,000
   d. $7,500

6. Assume that a drill press is rebuilt during its sixth year of use so that its useful life is extended 5 years beyond the original estimate of 10 years. In this case, the cost of rebuilding the drill press should be charged to the appropriate:

    a. expense account

    b. accumulated depreciation account

    c. asset account

    d. liability account

7. Old equipment which cost $11,000 and has accumulated depreciation of $6,300 is given, along with $9,000 in cash, for the same type of new equipment with a price of $15,600. At what amount should the new equipment be recorded?

    a. $15,600

    b. $15,300

    c. $13,700

    d. $9,000

8. Assume the same facts as in No. 7, except that the old equipment and $11,500 in cash is given for the new equipment. At what amount should the new equipment be recorded for financial accounting purposes?

    a. $16,200

    b. $15,600

    c. $11,500

    d. $10,900

9. In a lease contract, the party who legally owns the asset is the:

    a. contractor

    b. operator

    c. lessee

    d. lessor

10. Which of the following items would not be considered an intangible asset?

    a. lease

    b. patent

    c. copyright

    d. goodwill

EXERCISE 10-1

A plant asset acquired on January 2 at a cost of $420,000 has an estimated useful life of 8 years. Assuming that it will have a residual value of $20,000, determine the depreciation for each of the first two years (a) by the straight-line method and (b) by the declining-balance method, using twice the straight-line rate.

(a) Straight-line method   Depreciation

Year 1 . . . .   _____

Year 2 . . . .   _____

(b) Declining-balance method   Depreciation

Year 1 . . . .   _____

Year 2 . . . .   _____

EXERCISE 10-2

Bidwell Co. uses the units-of-production method for computing the depreciation on its machines. One machine, which cost $88,000, is estimated to have a useful life of 22,000 hours and no residual value. During the first year of operation, this machine was used a total of 5,200 hours. Record the depreciation of this machine on December 31, the end of the first year. (Omit explanation.)

JOURNAL   PAGE

	DATE	DESCRIPTION	POST. REF.	DEBIT	CREDIT	
1						1
2						2
3						3
4						4
5						5
6						6
7						7
8						8
9						9
10						10
11						11
12						12
13						13

EXERCISE 10-3

On March 8, Tilly's Wholesale decides to sell for $2,000 cash some fixtures for which it paid $4,000 and on which it has taken total depreciation of $2,500 to date of sale. Record this sale. (Omit explanation.)

JOURNAL

PAGE

	DATE	DESCRIPTION	POST. REF.	DEBIT	CREDIT	
1						1
2						2
3						3
4						4
5						5
6						6
7						7
8						8

EXERCISE 10-4

Mine-It Co. paid $2,400,000 for some mineral rights in Idaho. The deposit is estimated to contain 800,000 tons of ore of uniform grade. Record the depletion of this deposit on December 31, the end of the first year, assuming that 80,000 tons are mined during the year. (Omit explanation.)

JOURNAL

PAGE

	DATE	DESCRIPTION	POST. REF.	DEBIT	CREDIT	
1						1
2						2
3						3
4						4
5						5
6						6
7						7
8						8
9						9
10						10
11						11
12						12

EXERCISE 10-5

Stables Co. acquires a patent at the beginning of its calendar (fiscal) year for $100,000. Although the patent will not expire for another ten years, it is expected to be of value for only five years. Record the amortization of this patent at the end of the fiscal year. (Omit explanation.)

JOURNAL   PAGE _____

	DATE	DESCRIPTION	POST. REF.	DEBIT	CREDIT	
1						1
2						2
3						3
4						4
5						5
6						6
7						7
8						8
9						9
10						10
11						11
12						12
13						13
14						14
15						15
16						16
17						17
18						18
19						19
20						20
21						21
22						22
23						23
24						24
25						25
26						26
27						27
28						28
29						29

PROBLEM 10-1

Bishop Company purchased equipment on January 1, 19XA, for $80,000. The equipment is expected to have a useful life of 4 years or 15,000 operating hours, and a residual value of $5,000. The equipment was used 3,400 hours in 19XA, 4,000 hours in 19XB, 6,000 hours in 19XC, and 1,600 hours in 19XD.

Instructions: Determine the amount of depreciation expense for the years ended December 31, 19XA, 19XB, 19XC, and 19XD, for each method of depreciation in the table below.

Year	Straight-Line	Declining-Balance	Units-of-Production
19XA			
19XB			
19XC			
19XD			
Total			

PROBLEM 10-2

Getco Co. has a sales representative who must travel a substantial amount. A car for this purpose was acquired January 2, four years ago, at a cost of $20,000. It is estimated to have a total useful life of 4 years or 100,000 miles.

Instructions:

(1) Record the annual depreciation on Getco's car at the end of the first and third years of ownership, using the straight-line method, assuming no residual value, and using a December 31 year end. (Omit explanation.)

(2) Record the annual depreciation on Getco's car at the end of the first and third years of ownership, using the declining-balance method at twice the straight-line rate and a December 31 year end. (Omit explanation.)

(3) Record the annual depreciation on Getco's car at the end of the first and third years of ownership, using the units-of-production method, assuming no residual value, and using a December 31 year end. The car was driven 35,000 miles in the first year and 28,000 miles in the third year. (Omit explanation.)

JOURNAL   PAGE

	DATE	DESCRIPTION	POST. REF.	DEBIT	CREDIT	
1						1
2						2
3						3
4						4
5						5
6						6
7						7
8						8
9						9
10						10
11						11
12						12
13						13
14						14
15						15
16						16
17						17
18						18
19						19
20						20

PROBLEM 10-3

(a) Braso Co. is planning to trade in its present truck for a new model on April 30 of the current year. The existing truck was purchased May 1 three years ago at a cost of $15,000, and accumulated depreciation is $12,000 through April 30 of the current year. The new truck has a list price of $20,700. Ralston Motors agrees to allow Braso $3,500 for the present truck, and Braso agrees to pay the balance of $17,200 in cash.

Instructions: Record the exchange in general journal form according to acceptable methods of accounting for exchanges. (Omit explanation.)

JOURNAL   PAGE

	DATE	DESCRIPTION	POST. REF.	DEBIT	CREDIT	
1						1
2						2
3						3
4						4

(b) Assume the same facts as in (a), except that the allowance on the present truck is $1,000 and Braso agrees to pay the balance of $19,700 in cash.

Instructions:

(1) Record the exchange according to acceptable methods of accounting for exchanges.

(2) Record the exchange as in (1), except that the entry should be in conformity with the requirements of the Internal Revenue Code.

JOURNAL   PAGE

	DATE	DESCRIPTION	POST. REF.	DEBIT	CREDIT	
1						1
2						2
3						3
4						4
5						5
6						6
7						7
8						8
9						9
10						10
11						11
12						12

11 Payroll, Notes Payable, and Other Current Liabilities

QUIZ AND TEST HINTS

The following hints may be helpful to you in preparing for a quiz or a test over the material covered in Chapter 11.

1. A major focus of this chapter is on the computation of payroll. You should be able to compute total earnings, FICA tax, state and federal unemployment tax, and net pay and prepare the necessary journal entries. Review the chapter illustrations related to these computations.

2. The journal entries for vacation pay, pensions, and warranty expense are fairly easy to do. Spend a few minutes reviewing these entries.

3. Most instructors will ask some questions related to notes payable. You should be able to compute interest and prepare the necessary journal entries, including an adjusting entry for accrued interest. Also, carefully review the discounting of non-interest-bearing notes.

4. The Illustrative Problem in the Chapter Review is a good overall review of the types of journal entries you might have to prepare on a test or a quiz. Try to work the problem without looking at the solution. Check your answer. If you made any errors, review those sections of the chapter. If you still don't understand the answer, ask your instructor for help.

5. Review the Key Terms.

CHAPTER OUTLINE

I. **Payroll and Payroll Taxes.**
   A. The term payroll refers to a total amount paid to employees for services provided during a period. Payroll includes amounts paid as salary and wages.
   B. Payroll expenditures are usually significant for a business for several reasons:
      1. Employees are sensitive to payroll errors or irregularities, and maintaining good employee morale requires that the payroll be paid on a timely, accurate basis.
      2. Payroll expenditures are subject to various federal and state regulations.
      3. Payroll expenditures and related payroll taxes have a significant effect on the net income of most businesses.
   C. Salary and wage rates are determined, in general, by agreement between the employer and employees. Businesses engaged in interstate

commerce must follow the requirements of the Fair Labor Standards Act. This act requires a minimum rate of 1 1/2 times the regular rate for all hours worked in excess of 40 hours per week.

D. The employee earnings for a period are determined by multiplying the hours worked up to 40 hours by the regular rate, and any overtime hours by 1 1/2 times the regular rate.

E. The total earnings of an employee for a payroll period, including bonuses and overtime pay, are often called the gross pay. From this amount is subtracted one or more deductions to arrive at net pay.

   1. Most employers are required by the Federal Insurance Contributions Act (FICA) to withhold a portion of the earnings of each of their employees as a deduction.

   2. Except for certain types of employment, all employers must withhold a portion of the earnings of their employees for payment of the employee's liability for federal income tax.

   3. Other deductions, such as union dues, employee insurance, etc., may be authorized by employees.

F. Gross earnings for a payroll period less the payroll deductions yields the amount to be paid to the employee, or the net pay.

G. Because there is a ceiling on annual earnings subject to FICA tax, when the amount of FICA tax to withhold from an employee is determined for a period, it is necessary to refer to one of the following cumulative amounts:

   1. Employee gross earnings for the year up to, but not including, the current payroll period.

   2. Employee tax withheld for the year up to, but not including, the current payroll period.

H. There is no ceiling on the amount of earnings subject to withholding for income taxes and hence no need to consider the cumulative earnings.

I. Most employers are subject to federal and state taxes based on the amount paid their employees. Such taxes are an operating expense of the business.

   1. Employers are required to contribute to the Federal Insurance Contributions Act (FICA) program for each employee. The tax rates are the same as those for employees.

   2. Employers also are subject to federal and state unemployment compensation taxes on the pay of employees.

J. A few states also collect a state unemployment compensation tax from employees.

II. Accounting Systems for Payroll and Payroll Taxes.

A. The major parts common to most payroll systems are the payroll register, employee's earnings record, and payroll checks.

B. The multicolumn form used in assembling and summarizing the data needed at the end of each payroll period is called the payroll register. A payroll register will normally have columns for the following items:

1. Total hours worked.

2. Regular, overtime, and total earnings.

3. Deductions for FICA, federal income tax, and other deductions.

4. Total amount of deductions.

5. The net amount of take-home pay.

6. The check number of the payroll check issued to the employee.

7. Distribution columns for the accounts to be debited for the payroll expense.

C. The payroll register serves as the basis for preparing the journal entries to record the payroll and related payroll tax expenses.

D. Payment of the liability for payroll and payroll taxes is recorded in the same manner as payment of other liabilities.

E. It is important to note that the payroll taxes levied against employers become liabilities at the time the payroll is paid to employees, rather than at the time the liability to the employees is incurred.

F. Detailed payroll data must be maintained for each employee in a record called the employee's earnings record. Such a record maintains data on total hours worked, total earnings, deductions, and net pay.

G. One of the principal outputs of most payroll systems is a series of payroll checks at the end of each pay period for distribution to employees.

1. Most employers with a large number of employees use a special bank account and payroll checks designed specifically for payroll.

2. Currency may be used to pay payroll when cashing checks is difficult for employees.

H. Through the use of diagrams, interrelationships of the principal parts of a payroll system may be shown.

1. The outputs of the payroll system are the payroll register, payroll checks, employees' earnings records, and reports for tax and other purposes.

2. The basic data entering the payroll system are called the input of the system. Input data that remain relatively unchanged are characterized as constants. Those data that differ from period to period are termed variables.

I. The cash disbursement controls discussed in earlier chapters are applicable to payrolls. Thus, the use of the voucher system and the requirement that all payments be supported by vouchers are desirable.

J. Other controls include proper authorization for additions and deletions of employees, pay rate changes, and the maintenance of attendance records.

III. Employees' Fringe Benefits.

A. Many companies provide their employees a variety of benefits in addition to salary and wages earned. These benefits are called fringe benefits and include vacation pay and pensions.

B. To properly match revenue and expense, the employer should accrue the vacation pay liability as the vacation rights are earned.

C. The entry to accrue vacation pay is to debit Vacation Pay Expense and credit a liability, Vacation Pay Payable.

D. A pension represents a cash payment to retired employees. Rights to pension payments are earned by employees during their working years.

    1. A defined contribution plan requires that a fixed amount of money be invested for the employee's behalf during the employee's working years.

        a. In a defined contribution plan, the employer is required to make annual pension contributions, but there is no promise with regard to future pension payments.

        b. In a defined contribution plan, the employee bears the investment risk.

    2. A defined benefit plan promises employees a fixed annual pension benefit at retirement, based on years of service and compensation levels.

    3. The employer's cost of an employee's pension plan in a given period is called the net periodic pension cost. This cost is debited to Pension Expense. Cash is credited for the same amount.

    4. Any unfunded amount of a defined benefit plan is credited to Unfunded Pension Liability. If the unfunded pension liability is to be paid within one year, it will be classified as a current liability. That portion of the liability to be paid beyond one year is a long-term liability.

E. Other postretirement benefits in addition to the pension benefits may include dental care, eye care, medical care, life insurance, tuition assistance, tax services, and legal services for employees or their dependents.

F. Generally accepted accounting principles require postretirement benefit expenses to be recognized in the financial statements as employees earn the rights to the benefits.

    1. The amount of the annual expense is based upon health and longevity statistics of the workforce.

    2. The entry to recognize benefits earned in the current year is to debit Postretirement Benefits Expense. Cash is credited for the same amount if the benefits are fully funded. If the benefits are not fully funded, a postretirement benefits plan liability account is credited.

IV. Short-Term Notes Payable.

A. Notes may be issued to creditors to satisfy an account payable created earlier, or they may be issued at the time merchandise or other assets are purchased. The entries to record a note payable are:

   1. Debit Accounts Payable and credit Notes Payable for the issuance of a note to satisfy an account payable.

   2. Debit Cash or other asset and credit Notes Payable for notes initially issued.

B. Interest must be recognized on notes payable.

   1. An adjusting entry debiting Interest Expense and crediting Interest Payable must normally be made at the end of the year to record the accrual of any interest.

   2. When notes are paid at maturity, the entry is normally to debit Notes Payable, debit Interest Expense, and credit Cash for the maturity amount.

C. Notes may be issued when money is borrowed from banks. Such notes may be interest-bearing or non-interest-bearing.

   1. An interest-bearing note is recorded by debiting Cash and crediting Notes Payable for the face value of the note. At the due date, Notes Payable is debited for the face value of the note, Interest Expense is debited for the interest, and Cash is credited for the total amount due.

   2. When a non-interest-bearing note is issued to a bank, the bank discounts the note and remits the proceeds to the borrower.

   3. The entry to record the discounted note is to debit Cash for the proceeds, debit Interest Expense for the difference between the face value of the note and the proceeds received, and credit Notes Payable for the amount of the face of the note. If the note is paid at maturity, Notes Payable is debited for the face value and Cash is credited.

V. Product Warranty Liability.

A. At the time of sale, a company may grant a warranty on a product. If revenues and expenses are to be matched properly, a liability to cover the warranty must be recorded in the period of the sale.

B. The entry to accrue warranty liability is to debit Product Warranty Expense and credit Product Warranty Payable.

C. When a defective product is repaired, the repair cost should be recorded by debiting Product Warranty Payable and crediting Cash, Supplies, or another appropriate account.

ILLUSTRATIVE PROBLEM

Selected transactions of Grainger Company, completed during the fiscal year ended December 31, are as follows:

Mar.   **1.**   Purchased merchandise on account from Perry Co., $15,000.

Apr.   **10.**   Issued a 60-day, 12% note for $15,000 to Perry Co. on account.

June   **9.**   Paid Perry Co. the amount owed on the note of April 10.

Aug.   **1.**   Issued a 90-day, non-interest-bearing note for $30,000 to Atlantic Coast National Bank. The bank discounted the note at 15%.

Oct.   **30.**   Paid Atlantic Coast National Bank the amount due on the note of August 1.

Dec.   **27.**   Journalized the entry to record the biweekly payroll. A summary of the payroll record follows:

Salary distribution:		
Sales	$50,800	
Officers	25,800	
Office	6,400	$83,000
Deductions:		
FICA tax	$ 4,820	
Federal income tax withheld	13,280	
State income tax withheld	3,840	
Savings bond deductions	630	
Medical insurance deductions	960	23,530
Net amount		$59,470

        30.   Issued a check in payment of employees' federal income tax of $13,280 and FICA tax of $9,640 due.

        31.   Issued a check for $8,600 to the pension fund trustee to fully fund the pension cost for December.

        31.   Journalized an entry to record the employees' accrued vacation pay, $32,200.

        31.   Journalized an entry to record the estimated accrued product warranty liability, $41,360.

Instructions: Journalize the preceding transactions, using a general journal.

Solution

Mar.	1	Purchases	15,000	
		Accounts Payable--Perry Co.		15,000
April	10	Accounts Payable--Perry Co.	15,000	
		Notes Payable		15,000
June	9	Notes Payable	15,000	
		Interest Expense	300	
		Cash		15,300
Aug.	1	Cash	28,875	
		Interest Expense	1,125	
		Notes Payable		30,000
Oct.	30	Notes Payable	30,000	
		Cash		30,000
Dec.	27	Sales Salaries Expense	50,800	
		Officers Salaries Expense	25,800	
		Office Salaries Expense	6,400	
		FICA Tax Payable		4,820
		Employees Federal Income Tax Payable .		13,280
		Employees State Income Tax Payable . .		3,840
		Bond Deductions Payable		630
		Medical Insurance Payable		960
		Salaries Payable		59,470
	30	Employees Federal Income Tax Payable . . .	13,280	
		FICA Tax Payable	9,640	
		Cash		22,920
	31	Pension Expense	8,600	
		Cash		8,600
	31	Vacation Pay Expense	32,200	
		Vacation Pay Payable		32,200
	31	Product Warranty Expense	41,360	
		Product Warranty Payable		41,360

MATCHING

Instructions: A list of terms and related statements appear below. From the list of terms, select the one that relates to each statement. Print its identifying letter in the space provided.

A. Defined benefit plan
B. Defined contribution plan
C. Discount
D. Employee's earnings record
E. FICA tax
F. Funded plan

G. Net pay
H. Net periodic pension cost
I. Payroll register
J. Proceeds
K. Wages
L. W-4
M. W-2

_____ 1. The Employee's Withholding Allowance Certificate.

_____ 2. Remuneration for manual labor, computed on an hourly, weekly, or piecework basis.

_____ 3. Gross pay less payroll deductions; the amount the employer is obligated to pay the employee.

_____ 4. A tax used to finance federal programs for old-age and disability benefits and health insurance for the aged.

_____ 5. Multicolumn form used in assembling and summarizing the data needed at the end of each payroll period.

_____ 6. A detailed record of an employee's earnings for each payroll period and for the year.

_____ 7. A pension plan that requires a fixed amount of money be invested for the employee's behalf during the employee's working years.

_____ 8. A pension plan that promises employees a fixed annual pension benefit at retirement, based on years of service and compensation levels.

_____ 9. The employer's cost of an employee's pension plan in a given period.

_____ 10. The net amount available to a borrower of funds.

TRUE / FALSE

Instructions: Indicate whether each of the following statements is true or false by placing a check mark in the appropriate column.

	True	False

1. The total earnings of an employee for a payroll period are called gross pay. . . . . _____ _____

2. Only employers are required to contribute to the Federal Insurance Contributions Act program. . . . . _____ _____

3. All states require that unemployment compensation taxes be withheld from employees' pay. . . . . _____ _____

4. Most employers are also subject to federal and state payroll taxes based on the amount earned by their employees not the amount paid. _____ _____

5. The amounts withheld from employees' earnings have an effect on the firm's debits to the salary or wage expense accounts. . . . . _____ _____

6. All payroll taxes levied against employers become liabilities at the time the related remuneration is paid to employees. _____ _____

7. The recording procedures when special payroll checks are used are different from the procedures when the checks are drawn on the regular bank account. . . . . _____ _____

8. Depending on when it is to be paid, vacation liability may be classified in the balance sheet as either a current liability or a long-term liability. . . . . _____ _____

9. To properly match revenues and expense, employees' vacation pay should be accrued as a liability as the vacation rights are earned. . . . . _____ _____

10. In order for revenues and expenses to be matched properly, a liability to cover the cost of a product warranty must be recorded in the period when the product is repaired. . . . . _____ _____

11. When employees are paid and the voucher system is used, it is necessary to prepare a voucher for the net amount to be paid to the employees. . . . . _____ _____

12. All changes in the constants of the payroll system, such as changes in pay rates, should be properly authorized in writing. . . . . _____ _____

13. The net periodic pension cost of a defined benefit plan is debited to Pension Expense, the amount funded is credited to Cash, and any unfunded amount is credited to Unfunded Pension Revenue. . . . . _____ _____

14. Examples of postretirement benefits from an employer may include dental care, eye care, medical care, life insurance, tuition assistance, or tax services. . . . . _____ _____

15. The rate used by a bank in discounting a non-interest-bearing note is called the prime rate. . . . . _____ _____

MULTIPLE CHOICE

Instructions: Circle the best answer for each of the following questions.

1. An employee's rate of pay is $8 per hour, with time and a half for hours worked in excess of 40 during a week. If the employee works 50 hours during a week, and has FICA tax withheld at a rate of 7.5% and federal income tax withheld at a rate of 15%, the employee's net pay for the week is:

   a. $440

   b. $374

   c. $341

   d. $310

2. For good internal control over payroll, which of the following is not desirable?

   a. all payments are made in cash

   b. all additions of employees are authorized in writing

   c. attendance records are controlled

   d. employee identification cards are used for clocking in

3. Which of the following items would not be considered a fringe benefit?

   a. vacations

   b. employee pension plans

   c. health insurance

   d. FICA benefits

4. For proper matching of revenues and expenses, the estimated cost of fringe benefits must be recognized as an expense of the period during which the:

   a. employee earns the benefit

   b. employee is paid the benefit

   c. fringe benefit contract is signed

   d. fringe benefit contract becomes effective

5. The inputs into a payroll system may be classified as either constants or variables. All of the following are variables except for:

   a. number of hours worked

   b. vacation credits

   c. number of income tax withholding allowances

   d. number of days sick leave with pay

EXERCISE 11-1

Instructions: In each of the following situations, determine the correct amount.

(1) An employee of a firm operating under the Federal Wage and Hour Law worked 50 hours last week. If the hourly rate of pay is $14, what is the employee's gross earnings for the week?

(2) During the current pay period, an employee earned $2,000. Prior to the current period, the employee earned (in the current year) $69,500. If the FICA tax is a combined rate of 7.5% on the first $70,000 of annual earnings and a rate of 1.5% on annual earnings over $70,000, what is the amount to be withheld from the employee's pay this period?

(3) During the current pay period, an employee earned $3,000. Prior to the current period, the employee earned (in the current year) $137,800. Using the FICA rates and bases in (2), compute the amount to be withheld from the employee's pay this period.

(4) Using the rates and maximum bases in (2), compute the amount of FICA tax withheld from the pay of an employee who has earned $10,000 but has actually received only $9,700, with the remaining $300 to be paid in the next year.

EXERCISE 11-2

Instructions: Prepare the general journal entries to record each of the following items for Wiler Co. for the year ended December 31. (Omit explanations.)

(1) Accrued employee vacation pay at the end of the year is $3,225.

(2) The estimated product warranty liability at the end of the year is 3% of sales of $150,000.

(3) A partially funded pension plan is maintained for employees at an annual cost of $40,000. At the end of the year, $27,500 is paid to the fund trustee and the remaining accrued pension liability is recognized.

JOURNAL

PAGE

	DATE	DESCRIPTION	POST. REF.	DEBIT	CREDIT	
1						1
2						2
3						3
4						4
5						5
6						6
7						7
8						8
9						9
10						10
11						11
12						12
13						13
14						14
15						15
16						16
17						17
18						18
19						19
20						20
21						21
22						22
23						23
24						24

PROBLEM 11-1

The weekly gross payroll of O'Brien Co. on December 7 amounts to $50,000, distributed as follows: sales salaries, $34,000; office salaries, $16,000. The following amounts are to be withheld: FICA tax $3,750; employees' income tax, $7,500; union dues, $900; and United Way, $450.

Instructions: Omitting explanations, prepare general journal entries to:

(1) Record the payroll.

(2) Record the payment of the payroll.

(3) Record the employer's payroll taxes. Assume that the entire payroll is subject to FICA tax at 7.5%, federal unemployment tax of .8%, and state unemployment tax at 5.4%.

(4) Record the employer's payroll taxes. Assume that $40,000 of payroll is subject to FICA at 7.5% and $10,000 at the FICA rate of 1.5%. Assume that none of the payroll is subject to federal or state unemployment tax.

JOURNAL
PAGE _____

	DATE	DESCRIPTION	POST. REF.	DEBIT	CREDIT	
1						1
2						2
3						3
4						4
5						5
6						6
7						7
8						8
9						9
10						10
11						11
12						12
13						13
14						14
15						15
16						16
17						17
18						18
19						19
20						20
21						21

PROBLEM 11-2

Instructions: For each of the employees listed below, compute the taxes indicated as well as the total of each tax. Assume the FICA tax is a combined rate of 7.5% on the first $70,000 of annual earnings and a rate of 1.5% on annual earnings over $70,000; a state unemployment tax rate of 5.4% on a maximum of $7,000; and a federal unemployment tax rate of .8% on a maximum of $7,000.

| Employee | Annual Earnings | Employee's FICA Tax | Employer's Taxes | | | |
			FICA	State Unemployment	Federal Unemployment	Total
Avery	$ 12,000					
Johnson	5,000					
Jones	59,000					
Smith	73,000					
Wilson	141,000					
Total	$ 290,000					

PROBLEM 11-3

Instructions: Prepare the general journal entries to record the following transactions. (Omit explanations.)

(1) Audrey Newman issued a 90-day, 12% note for $2,000 to Mayday Co. for a $2,000 overdue account.

(2) Newman paid the note in (1) at maturity.

(3) Paula Wheat borrowed $8,000 from the bank and gave the bank a 90-day, 11% note.

(4) Wheat paid the note in (3) at maturity.

(5) Randy Lucky borrowed $6,000 from the bank, giving a 60-day, non-interest-bearing note which was discounted at 9%.

(6) Lucky paid the note recorded in (5) at maturity.

JOURNAL

PAGE ____

	DATE	DESCRIPTION	POST. REF.	DEBIT	CREDIT	
1						1
2						2
3						3
4						4
5						5
6						6
7						7
8						8
9						9
10						10
11						11
12						12
13						13
14						14
15						15
16						16
17						17
18						18
19						19
20						20
21						21
22						22
23						23

JOURNAL

PAGE

	DATE		DESCRIPTION	POST. REF.	DEBIT	CREDIT	
1							1
2							2
3							3
4							4
5							5
6							6
7							7
8							8
9							9
10							10
11							11
12							12
13							13
14							14
15							15
16							16
17							17
18							18
19							19
20							20
21							21
22							22
23							23
24							24
25							25
26							26
27							27
28							28
29							29
30							30
31							31
32							32

12 Concepts and Principles

QUIZ AND TEST HINTS

The following hints may be helpful to you in preparing for a quiz or a test over the material covered in Chapter 12.

1. The chapter focuses on the ten concepts and principles of accounting. Carefully review the significance of each concept and principle. There is a significant amount of new terminology. Be sure to review the Key Terms.

2. The information in this chapter lends itself to both true-false and multiple-choice questions. Computational problems will involve either the installment method or percentage-of-completion method of recognizing revenue. Review the chapter illustrations for each of these methods. The Illustrative Problem in the Chapter Review provides a good review of the installment method.

CHAPTER OUTLINE

I. **Nature of Concepts and Principles.**

   A. Accounting concepts and principles provide the framework for the practice of accounting.

   B. The primary criterion for the establishment of an accounting concept or principle is its general acceptance among users of financial statements and members of the accounting profession.

   C. The Financial Accounting Standards Board (FASB) is currently the primary body developing accounting concepts and principles in the United States.

      1. After issuing discussion memoranda and preliminary proposals and evaluating comments from interested parties, the FASB issues *Statements of Financial Accounting Standards*, which become part of generally accepted accounting principles.

      2. The FASB also issues *Interpretations* which have the same authority as the standards.

      3. Presently, the FASB is in the process of developing a broad conceptual framework for financial accounting through the issuance of *Statements of Financial Accounting Concepts*. To date, six statements have been issued.

   D. The Governmental Accounting Standards Board (GASB) was formed in 1984 to establish accounting standards to be followed by state and municipal governments.

E. Accounting organizations that are influential in the establishment of accounting principles include the American Institute of Certified Public Accountants (AICPA), the Institute of Management Accountants (IMA), and the American Accounting Association (AAA). Each of these organizations publishes a monthly or quarterly periodical and issues other publications in the form of research studies, technical opinions, and monographs.

F. Governmental agencies with an interest in the development of accounting principles include the Securities and Exchange Commission (SEC) and the Internal Revenue Service (IRS).

G. Other regulatory agencies exercise a major influence over the accounting principles of the industries under their jurisdiction. For example, the Controller of the Currency and the Federal Deposit Insurance Corporation greatly influence generally accepted accounting principles used by banks.

H. As a result of the increasing global business activity, attention has been focused on developing uniform international accounting standards.

    1. The primary group involved in developing international accounting standards is the International Accounting Standards Committee (IASC).

    2. The IASC functions very similarly to the FASB.

    3. The IASC has no enforcement powers. Instead, the members pledge to use their best efforts to advocate the adoption of the *Standards* in their own countries.

II. Statements of Financial Accounting Concepts.

A. The FASB's *Statements of Financial Accounting Concepts* are the framework for financial accounting.

B. The primary objective of financial statements is to provide useful information to investors, managers, creditors, and others.

C. The basic elements of the financial statements are assets, liabilities, owner's equity, revenue, and expenses.

D. *Statement of Concepts No. 2* identifies the following characteristics of accounting information.

    1. Financial statements should be useful. This is the most important characteristic of financial statements.

    2. Financial statements must be understandable and clear in their presentation.

    3. Financial statements must be relevant to the decision-making needs of users such as investors and creditors.

    4. Financial statements should be reliable.

    5. Financial statements should be objective in nature so that they can be verified by others.

6. Financial statements should also be prepared for an accounting period that is timely to user needs.

7. Financial statements should be neutral in content and presentation and should not be biased towards any one purpose or user.

8. Financial statements should be complete, with full disclosure.

9. Financial statements should be comparable or consistent so that the statements can be compared over time.

III. Business Entity Concept.

A. The business entity concept assumes that a business is separate and distinct from the persons who supply its assets, regardless of the legal form of the entity.

B. The business entity concept is implied by the accounting equation. The business owns the assets and must account for the use of the assets to the various equity holders (owners and creditors).

IV. Going Concern Concept.

A. The going concern concept assumes that a business entity expects to continue in business at a profit for an indefinite period of time.

B. The going concern concept justifies recording plant assets at cost and depreciating them without reference to their current realizable (market) values.

C. Doubt as to the continued existence of a firm may be disclosed in a note to the financial statements.

D. When there is pervasive evidence that a business entity has a limited life, the accounting procedures should reflect the expected terminal date of the entity. For example, the financial statements should be prepared from a "quitting concern" or liquidation point of view rather than a "going concern" point of view.

V. Objectivity Principle.

A. To maintain the confidence of the many users of the financial statements, entries in the accounting records and the data reported on financial statements must be based on objective evidence.

B. Judgments, estimates, and other subjective factors must be used in preparing financial statements. In such cases, the most objective evidence should be used.

VI. Unit of Measurement Concept.

A. All business transactions are recorded in terms of dollars. It is only through the use of dollar amounts that the diverse transactions and activities of a business may be measured, reported, and periodically compared.

B. The scope of accounting reports is generally limited to those factors that can be expressed in monetary terms.

C. As a unit of measurement, the value of the dollar, called its purchasing power, continually changes. However, assuming that the dollar is stable allows for greater objectivity in preparing financial statements.

   1. One method of supplementing the historical-dollar statements is to report current cost data.

   a. Current cost is the amount of cash that would have to be paid currently to acquire assets of the same age and same condition as existing assets.

   b. The use of current costs permits the identification of gains and losses that result from holding assets during periods of changes in price levels.

   c. The major disadvantage in the use of current costs is the lack of standards for determining such costs.

   2. Constant dollar data may also be used for supplementing historical-dollar financial statements.

   a. Constant dollar data are historical costs that have been restated to constant dollars through use of a price-level index.

   b. A price-level index is the ratio of the total cost of a group of goods at a specific time to the total cost of the same group of goods at an earlier base time.

D. Current cost or constant dollar data are optional disclosures.

VII. Accounting Period Concept.

A. A complete and accurate reporting of a business's success or failure cannot be obtained until it discontinues operations, converts its assets into cash, and pays off its debts.

B. Because many decisions must be made by management and interested outsiders throughout the life of a business entity, periodic reports are prepared on operations, financial position, and cash flows.

VIII. Matching Concept.

A. Determining periodic net income is a two-fold process of matching (1) revenue for the period with (2) expenses incurred in generating the revenues. The difference between the revenues and expenses is the net income or net loss for the period.

B. Various criteria are acceptable for determining when revenue is recognized. Generally, the criteria used should agree with any contractual terms with the customer and should be based on objective evidence.

   1. Revenue from the sale of merchandise is usually determined by the point-of-sale method, under which revenue is recognized at the time title passes to the buyer.

2. The recognition of revenue may be delayed until payment is received. When this criterion is used, revenue is considered to be recognized at the time the cash is collected, regardless of when the sale was made. This method, referred to as the cash basis, has the practical advantage of simplicity, and may be used by professional services businesses.

3. Under the installment method of determining revenue (used primarily in the retail field), each receipt of cash is considered to be revenue and composed of part cost of merchandise sold and part gross profit on the sale.

4. For long-term construction projects, revenue and expenses may be recognized using either the completed-contract method or the percentage-of-completion method.

   a. Under the completed-contract method, no revenue or expense is recognized on long term construction projects until the project is completed.

   b. Under the percentage-of-completion method, the revenue to be recognized and the income for the period are determined by the estimated percentage of the contract that has been completed during the period. This estimated percentage can be developed by comparing the incurred costs with the most recent estimates by engineers, architects, or other qualified personnel of the progress of the work performed.

C. Expenses are the using up of assets to generate revenues. The amount of an asset's cost that is used up is a measure of the expense.

1. Each expense must be matched against its related revenue in order to properly determine the amount of net income or net loss for the period.

2. Adjusting entries at the end of the period are often required to properly match revenues and expenses.

IX. Adequate Disclosure Concept.

A. Under the adequate disclosure concept, financial statements and their related footnotes or other disclosures should contain all the relevant data essential to the user's understanding of the entity's financial status.

B. When there are several acceptable alternative accounting methods that could have a significant effect on amounts reported on the statements, the particular method used should be disclosed.

C. In situations where an accounting estimate has been changed, any material effect of the change on net income should be disclosed in the financial statements for the year of the change.

D. Contingent liabilities are potential obligations that will become liabilities only if certain events occur in the future.

1. If the amount of the contingent liability is probable and can be reasonably estimated, it should be recorded in the accounts.

2. If the amount of the contingent liability cannot be reasonably estimated, the details of the contingency should be disclosed.

3. The most common contingent liabilities disclosed in notes to financial statements concern litigation, guarantees, and discounting receivables.

E. A financial instrument is cash, a security that evidences ownership interest in an entity, or a contract that imposes certain obligations and rights upon another entity. Generally accepted accounting principles require specific disclosures related to financial instruments.

1. Disclosures for financial instruments include the market (fair) value of the financial instruments.

2. Any unusual risks related to the financial instruments in excess of the amounts reported in the financial statements must also be disclosed.

3. Finally, any unusual credit risks related to the financial instruments must also be reported.

F. To help financial statement users assess operating results of companies involved in more than one type of business activity or market, the financial statements should disclose information by segments. The information reported for each major segment includes: revenue, income from operations, and identifiable assets related to the segment.

G. Significant events occurring after the close of the period should be disclosed.

X. Consistency Concept.

A. The concept of consistency does not completely prohibit changes in accounting principles used. However, changes in accounting principles must be justified and should be fully disclosed in the financial statements.

B. Different accounting methods may be used throughout a business, such as the use of different depreciation methods for different classes of assets or different inventory methods for different classes of inventory.

XI. Materiality Concept.

A. The concept of materiality refers to the relative importance of an event, accounting method, or change in methods that affects items on the financial statements.

B. In assessing materiality of an item, the size of the item, its nature, and relationship to other items in the financial statements should be considered.

C. The concept of materiality may also be applied to the recording of transactions. For example, small expenditures for plant assets may be treated as an expense of the period rather than as an asset.

XII. Conservatism Concept.

A. The concept of conservatism means that in selecting among alternatives, the method or estimates that yield the lesser amount of net income or asset value should be selected.

B. The conservatism concept is no longer considered to be the dominant factor in selecting among alternatives.

XIII. Role of Auditing of Financial Statements.

A. The role of auditing is to add credibility to the financial statements by having an independent, outside party attest to the fairness of the selection and use of accounting concepts in preparing the financial statements.

B. All public corporations are required to have an annual, independent audit of their financial statements by a certified public accountant (CPA).

C. Other companies may be required to have their financial statements audited by banks or other financial institutions.

D. Independent auditors use generally accepted accounting principles and concepts in assessing the fairness of a company's financial statements.

E. Upon completing an audit, the auditor issues an Independent Auditors' Report. This report accompanies the financial statements when they are distributed to outside users.

F. The normal audit report includes the following three paragraphs:

1. An introductory paragraph identifying the financial statements audited.

2. A scope paragraph describing the nature of the audit.

3. An opinion paragraph presenting the auditor's opinion as to the fairness of the statements.

G. In some circumstances, the normal audit report is not issued.

1. Auditors may add a paragraph to the unqualified or clean opinion to call attention to an important event or fact.

2. If the financial statements do not conform to generally accepted accounting principles. A qualified opinion is issued, and the reason for it is briefly described.

3. If the financial statements contain an extreme departure from accepted principles, an adverse or negative opinion is issued and the reason for the opinion described.

4. If the auditor is unable to reach an opinion on the financial statements, a disclaimer of opinion is issued.

ILLUSTRATIVE PROBLEM

Town and Country Furniture Company makes all sales on the installment basis and recognizes revenue at the point of sale. Condensed income statements and the amounts collected from customers for each of the first three years of operations are as follows:

	1994	1995	1996
Sales	$ 190,000	$240,000	$ 170,000
Cost of merchandise sold	133,000	163,200	122,400
Gross profit	$ 57,000	$ 76,800	$ 47,600
Operating expenses	33,900	41,500	30,000
Net income	$ 23,100	$ 35,300	$ 17,600
Collected from sales of first year	$ 50,000	$110,000	$ 30,000
Collected from sales of second year		80,000	120,000
Collected from sales of third year			60,000

Instructions

1. Determine the gross profit percentages for each year.

2. Using the installment method, determine the amount of net income or loss that would have been reported in each year.

Solution

1. Gross profit percentages:
   1994: $57,000 / $190,000 = 30%
   1995: $76,800 / $240,000 = 32%
   1996: $47,600 / $170,000 = 28%

2.	1994	1995	1996
Gross profit realized on collections from sales of:			
1994: 30% x $50,000	$ 15,000		
1994: 30% x $110,000		$ 33,000	
1994: 30% x $30,000			$ 9,000
1995: 32% x $80,000		25,600	
1995: 32% x $120,000			38,400
1996: 28% x $60,000			16,800
Total gross profit realized	$ 15,000	$ 58,600	$ 64,200
Operating expenses	33,900	41,500	30,000
Net income (loss)	$(18,900)	$ 17,100	$ 34,200

MATCHING

Instructions: A list of terms and related statements appear below. From the list of terms, select the one that relates to each statement. Print its identifying letter in the space provided.

A. Adequate disclosure	I. Going concern concept
B. Business entity concept	J. Installment method
C. Completed-contract method	K. Matching
D. Conservatism	L. Materiality concept
E. Consistency concept	M. Percentage-of-completion method
F. Current cost data	N. Point-of-sale method
G. FASB	O. SEC
H. General price-level data	

_____ 1. The concept that assumes that a business is separate and distinct from the persons who supply its assets.

_____ 2. The concept that assumes that a business entity has a reasonable expectation of continuing in business at a profit for an indefinite period of time.

_____ 3. Data indicating the amount of cash that would have to be paid currently to acquire assets of the same age and in the same condition as existing assets.

_____ 4. Data indicating historical cost amounts that have been converted to constant dollars.

_____ 5. A method under which revenue is recognized at the time title passes to the buyer.

_____ 6. A method under which each receipt of cash is considered to be revenue and to be composed of partial amounts of (1) the cost of merchandise sold and (2) gross profit on the sale.

_____ 7. A method under which revenue is recognized over the entire life of a long-term contract.

_____ 8. The concept that enables financial statement users to assume that successive financial statements of a business are based on the same generally accepted accounting principles.

_____ 9. The concept that permits accountants to treat small expenditures for plant assets as an expense rather than an asset.

_____ 10. The attitude that leads accountants to prefer the method or procedure that yields the lesser amount of net income or of asset value.

_____ 11. The concept that financial statements and their accompanying footnotes should contain all of the pertinent data believed essential to the reader's understanding of a business's financial status.

_____ 12. The method that recognizes revenue from long-term construction contracts when the project is completed.

_____ 13. The current authoritative body for the development of accounting principles for all entities except state and municipal governments.

_____ 14. The principle of accounting that all revenues should be matched with the expenses incurred in earning those revenues during a period of time.

_____ 15. The federal agency that exercises a dominant influence over the development of accounting principles for most companies whose securities are traded in interstate commerce.

TRUE / FALSE

Instructions: Indicate whether each of the following statements is true or false by placing a check mark in the appropriate column.

True   False

1. There is likely to be less differentiation between "management" and "owners" in a business as it increases in size and complexity. . . . .   _____ _____

2. The "principles" used in accounting are similar to the natural laws relating to the physical sciences. . . . .   _____ _____

3. General acceptance among the members of the accounting profession is the criterion for determining an accounting principle. . . . .   _____ _____

4. Responsibility for the development of accounting principles has rested primarily with the federal government. . . . . .   _____ _____

5. The FASB is a governmental agency under the SEC. . . .   _____ _____

6. The FASB's *Statements of Financial Accounting Concepts* are intended to provide a broad conceptual framework for accounting. . . . .   _____ _____

7. The AICPA has responsibility for establishing the accounting standards to be followed by state and municipal governments. . . . .   _____ _____

8. The SEC is a branch of the IRS. . . . .   _____ _____

9. The business entity concept used in accounting for a sole proprietorship is the same as the legal concept of a sole proprietorship. . . . .   _____ _____

10. The going concern assumption supports the treatment of virtually unsalable prepaid expenses as assets. . . . . . .   _____ _____

11. In a going concern, plant assets usually are recorded on the balance sheet at their estimated realizable values. . .   _____ _____

12. According to the objective evidence principle, entries in the accounting records and data reported on financial statements must be based on objectively determined evidence. . . . .   _____ _____

True   False

13. The major disadvantage in the use of current costs is the absence of established standards and procedures for determining such costs. . . . .   _____ _____

14. Large, publicly held companies are required to disclose both current cost and constant dollar information annually.   _____ _____

15. A complete and accurate picture of a business's success or failure cannot be obtained until it discontinues operations, converts its assets into cash, and pays off its debts. . . . .   _____ _____

16. In recent years, financial statement emphasis has shifted from the income statement to the balance sheet. . . . . .   _____ _____

17. Revenue from the sale of goods generally is considered to be recognized at the time title passes to the buyer. . . . .   _____ _____

18. Revenue from the sale of services is normally recognized when the services have been performed. . . . .   _____ _____

19. On the cash basis, revenue is considered to be earned at the time the cash is collected, regardless of when the sale was made. . . . .   _____ _____

20. The percentage-of-completion method usually is more objective than the point-of-sale method. . . . .   _____ _____

21. The amount of cash or equivalent given to acquire property or service is referred to as its cost. . . . .   _____ _____

22. The IRS's laws and regulations for preparing federal tax returns coincide with the generally accepted accounting principles used for preparing financial statements. . . . . .   _____ _____

23. Criteria for standards of disclosure must be based on objective facts rather than on value judgments. . . . . . .   _____ _____

24. When there are several acceptable alternative accounting methods that could have a significant effect on amounts reported on the statements, the particular method used should be disclosed. . . . .   _____ _____

25. It is acceptable to revise accounting estimates based on additional information or subsequent developments. . . . .   _____ _____

26. If the amount of a contingent liability is probable and can be reasonably estimated, it should be recorded in the accounts.   _____ _____

27. The concept of consistency prohibits changes in accounting principles employed.   _____ _____

28. The consistency concept requires that a specific accounting method be applied uniformly throughout a business. . . . .   _____ _____

29. If a lawsuit is filed against a company, the amount of the lawsuit must be recorded in the account as a liability and reported on the financial statements. . . . .   _____ _____

30. If company A guarantees a loan for company B, company A is obligated to pay the loan if company B fails to make payment. . . . .   _____ _____

MULTIPLE CHOICE

Instructions: Circle the best answer for each of the following questions.

1. At the present time, the dominant body in the development of generally accepted accounting principles is the:
   a. AICPA
   b. FASB
   c. APB
   d. GASB

2. The statements of generally accepted accounting principles issued by the FASB are called:
   a. Statements of Accounting Principles
   b. Statements of FAF
   c. Statements of Financial Accounting Standards
   d. FASB Opinions

3. Of the various governmental agencies with an interest in the development of accounting principles, the one that has been the most influential has been the:
   a. SEC
   b. IRS
   c. GASB
   d. FEI

4. For a number of reasons, including custom and various legal requirements, the maximum interval between accounting reports is:
   a. one month
   b. three months
   c. one year
   d. three years

5. When circumstances are such that the collection of receivables is not reasonably assured, a method of determining revenue that may be used is called the:
   a. installment method
   b. post-sale method
   c. gross profit method
   d. point-of-sale method

6. If property other than cash is given to acquire property, the cost of the acquired property is considered to be the:
   a. net realizable value of the acquired property
   b. current cost of the property given
   c. list price of the acquired property
   d. cash equivalent of the property given

7. If a business suffers a major loss from a fire between the end of the year and the issuance of the financial statements, the business should:

   a. not mention the loss in the statements because it occurred in a different accounting period

   b. disclose the loss in a note to the statements

   c. not mention the loss in the statements, but put out a separate announcement of the loss

   d. record the loss in the accounting records and in the statements

8. For each significant reporting segment of a business, a business is required to disclose each of the following except:

   a. revenue

   b. income from operations

   c. identifiable assets associated with the segment

   d. identifiable liabilities associated with the segment

9. Of the following accounting concepts, the least important one in choosing among alternative accounting methods is:

   a. conservatism

   b. objectivity

   c. consistency

   d. materiality

10. All of the following are examples of contingent liabilities disclosed in notes to the financial statements except for:

    a. litigation

    b. guarantees

    c. receiving donated real estate

    d. discounting receivables

11. Entries in the accounting records and data reported on financial statements should be based on objective evidence. Of the following items of evidence, the least objective one is:

    a. bank statements

    b. vouchers for purchases

    c. physical counts of inventory

    d. estimates by the credit manager about the collectibility of accounts receivable

12. When, in the opinion of an independent auditor, the financial statements contain an extreme departure from generally accepted accounting principles, the auditor would issue:

    a. a normal report accompanied by a supplemental report describing the departure

    b. a report containing an adverse opinion

    c. a report containing a disclaimer of opinion

    d. a report containing a qualified opinion

EXERCISE 12-1

During the current year, Wilton Construction Company contracted to build a new baseball stadium for the local university. The total contract price was $20,000,000 and the estimated construction costs were $16,500,000. At the end of the current year, the project was estimated to be 25% completed and the costs incurred totaled $4,100,000.

Instructions: Using the percentage-of-completion method of recognizing revenue, determine the following amounts for the current year:

(1) Revenue from the contract . . . . $ _____

(2) Cost associated with the contract . . . . $ _____

(3) Income from the contract recognized for the current year $ _____

EXERCISE 12-2

Pasquale Co.'s net income for its first year of operations is $76,350, based on FIFO inventory and straight-line depreciation. Pasquale is considering making two accounting changes in the current year, as follows:

(1) From straight-line to declining-balance depreciation at twice the straight-line rate. Straight-line depreciation is $10,000, whereas declining-balance depreciation would be $12,000.

(2) From FIFO to LIFO inventory. FIFO inventory cost is $19,000, whereas LIFO inventory cost would be $13,800.

Instructions: In the space provided below, compute the net income for the first year of operations if the two accounting changes had been made.

Net income using straight-line and FIFO . . . . $ 76,350

(1) Effect of depreciation expense . . . . $ _____

(2) Effect of inventory change . . . . $ _____

(3) Revised net income . . . . $ _____

EXERCISE 12-3

Rista Co. reported net income for the current year of $37,600. In reviewing Rista's records, you discover the following items for which no adjustments were made at the end of the period.

(1) Supplies of $13 were on hand. All supplies had been expensed.

(2) Interest expense of $15 had accrued for 3 days on a note payable.

(3) Delivery charges of $6 on packages received in the current period were not entered until paid in the following period.

(4) Petty cash expenditures of $20 were not entered, because reimbursement of petty cash was not made at the end of the period.

Instructions:

(1) In the spaces provided below, compute the net income of Rista Co. for the year if adjustments were made for these items:

(a)	Reported net income	$	37,600
(b)	Supplies	$	_____
(c)	Interest expense	$	_____
(d)	Delivery charges	$	_____
(e)	Petty cash expenditures	$	_____
(f)	Revised net income	$	_____

(2) What accounting concept would support Rista's not making these adjustments?

PROBLEM 12-1

Instructions: In each of the following situations, determine the correct amounts.

(1) Ten years ago, Delaney Co. bought a building for $400,000. The company has taken depreciation of $15,000 a year on this building. Recently, the building was appraised at $300,000. Another firm offered to buy the building for $325,000. Delaney Co. should report this building on its balance sheet at the amount of $ _____

(2) On January 1, Hillman Company paid $13,350 for a 3-year insurance policy. The company should report insurance expense for the second year in the amount of . . . . $ _____

(3) Charo Company was organized on January 1. All sales are made on the installment plan and gross profits are calculated by the installment method. During the first year, sales amounted to $2,100,000; cost of sales, $1,365,000; and collections, $1,344,000. The gross profit for the first year was . . . . $ _____

(4) Dutch Sales Company, organized January 1, makes all sales on the installment plan but calculates gross profits by using the point-of-sale method. During the first year, the company's sales amounted to $2,100,000; cost of sales, $1,365,000; and collections on installments, $1,344,000. The gross profit for the year was . . . . $ _____

(5) V. Milano established a sole proprietorship business. During the first month, she wrote checks for $12,000 on the business bank account. Of this amount, she spent $6,750 for personal needs and $5,250 for office equipment for the business. As a result of these transactions, the net worth of the business was decreased by . . . . $ _____

13 Partnership Formation, Income Division, and Liquidation

QUIZ AND TEST HINTS

The following hints may be helpful to you in preparing for a quiz or a test over the material covered in Chapter 13.

1. Review the Key Terms that may be tested using true-false or multiple-choice questions.

2. You should be able to prepare journal entries for formation and dissolution of a partnership. Pay particular attention to the payment of a bonus on the admission of a new partner.

3. Expect at least one question involving distribution of partnership net income among the partners. This question may involve salary allowances and interest allowances on partners' capital balances. Remember, if the partnership agreement does not indicate how income is shared among the partners, it is shared equally. Also, be able to prepare the journal entries distributing a partnership net income or loss. The entry for distributing net income debits Income Summary and credits the partners' capital accounts.

4. If your instructor assigned a homework problem involving partnership liquidation or covered it in class, you may see a question related to liquidating a partnership. Review the chapter illustrations and the Illustrative Problem in the Chapter Review.

CHAPTER OUTLINE

I. **Characteristics of Partnerships.**

   A. The Uniform Partnership Act defines a partnership as an association of two or more persons to carry on as co-owners a business for profit.

   B. Partnerships have several characteristics that have accounting implications.

   1. A partnership has a limited life. Dissolution of a partnership occurs whenever a partner ceases to be a member of the firm for any reason, or a new partner is admitted.

   2. Most partnerships are general partnerships, in which the partners have unlimited liability. Each partner is individually liable to creditors for debts incurred by the partnership.

   3. In some states, a limited partnership may be formed in which the liability of some partners may be limited to the amount of their capital

investment. However, a limited partnership must have at least one general partner who has unlimited liability.

4. Partners have co-ownership of partnership property. The property invested in a partnership by a partner becomes the property of all the partners jointly.

5. The mutual agency characteristic of a partnership means that each partner is an agent of the partnership with the authority to enter into contracts for the partnership. Thus, the acts of each partner bind the partnership and become the responsibility of all partners.

6. A significant right of partners is participation in income of the partnership. Net income and net loss are distributed among the partners according to their agreement. In the absence of any agreement, all partners share equally.

7. Although partnerships are nontaxable entities and therefore do not pay federal income taxes, they must file an information return with the Internal Revenue Service.

8. A partnership is created by a contract containing all the elements essential to any other enforceable contract. This contract is known as the articles of partnership or partnership agreement.

D. The advantages of a partnership form of organization include the following:

1. A partnership is relatively easy and inexpensive to organize, requiring only an agreement between two or more persons.

2. A partnership has the advantage of being able to bring together more capital, more managerial skills, and more experience than a sole proprietorship.

3. A partnership is a nontaxable entity; the combined income taxes paid by the individual partners may be lower than the income taxes that would be paid by a corporation.

E. The disadvantages of a partnership form of organization are as follows:

1. The partnership life is limited.

2. Each partner has unlimited liability.

3. One partner can bind the partnership to contracts.

4. Raising large amounts of capital is more difficult for a partnership than for a corporation.

F. The day-to-day accounting for a partnership is similar to other forms of business organization, except in the areas of formation, income distribution, dissolution, and liquidation of partnerships.

II. **Formation of a Partnership**.

A. A separate entry is made for the investment of each partner in a partnership.

1. The various assets contributed by a partner are debited to the proper asset accounts.

2. If liabilities are assumed by the partnership, the liability accounts are credited.

3. The partner's capital account is credited for the net amount.

B. The monetary amounts at which noncash assets are recorded by a partnership are those agreed upon by the partners. The agreed upon values normally represent current market values.

C. Receivables contributed to the partnership are recorded at their face amount, with a credit to a contra account if provision is to be made for possible future uncollectibility.

III. Dividing Net Income or Net Loss.

A. Distribution and division of income or loss among partners should be in accordance with the partnership agreement. If the partnership agreement is silent on the matter, the law provides that all partners should share equally.

B. As a means of recognizing differences in ability and in amount of time devoted to the business, the partnership agreement may provide for the division of a portion of net income to the partners in the form of a salary allowance.

1. A clear distinction must be made between division of net income, which is credited to the capital accounts, and payments to the partners, which are debited to the drawing accounts.

2. In most cases, the amount of net income distributed to each partner's capital account at the end of the year will differ from the amount the partner withdraws during the year.

C. Partners may agree to allow salaries based on the services rendered and also to allow interest on their capital investments. The remainder is then divided as agreed.

D. If net income is less than the total of special allowances (salaries and interest), the remaining balance to be distributed will be a negative figure that must be divided among the partners as though it were a net loss.

E. The division of net income should be disclosed in the financial statements prepared at the end of the fiscal period.

F. The changes in the owner's equity of a partnership during the period should also be presented in a statement of owner's equity.

IV. Partnership Dissolution.

A. One of the basic characteristics of the partnership form of organization is its limited life. Any change in the personnel of the ownership dissolves the partnership.

B. Dissolution of the partnership is not necessarily followed by the winding up of the affairs of the business. In many cases, the remaining partners may continue to operate the business. When this happens, a new partnership is formed and a new partnership agreement is prepared.

C. An additional person may be admitted to a partnership only with the consent of all the current partners.

D. An additional partner may be admitted to a partnership through either of two procedures:

1. A new partner may be admitted with the purchase of an interest from one or more of the current partners. In this case, neither the total assets nor the total owner's equity of the business is affected. The purchase price of the partnership share is paid directly to the selling partner or partners. The only accounting entry needed is to transfer the proper amounts of owner's equity from the capital accounts of the selling partner or partners to the capital account established for the incoming partner.

2. A new partner may be admitted to the partnership through the contribution of assets directly to the partnership. In this case, both the total assets and the total owner's equity of the business are increased. The assets contributed to the partnership are debited and the capital account of the incoming partner is credited.

E. Whenever a new partner is admitted to a partnership, the existing assets of the partnership should be adjusted to their fair market value. The net amount of the increases and decreases in asset values are then allocated to the capital accounts of the old partners according to their income-sharing ratio. It is important that the assets be stated in terms of current prices at the time of admission of the new partner. Failure to recognize current prices may result in the new partner participating in gains or losses that arose in prior periods.

F. When a new partner is admitted to a partnership, the incoming partner may pay a bonus to the existing partners to join the partnership. The amount of any bonus paid to the partnership is distributed among the existing partners' capital accounts.

G. When a new partner is admitted to a partnership, the incoming partner may be paid a bonus to join the partnership. The amount of the bonus is debited to the capital accounts of the existing partners and credited to the capital account of the new partner.

H. When a partner retires or for some reason wishes to withdraw from the firm, one or more of the remaining partners may purchase the withdrawing partner's interest and the business may continue uninterrupted.

1. The settlement of the purchase and sale is made between the partners as individuals, in a manner similar to the admission of a new partner by purchase of interest, and thus is not recorded by the partnership.

2. The only entry required by the partnership is a debit to the capital account of the partner withdrawing and a credit to the capital account of the partner or partners acquiring the interest.

I.   When a partner retires or for some other reason wishes to withdraw from the firm, the settlement with the withdrawing partner may be made by the partnership.

1.   The effect of this withdrawal is to reduce the assets and the owner's equity of the firm.

2.   To determine the ownership equity of the withdrawing partner, the asset accounts should be adjusted to current market prices. The net amount of the adjustment should be divided among the capital accounts of the partners according to the income-sharing ratio.

3.   The entry to record the withdrawal is to debit the capital account of the withdrawing partner and credit the assets paid or liability incurred to the withdrawing partner.

J.   The death of a partner dissolves the partnership. In the absence of any agreement, the accounts should be closed as of the date of death, and the net income for the part of the year should be transferred to the capital accounts.

1.   The partnership agreement may indicate that the accounts remain open to the end of the fiscal year or until the affairs are wound up, if that should occur earlier.

2.   The net income of the entire period is then divided, as provided by the agreement, between the periods occurring before and after the partner's death.

3.   The balance in the capital account of the deceased partner is transferred to a liability account with the deceased's estate.

V. Liquidating Partnerships.

A.   When a partnership goes out of business, it usually sells the assets, pays the creditors, and distributes the remaining cash or other assets to the partners. This winding-up process is called liquidation.

B.   During the process of liquidation, the sale of assets is called realization. As cash is realized, it is applied first to the payment of the claims of creditors.

C.   Any gains or losses realized from the sale of assets should be distributed to the capital accounts of the partners in their income-sharing ratios.

D.   After all liabilities have been paid, the remaining cash should be distributed to the partners according to the balances in their capital accounts. Under no circumstances should the income-sharing ratio be used as a basis for distributing cash to the partners after payment of liabilities.

E.   If the share of a loss from the realization of assets exceeds a partner's ownership equity (capital account balance),the resulting debit balance in the partner's capital account is called a deficiency.

1.   Pending collection from the deficient partner, the partnership cash will not be sufficient to pay the other partners in full.

2. The affairs of the partnership are not completely wound up until the claims against the partners are settled. Payments to the firm by the deficient partner are credited to that partner's capital account. Any cash thus collected is distributed to the remaining partners.

3. Any uncollectible deficiency from a partner becomes a loss to the partnership and is written off against the capital accounts of the remaining partners according to their income-sharing ratios.

F. The type of error most likely to occur in the liquidation of a partnership is an improper distribution of cash to the partners. Errors of this type result from confusing the distribution of cash with the division of gains and losses on realization.

1. Gains and losses on realization result from the disposal of assets to outsiders. These gains and losses should be divided among the capital accounts in the same manner as net income or net loss from normal business operations, using the income-sharing ratio.

2. The distribution of cash (or other assets) to the partners upon liquidation is the exact reverse of the contribution of assets by the partners at the time the partnership was established. The distribution of assets to partners is equal to the credit balances of the partners' capital accounts after all gains and losses on realization have been divided and allowances have been made for any potential partner deficiencies.

ILLUSTRATIVE PROBLEM

Ryan, Shaw, and Todd, who share in income and losses in the ratio of 4:2:4, decided to discontinue operations as of April 30 and liquidate their partnership. After the accounts were closed on April 30, the following trial balance was prepared:

Cash	$ 8,100	
Noncash Assets	70,600	
Liabilities		$ 27,500
Ryan, Capital		23,300
Shaw, Capital		12,100
Todd, Capital		15,800
Total	$ 78,700	$ 78,700

Between May 1 and May 18, the noncash assets were sold for $20,600, and the liabilities were paid.

Instructions

1. Assuming that the partner with the capital deficiency pays the entire amount owed to the partnership, prepare a statement of partnership liquidation.

2. Journalize the entries to record (a) the sale of the assets, (b) the division of loss on the sale of the assets, (c) the payment of the liabilities, (d) the receipt of the deficiency, and (e) the distribution of cash to the partners.

Solution

1.

Ryan, Shaw, and Todd
Statement of Partnership Liquidation
For Period May 1-18, 19--

		Noncash		Capital Ryan	Shaw	Todd
	Cash +	Assets	= Liabilities +	(40%) +	(20%) +	(40%)
Balances before realization	$ 8,100	$70,600	$27,500	$23,300	$12,100	$15,800
Sale of assets and division of loss	+20,600	-70,600	----	-20,000	-10,000	-20,000
Balances after realization	$28,700	0	$27,500	$ 3,300	$ 2,100	$ 4,200 (Dr.)
Payment of liabilities . .	-27,500	----	-27,500	----	----	----
Balances after payment of liabilities	$ 1,200	0	0	$ 3,300	$ 2,100	$ 4,200 (Dr.)
Receipt of deficiency . .	+ 4,200	----	----	----	----	+ 4,200
Balances	$ 5,400	0	0	$ 3,300	$ 2,100	0
Distribution of cash to partners	- 5,400	----	----	- 3,300	- 2,100	----
Final balances	0	0	0	0	0	0

2. a. Cash   20,600
     Loss and Gain on Realization   50,000
          Noncash Assets   70,600

b. Ryan, Capital   20,000
     Shaw, Capital   10,000
     Todd, Capital   20,000
          Loss and Gain on Realization   50,000

c. Liabilities   27,500
          Cash   27,500

d. Cash   4,200
          Todd, Capital   4,200

e. Ryan, Capital   3,300
     Shaw, Capital   2,100
          Cash   5,400

MATCHING

Instructions: A list of terms and related statements appear below. From the list of terms, select the one that relates to each statement. Print its identifying letter in the space provided.

A. Articles of partnership
B. Deficiency
C. General partnership
D. Income statement
E. Limited life

F. Limited partnership
G. Liquidation
H. Mutual agency
I. Partnership
J. Realization

_____ 1. A type of partnership in which the partners have unlimited liability.

_____ 2. A type of partnership in which the liability of some partners may be restricted to the amount of their capital investment.

_____ 3. A characteristic of a partnership that means that each partner has the authority to enter into contracts for the partnership.

_____ 4. Another name for the partnership agreement or contract among the partners.

_____ 5. A disadvantage of a partnership.

_____ 6. A financial statement in which the details of the division of partnership net income would be disclosed.

_____ 7. An unincorporated business of two or more persons to carry on as co-owners a business for profit.

_____ 8. The winding-up process of a partnership may generally be called (?).

_____ 9. When a partnership is going out of business, the sale of assets is called (?).

_____ 10. When a partnership is going out of business and the loss chargeable to a partner exceeds that partner's ownership equity, the resulting debit balance in the capital account is called a(n) (?).

TRUE / FALSE

Instructions: Indicate whether each of the following statements is true or false by placing a check mark in the appropriate column.

	True	**False**

1. Partners are legally employees of the partnership and their capital contributions are considered a loan. . . . .   _____ _____

2. Each general partner is individually liable to creditors for debts incurred by the partnership. . . . .   _____ _____

3. Salary allowances are treated as divisions of partnership net income and are credited to the partners' capital accounts. . . . .   _____ _____

4. The property invested in a partnership by a partner remains identified as that partner's property. . . . .   _____ _____

5. A partner's claim against the assets of the partnership in the event of dissolution is measured by the amount of the partner's initial investment. . . . .   _____ _____

6. A written contract is necessary to the legal formation of a partnership. . . . .   _____ _____

7. At the time a partnership is formed, the market values of the assets should be considered in determining each partner's investment. . . . .   _____ _____

8. In the absence of an agreement for income or loss distributions among the partners, the partners should share income equally, even if there are differences in their capital contributions. . . . .   _____ _____

9. Regardless of whether partners' salaries and interest are treated as expenses of the partnership or as a division of net income, the total amount allocated to each partner will not be affected. . . . .   _____ _____

10. A partnership is required to pay federal income taxes. . . .   _____ _____

11. Any change in the personnel of the ownership results in a dissolution of a partnership. . . . .   _____ _____

12. A new partner may be admitted to a partnership with the consent of the majority of the old partners. . . . .   _____ _____

13. A partner's interest may be disposed of only with the consent of the remaining partners. . . . .   _____ _____

14. When a new partner is admitted by purchasing an interest from one or more of the old partners, the purchase price is recorded in the accounts of the partnership. . . . .   _____ _____

15. It is appropriate to adjust the old partnership assets to current market values at the time a new partner is admitted.   _____ _____

16. At the time a new partner is admitted, a bonus may be paid to the incoming partner. . . . .   _____ _____

17. A person may be admitted to a partnership by purchasing an interest from one or more of the existing partners. The only entry required by the partnership is to transfer owner's equity amounts from the capital accounts of the selling partners to the capital account of the new partner. . . . . .   _____ _____

18. As cash is realized from the sale of assets during the liquidation of a partnership, the cash is applied first to the payment of the claims of the limited partners. . . . .   _____ _____

19. If the distribution of the loss on the sale of non-cash assets when a partnership goes out of business causes a partner's account to have a debit balance, this balance represents a claim of the partnership against the partner. . . . .   _____ _____

20. If a deficiency of a partner is uncollectible, this represents a loss which is written off against the capital balances of the remaining partners. . . . .   _____ _____

MULTIPLE CHOICE

Instructions: Circle the best answer for each of the following questions.

1. If a partnership agreement is silent on dividing net income or net losses, the partners:
    a. divide income/losses according to their original capital investments
    b. divide income/losses equally
    c. divide income/losses according to skills possessed by each partner
    d. divide income/losses on the basis of individual time devoted to the business

2. Which of the following is not an advantage of a partnership?
    a. It is possible to bring together more capital than in a sole proprietorship
    b. Partners' income taxes may be less than the income taxes would be on a corporation
    c. It is possible to bring together more managerial skills than in a sole proprietorship
    d. Each partner has limited liability

3. When a new partner is admitted to the partnership by a contribution of assets to the partnership:
    a. neither the total assets nor the total owner's equity of the business is affected
    b. only the total assets are affected
    c. only the owner's equity is affected
    d. both the total assets and the total owner's equity are increased

4. When a partner retires and the settlement with the partner is made by the partnership, the effect is to:
    a. reduce the assets and the owner's equity of the firm
    b. reduce the assets and increase the owner's equity of the firm
    c. increase the liabilities and the owner's equity of the firm
    d. leave the assets and the owner's equity unchanged

5. If there is a loss on the sale of noncash assets when a partnership goes out of business, the loss should be divided among the partners:
    a. according to their original capital investments
    b. according to their current capital balances
    c. according to their income-sharing ratio
    d. equally

EXERCISE 13-1

Ruth Cutco and Darrell Robbs formed a partnership. Cutco invested $100,000 cash and merchandise valued at $80,000. Robbs invested $10,000 cash, land valued at $115,000, equipment valued at $45,000, and merchandise valued at $5,000.

Instructions: Prepare the entries to record the investments of Cutco and Robbs on the partnership books. Use the current date.

JOURNAL   PAGE

	DATE	DESCRIPTION	POST. REF.	DEBIT	CREDIT	
1						1
2						2
3						3
4						4
5						5
6						6
7						7
8						8
9						9
10						10
11						11
12						12
13						13
14						14
15						15
16						16
17						17
18						18
19						19
20						20
21						21
22						22
23						23
24						24
25						25
26						26
27						27
28						28

EXERCISE 13-2

Ann Hartly, Barry Smetz, and Lynette Grasso are partners having capitals of $100,000, $55,000, and $35,000 respectively. They share net income equally.

Instructions: Prepare the entries to record each of the following situations. (Omit explanations.)

(1) On June 30, John Schafer is admitted to the partnership by purchasing one-fifth of the respective capital interests of the three partners. He pays $30,000 to Hartly, $15,000 to Smetz, and $10,000 to Grasso.

JOURNAL PAGE

	DATE	DESCRIPTION	POST. REF.	DEBIT	CREDIT	
1						1
2						2
3						3
4						4

(2) On July 1, Laura Masko is admitted to the partnership for an investment of $50,000, and the parties agree to pay a bonus of $21,000 to Masko.

JOURNAL PAGE

	DATE	DESCRIPTION	POST. REF.	DEBIT	CREDIT	
1						1
2						2
3						3
4						4
5						5
6						6
7						7
8						8
9						9
10						10
11						11
12						12
13						13
14						14
15						15
16						16

EXERCISE 13-3

Arway, Batts and Carlone are partners having capital balances of $65,000, $55,000, and $40,000 respectively. The partners share net income equally. Carlone has decided to leave the partnership.

Instructions: Prepare the entries to record each of the following situations. (Omit explanations.)

(1) The partners agree that the inventory of the partnership should be increased by $12,750 to recognize its fair market value. Arway buys Carlone's interest in the partnership for $53,000.

JOURNAL   PAGE

	DATE	DESCRIPTION	POST. REF.	DEBIT	CREDIT	
1						1
2						2
3						3
4						4
5						5
6						6
7						7

(2) The partners agree that the inventory of the partnership should be increased by $6,000 to recognize its fair market value. The partnership pays Carlone cash for her interest as reflected by the balance in her capital account.

JOURNAL   PAGE

	DATE	DESCRIPTION	POST. REF.	DEBIT	CREDIT	
1						1
2						2
3						3
4						4
5						5
6						6
7						7
8						8
9						9
10						10
11						11
12						12

PROBLEM 13-1

On January 2 of the current year, Bulley and Scram formed a partnership in which Bulley invested $300,000 and Scram invested $700,000. During the year, the partnership had a net income of $200,000.

Instructions: Show how this net income would be distributed under each of the following conditions:

(1) The partnership agreement says nothing about the distribution of net income.

Bulley's share	$	_____
Scram's share	$	_____
Total	$	_____

(2) The partnership agreement provides that Bulley and Scram are to share net income in a 2:3 ratio respectively.

Bulley's share	$	_____
Scram's share	$	_____
Total	$	_____

(3) The partnership agreement provides that Bulley and Scram are to share net income in accordance with the ratio of their original capital investments.

Bulley's share	$	_____
Scram's share	$	_____
Total	$	_____

(4) The partnership agreement provides that Bulley is to be allowed a salary of $30,000 and Scram a salary of $50,000 with the balance of net income distributed equally.

Division of Net Income	Bulley	Scram	Total
Salary allowance	$	$	$
Remaining income			
Net income	$	$	$ 200,000

(5) The partnership agreement provides that interest at 5% is to be allowed on the beginning capital and that the balance is to be distributed equally.

Division of Net Income	Bulley	Scram	Total
Interest allowance	$	$	$
Remaining income			
Net income	$	$	$ 200,000

(6) The partnership agreement provides that Bulley is to be allowed a salary of $15,000 and Scram a salary of $25,000; that interest at 5% is to be allowed on beginning capital; and that the balance is to be distributed equally.

Division of Net Income	Bulley	Scram	Total
Salary allowance	$	$	$
Interest allowance			
Remaining income			
Net income	$	$	$ 200,000

(7) The partnership agreement provides that Bulley is to be allowed a salary of $80,000 and Scram a salary of $78,000; that interest at 5% is to be allowed on beginning capital; and that the balance is to be distributed equally.

Division of Net Income	Bulley	Scram	Total
Salary allowance	$	$	$
Interest allowance			
Total	$	$	$
Excess of allowances over income . .			
Net income	$	$	$ 200,000

PROBLEM 13-2

Prior to the liquidation of the partnership of Triste, Sandpipe, and Hinkle, the ledger contained the following accounts and balances: Cash, $100,000; Noncash Assets, $300,000; Liabilities, $120,000; Triste, Capital, $90,000; Sandpipe, Capital, $60,000; and Hinkle, Capital, $130,000. Assume that the noncash assets are sold for $400,000. Triste, Sandpipe, and Hinkle share profits in a 30:50:20 ratio.

Instructions:

(1) Complete the following schedule showing the sale of assets, payment of liabilities, and distribution of the remaining cash to the partners.

| | | Noncash | | Capital | | |
	Cash +	Assets	= Liabilities +	Triste (30%) +	Sandpipe (50%) +	Hinkle (20%)
Balances before realization	$100,000	$300,000	$120,000	$90,000	$60,000	$130,000
Sale of noncash assets and division of gain						
Balances after realization						
Payment of liabilities						
Balances after payment of liabilities						
Distribution of cash to partners						
Final balances						

(2) Assume that the noncash assets are sold for $130,000 and that the partner with a debit balance pays the entire deficiency. Complete the following schedule showing the sale of assets, payment of liabilities, and distribution of the remaining cash to the partners.

| | | Noncash | | Capital | | |
	Cash +	Assets	= Liabilities +	Triste (30%) +	Sandpipe (50%) +	Hinkle (20%)
Balances before realization	$100,000	$300,000	$120,000	$90,000	$60,000	$130,000
Sale of noncash assets and division of loss						
Balances after realization						
Payment of liabilities						
Balances after payment of liabilities						
Receipt of deficiancy						
Balances						
Distribution of cash to partners						
Final balances						

(3) Prepare the journal entries to record the liquidation of the partnership based on the facts in (2). Use the current date. (Omit explanations.)

JOURNAL   PAGE

	DATE		DESCRIPTION	POST. REF.	DEBIT	CREDIT	
1							1
2							2
3							3
4							4
5							5
6							6
7							7
8							8
9							9
10							10
11							11
12							12
13							13
14							14
15							15
16							16
17							17
18							18
19							19
20							20
21							21
22							22
23							23
24							24
25							25
26							26
27							27
28							28
29							29
30							30

SOLUTIONS

CHAPTER 1

MATCHING

1.	G	6.	C	11.	H
2.	D	7.	A	12.	E
3.	F	8.	M	13.	I
4.	J	9.	N	14.	P
5.	O	10.	B	15.	K

TRUE/FALSE

1.	T	6.	F
2.	F	7.	F
3.	F	8.	T
4.	F	9.	F
5.	F	10.	F

MULTIPLE CHOICE

1.	d
2.	c
3.	b
4.	d
5.	c

EXERCISE 1-1

	A	L	OE
1.	+	o	+
2.	+	+	o
3.	+	o	+
4.	+	o	+
5.	-	o	-
6.	+,-	o	o
7.	+,-	o	o
8.	-	-	o
9.	-	-	o
10.	-	o	-

PROBLEM 1-1

	Assets			= Liabilities	+ Owner's Equity
	Cash	+ Supplies	+ Land	= Accts. Pay.	+ Ed Casey, Capital
1.	$40,000				$40,000 I
2.		+$2,000		+$2,000	
Bal.	$40,000	$2,000		$2,000	$40,000
3.	-14,000		+$14,000		
Bal.	$26,000	$2,000	$14,000	$2,000	$40,000
4.	- 1,800			-1,800	
Bal.	$24,200	$2,000	$14,000	$ 200	$40,000
5.	- 2,000				- 2,000 D
Bal.	$22,200	$2,000	$14,000	$ 200	$38,000
6.	- 2,800				- 2,800 E
Bal.	$19,400	$2,000	$14,000	$ 200	$35,200
7.				+ 900	- 900 E
Bal.	$19,400	$2,000	$14,000	$1,100	$34,300
8.	+10,000				+10,000 I
Bal.	$29,400	$2,000	$14,000	$1,100	$44,300
9.	+ 500				+ 500 R
Bal.	$29,900	$2,000	$14,000	$1,100	$44,800
10.		- 600			- 600 E
Bal.	$29,900	$1,400	$14,000	$1,100	$44,200
	=======	=======	========	=======	========

PROBLEM 1-2

(1)
```
                         Tom's Painting Service
                            Income Statement
                      For Year Ended December 31, 19--
----------------------------------------------------------------------
Sales                                            $27,450
Operating Expenses:
  Supplies expense                    $5,450
  Advertising expense                  4,825
  Truck rental expense                 1,525
  Utilities expense                      700
  Misc. expense                        1,400       13,900
                                      ------      -------
Net income                                       $13,550
                                                 =======
```

(2)
```
                         Tom's Painting Service
                       Statement of Owner's Equity
                      For Year Ended December 31, 19--
----------------------------------------------------------------------
Investment, Jan. 1, 19--                          $ 4,000
Additional investment by owner        $ 2,000
Income for the year                    13,550
Less withdrawal                        (1,000)
                                      --------
Increase in owner's equity                         14,550
                                                  -------
Tom Wallace, capital, Dec. 31, 19--               $18,550
                                                  =======
```

(3)
```
                         Tom's Painting Service
                            Balance Sheet
                          December 31, 19--
----------------------------------------------------------------------
     Assets                              Liabilities
Cash                    $10,050   Accounts payable              $ 4,450
Accounts receivable       8,950      Owner's Equity
Supplies                  4,000   Tom Wallace, capital           18,550
                        -------                                 -------
Total assets            $23,000   Total liab. & owner's eq.     $23,000
                        =======                                 =======
```

CHAPTER 2

MATCHING		TRUE/FALSE		MULTIPLE CHOICE	
1. H	7. I	1. F	6. F	1. b	6. b
2. G	8. D	2. T	7. F	2. d	7. b
3. K	9. E	3. T	8. F	3. b	8. d
4. C	10. J	4. F	9. T	4. c	9. c
5. B	11. L	5. T	10. F	5. a	10. b
6. F	12. A				

EXERCISE 2-1

Transactions	Account Debited		Account Credited	
	Type	Effect	Type	Effect
(1)	asset	+	capital	+
(2)	asset	+	liability	+
(3)	asset	+	liability	+
(4)	asset	+	revenue	+
(5)	liability	-	asset	-
(6)	expense	+	liability	+
(7)	asset	+	asset	-
(8)	drawing	+	asset	-

PROBLEM 2-1

(1)

June 1	Cash		11	5,000	
	Equipment		18	14,500	
	Vehicles		19	21,000	
	Joan Star, Capital		31		40,500
16	Equipment		18	5,500	
	Accounts Payable		21		5,500
28	Supplies		12	500	
	Accounts Payable		21		500
30	Accounts Payable		21	2,100	
	Cash		11		2,100

(2)

Account   Cash   Account No. 11

Date	Item	Post. Ref.	Debit	Credit	Balance Debit	Credit
19--						
June 1		1	5,000		5,000	
30		1		2,100	2,900	

Account   Supplies   Account No. 12

Date	Item	Post. Ref.	Debit	Credit	Balance Debit	Credit
19--						
June 28		1	500		500	

Account   Equipment   Account No. 18

Date	Item	Post. Ref.	Debit	Credit	Balance Debit	Credit
19--						
June 1		1	14,500		14,500	
16		1	5,500		20,000	

Account   Vehicles   Account No. 19

Date	Item	Post. Ref.	Debit	Credit	Balance Debit	Credit
19--						
June 1		1	21,000		21,000	

Account   Accounts Payable   Account No. 21

Date	Item	Post. Ref.	Debit	Credit	Balance Debit	Credit
19--						
June 16		1		5,500		5,500
28		1		500		6,000
30		1	2,100			3,900

Account   Joan Star, Capital   Account No. 31

Date	Item	Post. Ref.	Debit	Credit	Balance Debit	Credit
19--						
June 1		1		40,500		40,500

(3)

Star Service Company
Trial Balance
June 30, 19--

Cash	2,900	
Supplies	500	
Equipment	20,000	
Vehicles	21,000	
Accounts Payable		3,900
Joan Star, Capital		40,500
	44,400	44,400

PROBLEM 2-2

(1)

	Cash					Accounts Payable		
(a)	20,000	(b)	2,500		(k)	240	(f)	200
(d)	19,600	(c)	1,000		(m)	2,000	(g)	10,400
		(e)	1,100				(j)	240
		(g)	2,600					
		(h)	5,000			Judy Turner, Capital		
		(i)	800				(a)	33,200
		(k)	240					
		(l)	1,700			Judy Turner, Drawing		
		(m)	2,000		(h)	5,000		
		(n)	5,000					
		(o)	500			Legal Fees		
							(d)	19,600

	Office Supplies					Rent Expense	
(c)	1,000				(b)	2,500	
(f)	200						

	Prepaid Insurance					Salary Expense	
(l)	1,700				(e)	1,100	

	Library				Telephone Expense	
(n)	5,000			(j)	240	

	Office Equipment				Auto Repairs & Maintenance Expense	
(a)	13,200			(i)	800	

	Auto				Janitor Expense	
(g)	13,000			(o)	500	

(2)

Judy Turner
Trial Balance
January 31, 19--

Cash	17,160	
Office Supplies	1,200	
Prepaid Insurance	1,700	
Library	5,000	
Office Equipment	13,200	
Auto	13,000	
Accounts Payable		8,600
Judy Turner, Capital		33,200
Judy Turner, Drawing	5,000	
Legal Fees		19,600
Rent Expense	2,500	
Salary Expense	1,100	
Telephone Expense	240	
Auto Repairs & Maintenance Expense	800	
Janitor Expense	500	
	61,400	61,400

PROBLEM 2-3

(a)	Prepaid Insurance		1,000	
	Prepaid Rent			1,000
	To correct erroneous debit to prepaid rent.			

(b)	Accounts Receivable		200	
	Accounts Payable			200
	To correct erroneous credit to accounts receivable.			

(c)	Drawing		3,000	
	Cash			3,000
	To correct erroneous entry debiting cash and crediting drawing.			

CONTINUING PROBLEM

(2) The complete ledger for the Continuing Problem is at the end of the solution for Chapter 6.

(1)

1996

Dec.	1	Rent Expense	532	400	
		Cash	110		400
		Paid office rent for December.			
	1	Van Expense	524	200	
		Cash	110		200
		Paid van lease for December.			
	2	Prepaid Insurance	118	600	
		Cash	110		600
		Purchased 1-year prop. ins. policy.			
	2	Fees Receivable	112	9,800	
		Fees Earned	410		9,800
		Billed clients for performances in Oct. and Nov.			
	4	Cash	110	1,000	
		Fees Receivable	112		1,000
		Received payment for billings.			
	8	Cash	110	1,200	
		Fees Earned	410		1,200
		Received cash for performance.			
	11	Subcontractors Payable	214	750	
		Cash	110		750
		Paid George the Mysterious amount owed.			
	14	Theater Services Payable	213	2,005	
		Cash	110		2,005
		Paid Chi-Town Theater amount owed.			
	15	Supplies & Props	116	185	
		Accounts Payable	211		185
		Purchased supplies and props on account.			
	16	Equipment - Stage	123	1,200	
		Cash	110		200
		Accounts Payable	211		1,000
		Purchased equipment on account with down payment.			

Dec.	17	Accounts Payable	211	1,100	
		Cash	110		1,100
		Paid creditors.			
	18	Cash	110	5,200	
		Fees Earned	410		5,200
		Received cash for December performances.			
	21	Cosmetics Expense	525	73	
		Cash	110		73
		Paid cash for cosmetics.			
	24	Cash	110	5,200	
		Fees Receivable	112		5,200
		Collected on December 2 billings.			
	29	Telephone Expense	534	95	
		Cash	110		95
		Paid telephone expense.			
	30	Subcontractor Expense	522	450	
		Cash	110		450
		Paid Jane the Fantastic for performance.			
	31	Furniture & Fixtures	121	7,000	
		Cash	110		2,000
		Notes Payable	220		5,000
		Purchased furniture with cash and note.			
	31	Cosmetics Expense	525	125	
		Cash	110		125
		Paid cash for cosmetics.			
	31	Van Expense	524	150	
		Cash	110		150
		Paid for gas for year.			

(3)

Egor J. Gribbet
Trial Balance
December 31, 1996

Cash	9,956	
Fees Receivable	6,086	
Supplies & Props	1,268	
Office Supplies	789	
Prepaid Insurance	2,000	
Furniture & Fixtures	13,400	
Equipment - Stage	12,000	
Accounts Payable		1,580
Notes Payable		6,500
E. J. Gribbet, Capital		21,852
E. J. Gribbet, Drawing	400	
Fees Earned		31,300
Theater Services Expense	4,000	
Subcontractor Expense	2,460	
Van Expense	3,250	
Cosmetics Expense	428	
Rent Expense	4,800	
Telephone Expense	395	
	-------	-------
	61,232	61,232
	=======	=======

CHAPTER 3

MATCHING		TRUE/FALSE		MULTIPLE CHOICE
1. A	6. H	1. T	6. T	1. b
2. C	7. L	2. F	7. T	2. c
3. I	8. M	3. T	8. F	3. a
4. G	9. K	4. F	9. T	4. d
5. B	10. D	5. T	10. F	5. a

EXERCISE 3-1

(1)

```
                 Cash                              Insurance Expense
                   |May 1      5,400      Dec. 31  1,200 |


            Prepaid Insurance
May 1          5,400 |Dec. 31    1,200
```

(2) Unexpired insurance............... $4,200

(3) Insurance expense................. $1,200

EXERCISE 3-2

(1)

```
                 Cash                              Salary Expense
                   |Oct.  7      250      Oct.  7      250 |
                   |     14      250           14      250 |
                   |     21      250           21      250 |
                   |     28      250           28      250 |
                                              31       50 |


            Salaries Payable
                   |Oct.            50
```

(2) Salary expense................... $1,050

(3) Salaries payable................. $50

EXERCISE 3-3

```
            Unearned Rent                          Rent Income
Dec. 31      500 |Dec. 1     6,000                  |Dec. 31      500
```

Dec. 31   Unearned Rent   500
           Rent Income   500

EXERCISE 3-4

```
          Interest Receivable                    Interest Income
Dec. 31      320 |                                 |Dec. 31      320
```

Dec. 31   Interest Receivable...............   320
           Interest Income.................   320

PROBLEM 3-1

(1) and **(2)**

Bob's Service Company
Work Sheet
For Month Ended July 31, 19--

Account Title	Trial Balance Dr.	Cr.	Adjustments Dr.	Cr.	Adjusted Trial Balance Dr.	Cr.
Cash	9,218				9,218	
Accts. Rec.	7,277		(e) 2,100		9,377	
Supplies	2,750			(c) 1,750	1,000	
Prepaid Rent	8,712			(b) 726	7,986	
Tools/Equipment	21,829				21,829	
Acc. Depr.		1,535		(d) 400		1,935
Accounts Payable		7,117				7,117
Bob Jones, Cap.		37,417				37,417
Bob Jones, Draw.	3,234				3,234	
Service Fees		28,699		(e) 2,100		30,799
Salary Expense	15,929		(a) 2,000		17,929	
Misc. Expense	5,819				5,819	
	74,768	74,768				
Salaries Payable				(a) 2,000		2,000
Rent Expense			(b) 726		726	
Supplies Expense			(c) 1,750		1,750	
Depr. Expense			(d) 400		400	
			6,976	6,976	79,268	79,268

CONTINUING PROBLEM

(4) and **(5)** See the Solution for the Continuing Problem in Chapter 4.

CHAPTER 4

MATCHING		TRUE/FALSE		MULTIPLE CHOICE
1. K	6. F	1. F	6. T	1. a
2. A	7. J	2. F	7. F	2. a
3. H	8. N	3. T	8. F	3. c
4. M	9. I	4. T	9. T	4. b
5. G	10. L	5. F	10. T	5. c

EXERCISE 4-1

Aug. 31	Salary Expense	1,500	
	Salaries Payable		1,500
31	Rent Expense	560	
	Prepaid Rent		560
31	Supplies Expense	700	
	Supplies		700
31	Depreciation Expense	1,000	
	Accumulated Depreciation		1,000
31	Accounts Receivable	3,200	
	Repair Fees		3,200

EXERCISE 4-2

(1)

```
19--
Mar. 31     Service Fees                    50      19,225
               Income Summary               45                 19,225

       31    Income Summary                 45      13,980
               Salary Expense               58                  8,550
               Supplies Expense             67                  5,430
```

(2)

Account Income Summary   Account No.   45

Date	Item	Post. Ref.	Debit	Credit	Balance Debit	Credit
19--						
Mar. 31		8		19,225		19,225
31		8	13,980			5,245

Account Service Fees   Account No.   50

19--						
Mar. 15		5		4,850		4,850
31		6		14,375		19,225
31		8	19,225			-0-

Account Salary Expense   Account No.   58

19--						
Mar. 31		5	8,550		8,550	
31		8		8,550	-0-	

Account Supplies Expense   Account No.   67

19--						
Mar. 15		5	2,430		2,430	
25		6	1,720		4,150	
31		6	1,280		5,430	
31		8		5,430	-0-	

PROBLEM 4-1

(1)

Castle Shop
Work Sheet
For Month Ended April 30, 19--

Account Title	Trial Balance Dr.	Trial Balance Cr.	Adjustments Dr.	Adjustments Cr.	Adjusted Trial Balance Dr.	Adjusted Trial Balance Cr.	Income Statement Dr.	Income Statement Cr.	Balance Sheet Dr.	Balance Sheet Cr.
Cash	10,056				10,056				10,056	
Accts. Rec.	7,938		(e) 3,000		10,938				10,938	
Supplies	3,000			(a) 1,200	1,800				1,800	
Prepaid Rent	9,504			(b) 792	8,712				8,712	
Tools/Equipment	23,814				23,814				23,814	
Acc. Depr.		1,674		(c) 1,000		2,674				2,674
Accounts Payable		7,764				7,764				7,764
Unearned Fees		2,000	(f) 500			1,500				1,500
Castle, Cap.		38,818				38,818				38,818
Castle, Draw.	3,528				3,528				3,528	
Service Fees		31,308		(e) 3,000 (f) 500		34,808		34,808		
Wage Expense	17,376		(d) 2,000		19,376		19,376			
Misc. Expense	6,348				6,348		6,348			
	81,564	81,564								
Wages Payable				(d) 2,000		2,000				2,000
Rent Expense			(b) 792		792		792			
Supplies Expense			(a) 1,200		1,200		1,200			
Depr. Expense			(c) 1,000		1,000		1,000			
			8,492	8,492	87,564	87,564	28,716	34,808	58,848	52,756
Net Income							6,092			6,092
							34,808	34,808	58,848	58,848

(2)

```
                              Castle Shop
                            Income Statement
                     For Year Ended April 30, 19--
------------------------------------------------------------------------
Service fees                                              $34,808
Operating expenses:
  Wages expenses                         $19,376
  Supplies expense                         1,200
  Depreciation expense                     1,000
  Rent expense                               792
  Misc. expenses                           6,348
                                         -------
Total operating expenses                                  28,716
                                                         -------
Net income                                               $ 6,092
                                                         =======



                              Castle Shop
                      Statement of Owner's Equity
                     For Year Ended April 30, 19--
------------------------------------------------------------------------
Capital, May 1, 19--                                     $38,818
Income for the year                      $6,092
Less drawing for the year                 3,528
                                         ------
Increase in owner's equity                                 2,564
                                                         -------
Capital, April 30, 19--                                  $41,382
                                                         =======




                              Castle Shop
                             Balance Sheet
                             April 30, 19--
------------------------------------------------------------------------
          Assets                              Liabilities
Current assets:                      Current liabilities:
  Cash                    $10,056      Accounts payable        $7,764
  Accounts receivable      10,938      Wages payable            2,000
  Supplies                  1,800      Unearned fees            1,500
  Prepaid rent              8,712                              ------
                          -------      Total liabilities              $11,264
    Total current assets          $31,506
Plant assets:                                Owner's Equity
  Office equipment        $23,814      Castle, capital                 41,382
  Less accumulated depreciation 2,674  21,140                        -------
                          -------  -------
Total assets                      $52,646  Total liabilities and owner's equity  $52,646
                                  =======                              =======
```

PROBLEM 4-2

19--		Adjusting Entries		
Apr.	30	Supplies Expense	1,200	
		Supplies		1,200
	30	Rent Expense	792	
		Prepaid Rent		792
	30	Depreciation Expense	1,000	
		Accumulated Depreciation		1,000
	30	Wages Expense	2,000	
		Wages Payable		2,000
	30	Accounts Receivable	3,000	
		Service Fees		3,000
	30	Unearned Fees	500	
		Service Fees		500
		Closing Entries		
	30	Service Fees	34,808	
		Income Summary		34,808
	30	Income Summary	28,716	
		Wage Expense		19,376
		Misc. Expense		6,348
		Supplies Expense		1,200
		Depreciation Expense		1,000
		Rent Expense		792
	30	Income Summary	6,092	
		Castle, Capital		6,092
	30	Castle, Capital	3,528	
		Castle, Drawing		3,528

CONTINUING PROBLEM

(4), (5), (6)

Egor the Magician
Work Sheet
For the Year Ended December 31, 1996

Account Title	Trial Balance Dr.	Trial Balance Cr.	Adjustments Dr.	Adjustments Cr.	Adjusted Trial Balance Dr.	Adjusted Trial Balance Cr.	Income Statement Dr.	Income Statement Cr.	Balance Sheet Dr.	Balance Sheet Cr.
Cash	9,956				9,956				9,956	
Fees Receivable	6,086				6,086				6,086	
Supplies & Props	1,268			(b) 903	365				365	
Office Supplies	789			(a) 579	210				210	
Prepaid Insurance	2,000			(c)1,450	550				550	
Furn. & Fixtures	13,400				13,400				13,400	
Equipment--Stage	12,000				12,000				12,000	
Accounts Payable		1,580				1,580				1,580
Theater Services Payable				(e) 850		850				850
Subcontractors Payable				(f) 600		600				600
Notes Payable		6,500				6,500				6,500
E. J. Gribbet, Capital		21,852				21,852				21,852
E. J. Gribbet, Drawing	400				400				400	
Fees Earned		31,300				31,300		31,300		
Theater Services Exp.	4,000		(e) 850		4,850		4,850			
Subcontractor Exp.	2,460		(f) 600		3,060		3,060			
Van Expense	3,250				3,250		3,250			
Cosmetics Expense	428				428		428			
Rent Expense	4,800				4,800		4,800			
Telephone Expense	395				395		395			
	61,232	61,232								
Office Supplies Exp.			(a) 579		579		579			
Supplies & Props Exp.			(b) 903		903		903			
Insurance Expense			(c)1,450		1,450		1,450			
Interest Expense			(d) 105		105		105			
Interest Payable				(d) 105		105				105
Depr. Exp.--Furn. & Fix.			(g)2,680		2,680		2,680			
Accum. Depr.--Furn. & Fix.				(g)2,680		2,680				2,680
Depr. Exp.--Equip.			(h)2,400		2,400		2,400			
Accum. Depr.--Equip.				(h)2,400		2,400				2,400
			9,567	9,567	67,867	67,867	24,900	31,300	42,967	36,567
Net Income							6,400			6,400
							31,300	31,300	42,967	42,967

(7)

```
                          Egor the Magician
                          Income Statement
                  For the Year Ended December 31, 1996
-------------------------------------------------------------------------
Fees earned                                                        $31,300
Operating expenses:
   Theater services expense               $4,850
   Rent expense                            4,800
   Van expense                             3,250
   Subcontractor expense                   3,060
   Depreciation expense--furn. & fix.      2,680
   Depreciation expense--equipment         2,400
   Insurance expense                       1,450
   Supplies & props expense                  903
   Office supplies expense                   579
   Cosmetics expense                         428
   Telephone expense                         395
   Interest expense                          105
      Total operating expenses                                     24,900
Net income                                                        $ 6,400
                                                                  =======




                          Egor the Magician
                    Statement of Owner's Equity
                  For the Year Ended December 31, 1996
-------------------------------------------------------------------------
Egor J. Gribbet, capital, January 1, 1996                         $21,852
Income for the year                        $6,400
Less drawing for the year                     400
Increase in owner's equity                                          6,000
Egor J. Gribbet, capital, December 31, 1996                       $27,852
                                                                  =======
```

Egor the Magician
Balance Sheet
December 31, 1996

Assets

Current assets:
Cash	$9,956	
Fees receivable	6,086	
Supplies & props	365	
Office supplies	210	
Prepaid insurance	550	
Total current assets		$17,167

Plant assets:
Furniture & fixtures	$13,400	
Less accumulated depreciation	2,680	$10,720
Equipment--stage	$12,000	
Less accumulated depreciation	2,400	9,600
Total plant assets		20,320
Total assets		$37,487

Liabilities

Current liabilities:
Accounts payable	$ 1,580	
Theater services payable	850	
Subcontractors payable	600	
Interest payable	105	
Total current liabilities		$ 3,135

Long-term liabilities:
Notes payable		6,500
Total liabilities		$ 9,635

Owner's Equity

E. J. Gribbet, capital		27,852
Total liabilities and owner's equity		$37,487

(8)

1996		Adjusting Entries			
Dec.	31	Office Supplies Expense	531	579	
		Office Supplies	117		579
	31	Supplies & Props Expense	533	903	
		Supplies & Props	116		903
	31	Insurance Expense	529	1,450	
		Prepaid Insurance	118		1,450
	31	Interest Expense	710	105	
		Interest Payable	215		105
	31	Theater Services Expense	521	850	
		Theater Services Payable	213		850
	31	Subcontractor Expense	522	600	
		Subcontractors Payable	214		600
	31	Depr. Exp. - Furniture & Fix.	527	2,680	
		Accum. Depr. - Furn. & Fix.	122		2,680
	31	Depreciation Expense - Equip.	528	2,400	
		Accum. Depr. - Equipment	124		2,400

(9)

1996		Closing Entries			
Dec.	31	Fees Earned	410	31,300	
		Income Summary	312		31,300
	31	Income Summary	312	24,900	
		Theater Services Expense	521		4,850
		Subcontractor Expense	522		3,060
		Van Expense	524		3,250
		Cosmetics Expense	525		428
		Rent Expense	532		4,800
		Telephone Expense	534		395
		Office Supplies Expense	531		579
		Supplies & Props Expense	533		903
		Insurance Expense	529		1,450
		Interest Expense	710		105
		Depr. Expense--Furn. & Fix.	527		2,680
		Depr. Expense--Equip.	528		2,400
	31	Income Summary	312	6,400	
		E. J. Gribbet, Capital	310		6,400
	31	E. J. Gribbet, Capital	310	400	
		E. J. Gribbet, Drawing	311		400

CHAPTER 5

MATCHING		TRUE/FALSE			MULTIPLE CHOICE	
1. H	7. A	1. F	6. F	11. T	1. d	5. a
2. J	8. B	2. T	7. T	12. F	2. c	6. d
3. D	9. K	3. F	8. F	13. T	3. c	7. b
4. L	10. E	4. F	9. T	14. T	4. c	8. a
5. G	11. C	5. T	10. T	15. F		
6. F	12. I					

EXERCISE 5-1

Feb. 1 Purchases Journal
      6 Cash Receipts Journal
      8 General Journal
     11 Cash Payments Journal
     18 Revenue (Sales) Journal
     28 Cash Receipts Journal

EXERCISE 5-2

Revenue Journal

Date	Invoice No.	Account Debited	Post. Ref.	Accts. Rec. Dr. Fees Earned Cr.
19--				
Oct. 3	2883	Blanders Co.		8,250
4	2884	Montana Co.		5,000

Cash Receipts Journal

Date	Account Credited	Post. Ref.	Other Accounts Cr.	Accounts Receivable Cr.	Cash Dr.
19--					
Oct. 13	Blanders Co.			7,250	7,250
14	Montana Co.			5,000	5,000
25	Office Supplies		300		300
31	Fees Earned		39,600		39,600

General Journal

19--				
Oct. 8	Fees Earned		1,000	
	Accounts Receivable--Blanders Co.			1,000

EXERCISE 5-3

Purchases Journal

Date	Accounts Credited	Post. Ref.	Accounts Payable Cr.	Store Supplies Dr.	Office Supplies Dr.	Other Dr.
19--						
Mar. 2	Eastside Co.		1,250	1,250		
8	Bench Co.		600	600		
28	James & Co.		900	800		100

Cash Payments Journal

Date	Ck. No.	Account Debited	Post. Ref.	Other Accounts Dr.	Accounts Payable Dr.	Cash Cr.
19--						
Mar. 16	230	Bench Co.			600	600
20	231	Office Supplies		250		250
27	232	Eastside Co.			950	950

General Journal

Date			
19--			
Mar. 9	Accounts Payable--Eastside Co.	300	
	Store Supplies		300

PROBLEM 5-1

(1)

Revenue Journal

Date	Invoice No.	Accounts Debited	Post. Ref.	Accts. Rec. Dr. Fees Earned Cr.
19--				
Sept. 8	210	Robert Poon	√	1,220
12	225	Jeff Lucas	√	750
24	260	Pamela Stark	√	860
30	290	Steve Kocan	√	2,500
				5,330
				=====
				(113) (411)

(2) and (3)

GENERAL LEDGER

Accounts Receivable		113
Sept. 30	5,330	

Fees Earned		411
	Sept. 30	5,330

ACCOUNTS RECEIVABLE LEDGER

Steve Kocan	
Sept. 30	2,500

Robert Poon	
Sept. 8	1,220

Jeff Lucas	
Sept. 12	750

Pamela Stark	
Sept. 24	860

(4)

Steve Kocan	$2,500
Jeff Lucas	750
Robert Poon	1,220
Pamela Stark	860
Total accounts receivable	$5,330
	=======

PROBLEM 5-2

(1)

Purchases Journal

Date	Account Credited	Post. Ref.	Accounts Payable Cr.	Store Supplies Dr.	Office Supplies Dr.	Other Accounts Dr.		
						Account	Post. Ref.	Amount
19--								
Apr. 14	Mills Co.	✓	300	300				
16	Quick Co.	✓	175		175			
22	Mills Co.	✓	5,250			Store Equip.	121	5,250
30	Mills Co.	✓	280	280				
			6,005	580	175			5,250
			(211)	(115)	(116)			(✓)

(2) and (3)

GENERAL LEDGER

Store Supplies	115
Apr. 30 580	

Store Equipment	121
Apr. 22 5,250	

Office Supplies	116
Apr. 30 175	

Accounts Payable	211
	Apr. 30 6,005

ACCOUNTS PAYABLE LEDGER

Mills Co.	
	Apr. 14 300
	22 5,250
	30 280

Quick Co.	
	Apr. 16 175

(4)

Mills Co.	$ 5,830
Quick Co.	175
Total accounts payable	$ 6,005

PROBLEM 5-3

(1)

Store Supplies	3,650	Accounts Payable	15,890
Office Supplies	1,250		
Other Accounts	10,990		
Debit Totals	15,890	Credit Totals	15,890

(2)

Purchases Journal

Date	Account Credited	Post. Ref.	Accounts Payable Cr.	Store Supplies Dr.	Office Supplies Dr.	Other Accounts Dr.		
						Account	Post. Ref.	Amount
19--								
Oct. 29			7,620			Store Equip.	121	7,620
31			15,890	3,650	1,250			10,990
			(211)	(115)	(116)			

GENERAL LEDGER

Store Supplies	115
Oct. 31 3,650	

Store Equipment	121
Oct. 29 7,620	

Office Supplies	116
Oct. 31 1,250	

Accounts Payable	211
	Oct. 31 15,890

CHAPTER 6

MATCHING   TRUE/FALSE   MULTIPLE CHOICE
1. E   11. W   1. T   11. F   1. c   6. c
2. R   12. C   2. F   12. F   2. b   7. a
3. F   13. M   3. T   13. F   3. b   8. d
4. D   14. V   4. F   14. F   4. a   9. d
5. T   15. I   5. T   15. T   5. c   10. b
6. H   16. U   6. F   16. T
7. G   17. B   7. F   17. T
8. P   18. J   8. T   18. F
9. Q   19. N   9. T   19. F
10. K   20. S   10. F   20. T

EXERCISE 6-1

(1) Merchandise Inventory   4,900
         Accounts Payable   4,900

(2) Accounts Payable   4,900
         Cash   4,900

(3) Merchandise Inventory   3,580
         Accounts Payable   3,580

(4) Accounts Payable   900
         Merchandise Inventory   900

(5) Accounts Payable   2,680
         Cash   2,680

EXERCISE 6-2

(1) Accounts Receivable   3,150
         Sales   3,150

     Cost of Merchandise Sold   2,000
         Merchandise Invetory   2,000

(2) Cash   2,850
         Sales   2,850

     Cost of Merchandise Sold   1,380
         Merchandise Inventory   1,380

(3) Cash   3,050
     Credit Card Collection Expense   100
         Accounts Receivable   3,150

(4) Accounts Receivable   4,500
         Sales   4,500

     Accounts Receivable   150
         Cash   150

     Cost of Merchandise Sold   3,100
         Merchandise Inventory   3,100

(5) Sales Returns and Allowances   400
         Accounts Receivable   400

     Merchandise Inventory   275
         Cost of Merchandise Sold   275

(6) Cash   4,168
     Sales Discounts   82
         Accounts Receivable   4,250

EXERCISE 6-3

```
19--
Jan.    3    Merchandise Inventory          24,500
                Accounts Payable                         24,500

        5    Accounts Payable                4,900
                Merchandise Inventory                     4,900

       12    Accounts Receivable            50,000
                Sales                                    50,000

       12    Cost of Merchandise Sold       35,000
                Merchandise Inventory                    35,000

       13    Accounts Payable               19,600
                Cash                                     19,600

       15    Sales Returns and Allowances    8,000
                Accounts Receivable                       8,000

       15    Merchandise Inventory           5,600
                Cost of Merchandise Sold                  5,600

       22    Cash                           41,580
             Sales Discounts                   420
                Accounts Receivable                      42,000
```

PROBLEM 6-1

```
19--
Sept.   3    Merchandise Inventory           8,415
                Accounts Payable                          8,415

        4    Office Supplies                   800
                Cash                                        800

        6    Accounts Receivable             4,000
                Sales                                     4,000

        6    Cost of Merchandise Sold        3,000
                Merchandise Inventory                     3,000

        7    Accounts Payable                1,980
                Merchandise Inventory                     1,980

       10    Merchandise Inventory           5,000
                Cash                                      5,000

       12    Accounts Receivable             5,500
                Sales                                     5,500

       12    Cost of Merchandise Sold        3,200
                Merchandise Inventory                     3,200

       13    Accounts Payable                6,435
                Cash                                      6,435

       16    Cash                            3,920
             Sales Discounts                    80
                Accounts Receivable                       4,000
```

```
Sept.   20   Cash                                      5,200
             Nonbank Credit Card Expense                300
               Accounts Receivable                                5,500


        24   Accounts Receivable                       3,000
               Sales                                              3,000


        24   Cost of Merchandise Sold                  1,750
               Merchandise Inventory                              1,750


        26   Cash                                      2,200
               Sales                                              2,200


        26   Cost of Merchandise Sold                  1,400
               Merchandise Inventory                              1,400


        30   Sales Returns and Allowances 1,000
               Accounts Receivable                                1,000


        30   Merchandise Inventory                      600
               Cost of Merchandise Sold                            600
```

PROBLEM 6-2a

Miller Co.
Income Statement
For Year Ended March 31, 19--

```
-----------------------------------------------------------------------
Revenue from sales:
  Sales                                           $1,016,700
  Less: Sales returns and allowances                  13,010
    Net sales                                                   $1,003,690
Cost of merchandise sold                                           681,060
Gross profit                                                   $  322,630
Operating expenses:
  Selling expenses:
    Sales salaries expense             $ 78,250
    Delivery expense                     42,100
    Advertising expense                  13,090
    Depr. expense--delivery equip.        9,050
    Misc. selling expense                13,950
      Total selling expenses                       $  156,440
  Administrative expenses:
    Office salaries expense            $ 55,800
    Insurance expense                    16,000
    Office supplies expense               9,100
    Misc. administrative expenses         6,870
      Total administrative expenses                    87,770
Total operating expenses                                          244,210
Income from operations                                         $   78,420
Other income:
  Interest income                                                   1,020
Net income                                                     $   79,440
```

PROBLEM 6-2b

Miller Co.
Income Statement
For Year Ended March 31, 19--

Revenues:
  Net sales............................ $1,003,690
  Interest income......................   1,020
    Total revenues..................... $1,004,710
Expenses:
  Cost of merchandise sold............. $681,060
  Selling expenses.....................   156,440
  Administrative expenses..............   87,770
    Total expenses.....................   925,270
Net income............................... $ 79,440

PROBLEM 6-2c

Cost of Merchandise Sold................   4,200
  Merchandise Inventory.................   4,200

PROBLEM 6-3

Miller Co.
Statement of Owner's Equity
For Year Ended March 31, 19--

R.W. Miller, capital, April 1 19-- $193,650
Net income for year $79,440
Less withdrawls   30,000
Increase in owner's equity   49,440
R.W. Miller, capital, March 31, 19-- $243,090

PROBLEM 6-4

Miller Co.
Balance Sheet
March 31, 19--

Assets
Current assets:
  Cash $ 43,100
  Notes receivable   6,000
  Accounts receivable   107,780
  Interest receivable   520
  Merchandise inventory   115,800
  Office supplies   1,250
  Prepaid insurance   8,740
    Total current assets $283,190
Plant assets:
  Delivery equipment $ 60,150
    Less accumulated depreciation   22,950
    Total plant assets   37,200
Total assets $320,390
Liabilities
Current liabilities:
  Accounts payable $ 75,300
  Salaries payable   2,000
    Total current liabilities $ 77,300
Owner's Equity
R.W. Miller, capital   243,090
Total liabilities and owner's equity $320,390

CONTINUING PROBLEM

(10)

1997					
Jan.	2	Rent Expense Cash Paid office rent for January-June.	532 110	2,400	2,400
	2	Van Expense Cash Paid auto lease for year.	524 110	2,400	2,400
	2	Notes Payable Interest Payable Cash Paid note plus interest.	220 215 110	1,500 105	1,605
	22	Cash Fees Receivable Received payment for billings.	110 112	2,486	2,486
Feb.	11	Theater Services Payable Cash Paid amount owed to theater.	213 110	850	850
	24	Subcontractors Payable Cash Paid J.P. Magic amount owed.	214 110	600	600
Mar.	15	Supplies and Props Cash Paid cash for props.	116 110	840	840
	15	Salary Expense Cash Paid part-time salary.	520 110	800	800
	31	Cash Fees Earned Received cash for performances.	110 410	9,400	9,400
Apr.	11	Merchandise Inventory Accounts Payable Purchased merchandise from Magical Enterprises, 2/10, n/30.	115 211	4,704	4,704
	20	Accounts Payable Cash Paid for purchase of April 11.	211 110	4,704	4,704
May	15	Salary Expense Cash Paid part-time salary.	520 110	800	800

June	5	Accounts Receivable	111	2,200	
		Sales	411		2,200
		Sold merchandise to			
		Jerome's Toys,			
		2/10, n/30.			
	5	Cost of Merchandise Sold	510	1,200	
		Merchandise Inventory	115		1,200
		Cost of Merchandise			
		sold to Jerome's Toys.			
	5	Transportation Out	535	45	
		Cash	110		45
		Paid transportation			
		costs.			
	30	Cash	110	2,200	
		Accounts Receivable	111		2,200
		Received payment from			
		Jerome's Toys.			
July	1	Rent Expense	532	2,400	
		Cash	110		2,400
		Paid office rent			
		July-Dec.			
	1	Interest Expense	710	150	
		Cash	110		150
		Paid 6 months'			
		interest on note.			
	2	Telephone Expense	534	120	
		Cash	110		120
		Paid telephone expense.			
	10	Accounts Payable	211	500	
		Cash	110		500
		Paid creditors.			
	15	Accounts Receivable	111	2,850	
		Sales	411		2,850
		Sold merchandise to			
		Evan's Magic, 2/10, n/30.			
	15	Cost of Merchandise Sold	510	1,500	
		Merchandise Inventory	115		1,500
		Cost of Merch. sold			
		to Evan's Magic.			
	15	Salary Expense	520	800	
		Cash	110		800
		Paid part-time salary.			
	18	Merchandise Inventory	115	5,684	
		Accounts Payable	211		5,684
		Purchased merchandise			
		from Magical Enterprises,			
		2/10, n/eom.			
	20	Accounts Payable	211	392	
		Merchandise Inventory	511		392
		Returned merchandise			
		purchased on 7/18.			

July	24	Cash	110	2,793	
		Sales Discounts	413	57	
		Accounts Receivable	111		2,850
		Received payment on			
		sale of 7/15.			
	28	Accounts Payable	211	5,292	
		Cash	110		5,292
		Paid for purchase of 7/18.			
	31	Accounts Receivable	111	4,600	
		Sales	411		4,600
		Sold merchandise to			
		Toy Depot, n/30.			
	31	Cost of Merchandise Sold	510	2,500	
		Merchandise Inventory	115		2,500
		Cost of Merchandise sold			
		to Toy Depot.			
Aug.	1	Transportation Out	535	75	
		Cash	110		75
		Paid transportation			
		cost for 7/31 shipment.			
	3	Fees Receivable	112	9,200	
		Fees Earned	410		9,200
		Billed clients for			
		performances in June and July.			
	16	Sales Returns and Allowances	412	500	
		Accounts Receivable	111		500
		Issued credit memo on sale			
		of 7/31.			
	16	Merchanidise Inventory	115	325	
		Cost of Merchdise Sold	510		325
		Cost of Merchandise			
		returned by Toy Depot.			
	30	Cash	110	4,100	
		Accounts Receivable	111		4,100
		Received payment on			
		sale of 7/31.			
Sept.	1	Cash	110	9,200	
		Fees Receivable	112		9,200
		Received payment for			
		billings.			
	15	Cosmetics Expense	525	100	
		Cash	110		100
		Paid cash for cosmetics.			
	15	Salary Expense	520	800	
		Cash	110		800
		Paid part-time salary.			
Oct.	8	Subcontractors Expense	522	400	
		Cash	110		400
		Paid Jane the Fantastic			
		for performance.			
Nov.	13	Theater Services Expense	521	600	
		Cash	110		600
		Paid Apollo Theater for			
		its use.			

Nov.	15	Salary Expense	520	800	
		Cash	110		800
		Paid part-time salary.			
Dec.	2	Prepaid Insurance	118	600	
		Cash	110		600
		Prepaid 1-year property insurance policy.			
	2	Fees Receivable	112	8,100	
		Fees Earned	410		8,100
		Billed clients for performances in October and November.			
	11	Accounts Receivable	111	3,400	
		Sales	411		3,400
		Sold merchandise to Mystic Emporium, 2/10, n/30.			
	11	Cost of Merchandise Sold	510	2,170	
		Merchandise Inventory	115		2,170
	30	Telephone Expense	534	135	
		Cash	110		135
		Paid telephone expense.			
	31	E.J. Gribbet, Drawing	311	1,000	
		Cash	110		1,000
		Withdrawal by owner.			

(12) (13) (14)

Egor the Magician
Work Sheet
For the Year Ended December 31, 1997

	Trial Balance Dr.	Trial Balance Cr.	Adjustments Dr.	Adjustments Cr.	Adj. Trial Balance Dr.	Adj. Trial Balance Cr.	Income Statement Dr.	Income Statement Cr.	Balance Sheet Dr.	Balance Sheet Cr.
Cash	11,319				11,319				11,319	
Accounts Receivable	3,400				3,400				3,400	
Fees Receivable	11,700				11,700				11,700	
Merchandise Inventory	2,951			(c) 585	2,366				2,366	
Supplies & Props	1,205			(b) 945	260				260	
Office Supplies	210			(a) 110	100				100	
Prepaid Insurance	1,150			(d) 600	550				550	
Furniture & Fixtures	13,400				13,400				13,400	
Accum. Depr.--Furn. & Fixtures		2,680		(g)2,680		5,360				5,360
Equipment - Stage	12,000				12,000				12,000	
Accum. Depr.--Equipment		2,400		(h)2,400		4,800				4,800
Accounts Payable		1,080				1,080				1,080
Notes Payable		5,000				5,000				5,000
E.J. Gribbet, Capital		27,852				27,852				27,852
E.J. Gribbet, Drawing	1,000				1,000				1,000	
Fees Earned		26,700				26,700		26,700		
Sales		13,050				13,050		13,050		
Sales Returns and Allowances	500				500		500			
Sales Discounts	57				57		57			
Cost of Merchandise Sold	7,045		(c) 585		7,630		7,630			
Salary Expense	4,000		(f) 800		4,800		4,800			
Theater Services Expense	600				600		600			
Subcontractor Expense	400				400		400			
Van Expense	2,400				2,400		2,400			
Cosmetics Expense	100				100		100			
Rent Expense	4,800				4,800		4,800			
Telephone Expense	255				255		255			
Transportation Out	120				120		120			
Interest Expense	150		(e) 300		450		450			
	78,762	78,762								
Office Supplies Expense			(a) 110		110		110			
Supplies & Props Expense			(b) 945		945		945			
Insurance Expense			(d) 600		600		600			
Interest Payable				(e) 300		300				300
Salaries Payable				(f) 800		800				800
Depr. Exp.--Furn. & Fixtures			(g)2,680		2,680		2,680			
Depr. Exp.--Equipment			(h)2,400		2,400		2,400			
			8,420	8,420	84,942	84,942	28,847	39,750	56,095	45,192
Net Income							10,903			10,903
							39,750	39,750	56,095	56,095

(15)

```
                           Egor the Magician
                           Income Statement
                     For the Year Ended Dec. 31, 1997
------------------------------------------------------------------------
Fees earned                                                      $26,700
Sales                                                  $13,050
Less:   Sales returns and allowances         $500
        Sales discounts                         57         557
Net sales                                              $12,493
Cost of goods sold                                       7,630
Gross profit                                                      4,863
    Total net revenues                                          $31,563
Operating expenses:
    Selling expenses:
        Salary expense                      $ 4,800
        Rent expense                          4,800
        Depreciation expense--equipment       2,400
        Van expense                           2,400
        Supplies & props expense               945
        Theater services expense              600
        Subcontractor expense                 400
        Telephone expense                     255
        Transportation out                    120
        Cosmetics expense                     100
            Total selling expenses                     $16,820
    Administrative expenses:
        Depreciation expense
          --furniture & fixtures            $ 2,680
        Insurance expense                     600
        Office supplies expense               110
            Total administrative expenses                3,390
        Total operating expenses                                 20,210
Operating income                                                $11,353
Other expense:
    Interest expense                                                450
Net income                                                      $10,903
```

```
                           Egor the Magician
                       Statement of Owner's Equity
                     For the Year Ended Dec. 31, 1997
------------------------------------------------------------------------
E.J. Gribbet, capital, January 1, 1997                          $27,852
Income for the year                                    $10,903
Less withdrawals                                         1,000
Increase in owner's equity                                        9,903
E.J. Gribbet, capital, December 31, 1997                        $37,755
```

Egor the Magician
Balance Sheet
Dec. 31, 1997

Assets

Current assets:			
Cash		$11,319	
Accounts receivable		3,400	
Fees receivable		11,700	
Merchandise inventory		2,366	
Supplies & props		260	
Office supplies		100	
Prepaid insurance		550	
Total current assets			$29,695
Plant assets:			
Furniture & fixtures	$13,400		
Less accumulated depreciation	5,360	$ 8,040	
Equipment - stage	$12,000		
Less accumulated depreciation	4,800	7,200	
Total plant assets			15,240
Total assets			$44,935

Liabilities

Current liabilities:		
Accounts payable	$ 1,080	
Interest payable	300	
Salaries payable	800	
Total current liabilities		$2,180
Long-term liabilities:		
Notes payable		5,000
Total liabilities		$ 7,180

Owner's' Equity

E.J. Gribbet, capital	37,755
Total liabilities and owner's equity	$44,935

(16)

Adjusting Entries

Date		Account	No.	Debit	Credit
Dec.	31	Office Supplies Expense	531	110	
		Office Supplies	117		110
	31	Supplies & Props Expense	533	945	
		Supplies & Props	116		945
	31	Cost of Merchandise Sold	510	585	
		Merchandise Inventory	115		585
	31	Insurance Expense	529	600	
		Prepaid Insurance	118		600
	31	Interest Expense	710	300	
		Interest Payable	215		300
	31	Salary Expense	520	800	
		Salaries Payable	212		800
	31	Depreciation Expense - Furn. & Fix.	527	2,680	
		Accum. Depr. - Furn. & Fix.	122		2,680
	31	Depreciation Expense - Equipment	528	2,400	
		Accum. Depr. - Equipment	124		2,400

(17)

Closing Entries

Dec.	31	Fees Earned	410	26,700	
		Sales	411	13,050	
		Income Summary	312		39,750
	31	Income Summary	312	28,847	
		Sales Returns & Allowances	412		500
		Sales Discounts	413		57
		Cost of Merchandise Sold	510		7,630
		Salary Expense	520		4,800
		Theater Services Expense	521		600
		Subcontractor Expense	522		400
		Van Expense	524		2,400
		Cosmetics Expense	525		100
		Depreciation Expense--Furn. & Fix.	527		2,680
		Depreciation Expense--Equipment	528		2,400
		Insurance Expense	529		600
		Office Supplies Expense	531		110
		Rent Expense	532		4,800
		Supplies & Props Expense	533		945
		Telephone Expense	534		255
		Transportation Out	535		120
		Interest Expense	710		450
	31	Income Summary	312	10,903	
		E.J. Gribbet, Capital	310		10,903
	31	E.J. Gribbet, Capital	310	1,000	
		E.J. Gribbet, Drawing	311		1,000

(2) The following ledger is the complete ledger for the continuing problem,
     which extends over several chapters. In checking your answer for this chap-
     ter, ignore transactions other than those occurring in 1997. The other
     transactions will be posted to the ledger in later chapters.

Account   Cash   Account No.   110

DATE		ITEM	POST. REF.	DEBIT	CREDIT	BALANCE DEBIT	BALANCE CREDIT
1996							
Nov.	30	Balance	√			5,504	
Dec.	1		1		400	5,104	
	1		1		200	4,904	
	2		1		600	4,304	
	4		1	1,000		5,304	
	8		1	1,200		6,504	
	11		1		750	5,754	
	14		1		2,005	3,749	
	16		2		200	3,549	
	17		2		1,100	2,449	
	18		2	5,200		7,649	
	21		2		73	7,576	
	24		2	5,200		12,776	
	29		3		95	12,681	
	30		3		450	12,231	
	31		2		2,000	10,231	
	31		3		125	10,106	
	31		3		150	9,956	
1997							
Jan.	2		6		2,400	7,556	
	2		6		2,400	5,156	
	2		6		1,605	3,551	
	22		6	2,486		6,037	
Feb.	11		6		850	5,187	
	24		6		600	4,587	
Mar.	15		6		840	3,747	
	15		6		800	2,947	
	31		6	9,400		12,347	
Apr.	20		7		4,704	7,643	
May	15		7		800	6,843	
June	5		7		45	6,798	
	30		7	2,200		8,998	
July	1		7		2,400	6,598	
	1		7		150	6,448	
	2		8		120	6,328	
	10		8		500	5,828	
	15		8		800	5,028	
	24		8	2,793		7,821	
	28		8		5,292	2,529	
Aug.	1		9		75	2,454	
	30		9	4,100		6,554	
Sep.	1		9	9,200		15,754	
	15		9		100	15,654	
	15		9		800	14,854	
Oct.	8		10		400	14,454	
Nov.	13		10		600	13,854	
	15		10		800	13,054	
Dec.	2		10		600	12,454	
	30		10		135	12,319	
	31		10		1,000	11,319	

Account   Accounts Receivable   Account No.   111

DATE		ITEM	POST. REF.	DEBIT	CREDIT	BALANCE DEBIT	CREDIT
1997							
June	5		7	2,200		2,200	
	30		7		2,200	0	
July	15		8	2,850		2,850	
	24		8		2,850	0	
	31		9	4,600		4,600	
Aug.	16		9		500	4,100	
	30		9		4,100	0	
Dec.	11		10	3,400		3,400	

Account   Fees Receivable   Account No.   112

						BALANCE DEBIT	CREDIT
1996							
Nov.	30	Balance	√			2,486	
Dec.	2		1	9,800		12,286	
	4		1		1,000	11,286	
	24		2		5,200	6,086	
1997							
Jan.	22		6		2,486	3,600	
Aug.	3		9	9,200		12,800	
Sep.	1		9		9,200	3,600	
Dec.	2		10	8,100		11,700	

Account   Merchandise Inventory   Account No.   115

						BALANCE DEBIT	CREDIT
1997							
Apr.	11		7	4,704		4,704	
June	5		7		1,200	3,504	
July	15		8		1,500	2,004	
	18		8	5,684		7,688	
	20		8		392	7,296	
	31		9		2,500	4,796	
Aug.	16		9	325		5,121	
Dec.	11		10		2,170	2,951	
	31	Adjusting	11		585	2,366	

Account   Supplies & Props   Account No.   116

						BALANCE DEBIT	CREDIT
1996							
Nov.	30	Balance	√			1,083	
Dec.	15		2	185		1,268	
	31	Adjusting	4		903	365	
1997							
Mar.	15		6	840		1,205	
Dec.	31	Adjusting	11		945	260	

Account   Office Supplies   Account No.   117

						BALANCE DEBIT	CREDIT
1996							
Nov.	30	Balance	√			789	
Dec.	31	Adjusting	4		579	210	
1997							
Dec.	31	Adjusting	11		110	100	

Account   Prepaid Insurance   Account No.   118

DATE		ITEM	POST. REF.	DEBIT	CREDIT	BALANCE	
						DEBIT	CREDIT
1996							
Nov.	30	Balance	√			1,400	
Dec.	2		1	600		2,000	
	31	Adjusting	4		1,450	550	
1997							
Dec.	2		10	600		1,150	
	31	Adjusting	11		600	550	

Account   Furniture & Fixtures   Account No.   121

DATE		ITEM	POST. REF.	DEBIT	CREDIT	DEBIT	CREDIT
1996							
Nov.	30	Balance	√			6,400	
Dec.	31		2	7,000		13,400	

Account   Accum. Depr.--Furniture & Fixtures   Account No.   122

DATE		ITEM	POST. REF.	DEBIT	CREDIT	DEBIT	CREDIT
1996							
Dec.	31	Adjusting	4		2,680		2,680
1997							
Dec.	31	Adjusting	11		2,680		5,360

Account   Equipment--Stage   Account No.   123

DATE		ITEM	POST. REF.	DEBIT	CREDIT	DEBIT	CREDIT
1996							
Nov.	30	Balance	√			10,800	
Dec.	16		2	1,200		12,000	

Account   Accum. Depr.--Equipment-Stage   Account No.   124

DATE		ITEM	POST. REF.	DEBIT	CREDIT	DEBIT	CREDIT
1996							
Dec.	31	Adjusting	4		2,400		2,400
1997							
Dec.	31	Adjusting	11		2,400		4,800

Account   Accounts Payable   Account No.   211

DATE		ITEM	POST. REF.	DEBIT	CREDIT	DEBIT	CREDIT
1996							
Nov.	30	Balance	√				1,495
Dec.	15		2		185		1,680
	16		2		1,000		2,680
	17		2	1,100			1,580
1997							
Apr.	11		7		4,704		6,284
	20		7	4,704			1,580
July	10		8	500			1,080
	18		8		5,684		6,764
	20		8	392			6,372
	28		8	5,292			1,080

Account   Salaries Payable   Account No.   212

DATE		ITEM	POST. REF.	DEBIT	CREDIT	DEBIT	CREDIT
1997							
Dec.	31	Adjusting	11		800		800

Account   Theater Services Payable   Account No.   213

DATE		ITEM	POST. REF.	DEBIT	CREDIT	DEBIT	CREDIT
1996							
Nov.	30	Balance	√				2,005
Dec.	14		1	2,005			0
	31	Adjusting	4		850		850
1997							
Feb.	11		6	850			0

Account   Subcontractors Payable   Account No. 214

DATE		ITEM	POST. REF.	DEBIT	CREDIT	BALANCE DEBIT	BALANCE CREDIT
1996							
Nov.	30	Balance	√				750
Dec.	11		1	750			0
	31	Adjusting	4		600		600
1997							
Feb.	24		6	600			0

Account   Interest Payable   Account No. 215

DATE		ITEM	POST. REF.	DEBIT	CREDIT	BALANCE DEBIT	BALANCE CREDIT
1996							
Dec.	31	Adjusting	4		105		105
1997							
Jan.	2		6	105			0
Dec.	31	Adjusting	11		300		300

Account   Notes Payable   Account No. 220

DATE		ITEM	POST. REF.	DEBIT	CREDIT	BALANCE DEBIT	BALANCE CREDIT
1996							
Nov.	30	Balance	√				1,500
Dec.	31		2		5,000		6,500
1997							
Jan.	2		6	1,500			5,000

Account   E.J. Gribbet, Capital   Account No. 310

DATE		ITEM	POST. REF.	DEBIT	CREDIT	BALANCE DEBIT	BALANCE CREDIT
1996							
Nov.	30	Balance	√				21,852
Dec.	31	Closing	5		6,400		28,252
	31	Closing	5	400			27,852
1997							
Dec.	31	Closing	12		10,903		38,755
	31	Closing	12	1,000			37,755

Account   E.J. Gribbet, Drawing   Account No. 311

DATE		ITEM	POST. REF.	DEBIT	CREDIT	BALANCE DEBIT	BALANCE CREDIT
1996							
Nov.	30	Balance	√			400	
Dec.	31	Closing	5		400	0	
1997							
Dec.	31		10	1,000		1,000	
	31	Closing	12		1,000	0	

Account   Income Summary   Account No. 312

DATE		ITEM	POST. REF.	DEBIT	CREDIT	BALANCE DEBIT	BALANCE CREDIT
1996							
Dec.	31	Closing	4		31,300		31,300
	31	Closing	5	24,900			6,400
	31	Closing	5	6,400			0
1997							
Dec.	31	Closing	11		39,750		39,750
	31	Closing	12	28,847			10,903
	31	Closing	12	10,903			0

Account   Fees Earned   Account No.   410

DATE		ITEM	POST. REF.	DEBIT	CREDIT	BALANCE DEBIT	CREDIT
1996							
Nov.	30	Balance	√				15,100
Dec.	2		1		9,800		24,900
	8		1		1,200		26,100
	18		2		5,200		31,300
	31	Closing	4	31,300			0
1997							
Mar.	31		6		9,400		9,400
Aug.	3		9		9,200		18,600
Dec.	2		10		8,100		26,700
	31	Closing	11	26,700			0

Account   Sales   Account No.   411

DATE		ITEM	POST. REF.	DEBIT	CREDIT	BALANCE DEBIT	CREDIT
1997							
June	5		7		2,200		2,200
July	15		8		2,850		5,050
	31		9		4,600		9,650
Dec.	11		10		3,400		13,050
	31	Closing	11	13,050			0

Account   Sales Returns & Allowances   Account No.   412

DATE		ITEM	POST. REF.	DEBIT	CREDIT	BALANCE DEBIT	CREDIT
1997							
Aug.	16		9	500		500	
Dec.	31	Closing	12		500	0	

Account   Sales Discounts   Account No.   413

DATE		ITEM	POST. REF.	DEBIT	CREDIT	BALANCE DEBIT	CREDIT
1997							
July	24		8	57		57	
Dec.	31	Closing	12		57	0	

Account   Cost of Merchandise Sold   Account No.   510

DATE		ITEM	POST. REF.	DEBIT	CREDIT	BALANCE DEBIT	CREDIT
1997							
June	5		7	1,200		1,200	
July	15		8	1,500		2,700	
	31		9	2,500		5,200	
Aug.	16		9		325	4,875	
Dec.	11		10	2,170		7,045	
	31	Adjusting	11	585		7,630	
	31	Closing	12		7,630	0	

Account   Salary Expense   Account No.   520

DATE		ITEM	POST. REF.	DEBIT	CREDIT	BALANCE DEBIT	CREDIT
1997							
Mar.	15		6	800		800	
May	15		7	800		1,600	
July	15		8	800		2,400	
Sep.	15		9	800		3,200	
Nov.	15		10	800		4,000	
Dec.	31	Adjusting	11	800		4,800	
	31	Closing	12		4,800	0	

Account   Theater Services Expense   Account No.   521

DATE		ITEM	POST. REF.	DEBIT	CREDIT	BALANCE DEBIT	BALANCE CREDIT
1996							
Nov.	30	Balance	√			4,000	
Dec.	31	Adjusting	4	850		4,850	
	31	Closing	5		4,850	0	
1997							
Nov.	13		10	600		600	
Dec.	31	Closing	12		600	0	

Account   Subcontractor Expense   Account No.   522

DATE		ITEM	POST. REF.	DEBIT	CREDIT	BALANCE DEBIT	BALANCE CREDIT
1996							
Nov.	30	Balance	√			2,010	
Dec.	30		3	450		2,460	
	31	Adjusting	4	600		3,060	
	31	Closing	5		3,060	0	
1997							
Oct.	8		10	400		400	
Dec.	31	Closing	12		400	0	

Account   Van Expense   Account No.   524

DATE		ITEM	POST. REF.	DEBIT	CREDIT	BALANCE DEBIT	BALANCE CREDIT
1996							
Nov.	30	Balance	√			2,900	
Dec.	1		1	200		3,100	
	31		3	150		3,250	
	31	Closing	5		3,250	0	
1997							
Jan.	2		6	2,400		2,400	
Dec.	31	Closing	12		2,400	0	

Account   Cosmetics Expense   Account No.   525

DATE		ITEM	POST. REF.	DEBIT	CREDIT	BALANCE DEBIT	BALANCE CREDIT
1996							
Nov.	30	Balance	√			230	
Dec.	21		2	73		303	
	31		3	125		428	
	31	Closing	5		428	0	
1997							
Sep.	15		9	100		100	
Dec.	31	Closing	12		100	0	

Account   Depreciation Expense--Furniture & Fixtures   Account No.   527

DATE		ITEM	POST. REF.	DEBIT	CREDIT	BALANCE DEBIT	BALANCE CREDIT
1996							
Dec.	31	Adjusting	4	2,680		2,680	
	31	Closing	5		2,680	0	
1997							
Dec.	31	Adjusting	11	2,680		2,680	
	31	Closing	12		2,680	0	

Account   Depreciation Expense--Equipment   Account No.   528

DATE		ITEM	POST. REF.	DEBIT	CREDIT	BALANCE DEBIT	BALANCE CREDIT
1996							
Dec.	31	Adjusting	4	2,400		2,400	
	31	Closing	5		2,400	0	
1997							
Dec.	31	Adjusting	11	2,400		2,400	
	31	Closing	12		2,400	0	

Account   Insurance Expense   Account No.   529

DATE		ITEM	POST. REF.	DEBIT	CREDIT	BALANCE DEBIT	CREDIT
1996							
Dec.	31	Adjusting	4	1,450		1,450	
	31	Closing	5		1,450	0	
1997							
Dec.	31	Adjusting	11	600		600	
	31	Closing	12		600	0	

Account   Office Supplies Expense   Account No.   531

DATE		ITEM	POST. REF.	DEBIT	CREDIT	BALANCE DEBIT	CREDIT
1996							
Dec.	31	Adjusting	4	579		579	
	31	Closing	5		579	0	
1997							
Dec.	31	Adjusting	11	110		110	
	31	Closing	12		110	0	

Account   Rent Expense   Account No.   532

DATE		ITEM	POST. REF.	DEBIT	CREDIT	BALANCE DEBIT	CREDIT
1996							
Nov.	30	Balance	√			4,400	
Dec.	1		1	400		4,800	
	31	Closing	5		4,800	0	
1997							
Jan.	2		6	2,400		2,400	
July	1		7	2,400		4,800	
Dec.	31	Closing	12		4,800	0	

Account   Supplies & Props Expense   Account No.   533

DATE		ITEM	POST. REF.	DEBIT	CREDIT	BALANCE DEBIT	CREDIT
1996							
Dec.	31	Adjusting	4	903		903	
	31	Closing	5		903	0	
1997							
Dec.	31	Adjusting	11	945		945	
	31	Closing	12		945	0	

Account   Telephone Expense   Account No.   534

DATE		ITEM	POST. REF.	DEBIT	CREDIT	BALANCE DEBIT	CREDIT
1996							
Nov.	30	Balance	√			300	
Dec.	29		3	95		395	
	31	Closing	5		395	0	
1997							
July	2		8	120		120	
Dec.	30		10	135		255	
	31	Closing	12		255	0	

Account   Transportation Out   Account No.   535

DATE		ITEM	POST. REF.	DEBIT	CREDIT	BALANCE DEBIT	CREDIT
1997							
June	5		7	45		45	
Aug.	1		9	75		120	
Dec.	31	Closing	12		120	0	

Account   Interest Expense   Account No.   710

DATE		ITEM	POST. REF.	DEBIT	CREDIT	BALANCE DEBIT	CREDIT
1996							
Dec.	31	Adjusting	4	105		105	
	31	Closing	5		105		
1997							
July	1		7	150		150	
Dec.	31	Adjusting	11	300		450	
	31	Closing	12		450	0	

CHAPTER 7

MATCHING		TRUE/FALSE		MULTIPLE CHOICE
1. G	6. J	1. F	6. F	1. b
2. B	7. D	2. F	7. F	2. a
3. I	8. F	3. F	8. T	3. c
4. A	9. H	4. T	9. F	4. d
5. K	10. E	5. T	10. T	5. c

EXERCISE 7-1

(2)

Cash in Bank	1,920	
Notes Receivable		1,800
Interest Income		120

(3)

Miscellaneous Administrative Expense	28	
Cash in Bank		28

(6)

Accounts Payable - Charlie's Optical Supply	100	
Cash in Bank		100

EXERCISE 7-2

Jan. 8	Merchandise Inventory	4,900	
	Accounts Payable		4,900
10	Merchandise Inventory	11,880	
	Accounts Payable		11,880
20	Accounts Payable	11,880	
	Cash in Bank		11,880
Feb. 9	Accounts Payable	4,900	
	Discounts Lost	100	
	Cash in Bank		5,000

EXERCISE 7-3

(1)

Petty Cash	400.00	
Accounts Payable		400.00

(2)

Accounts Payable	400.00	
Cash in Bank		400.00

(3)

Office Supplies	80.25	
Miscellaneous Selling Expense	115.33	
Miscellaneous Administrative Expense	78.05	
Cash Short and Over		1.97
Accounts Payable		271.66

(4)

Accounts Payable	271.66	
Cash in Bank		271.66

PROBLEM 7-1

(1)   Dumont Co.
                                    Bank Reconciliation
                                    September 30, 19--

Balance according to bank statement $ 8,510
Add deposit not recorded   1,900
                                                                         $10,410
Deduct outstanding checks:
  No. 255 $325
  No. 280   100
  No. 295   700
Adjusted balance   1,125
                                                                         $ 9,285
                                                                         =======
Balance according to depositor's records $ 7,540
Add: Error in recording Check No. 289 $270
     Error in a deposit   720
     Note and interest collected by bank   780
                                                                           1,770
                                                                         $ 9,310
Deduct bank service charge   25
Adjusted balance $ 9,285
                                                                         =======

(2)
Sept. 30   Cash in Bank   1,745
           Miscellaneous Administrative Expense   25
               Accounts Payable   270
               Accounts Receivable   720
               Notes Receivable   700
               Interest Income   80

CHAPTER 8

MATCHING			TRUE/FALSE		MULTIPLE CHOICE	
1. B	6. G	11. O	1. T	6. F	11. F	1. b	6. a
2. F	7. L	12. N	2. T	7. T	12. F	2. c	
3. J	8. D	13. E	3. F	8. T	13. T	3. c	
4. A	9. H	14. P	4. T	9. F	14. T	4. d	
5. M	10. K	15. I	5. T	10. T	15. F	5. b	

EXERCISE 8-1

(1)
Mar. 31   Allowance for Doubtful Accounts   3,150
              Accounts Receivable - Jane Eades   3,150
(2)
May 8   Accounts Receivable - Jane Eades   3,150
              Allowance for Doubtful Accounts   3,150

    8   Cash   3,150
              Accounts Receivable - Jane Eades   3,150

EXERCISE 8-2

(1)
Aug. 31   Uncollectible Accounts Expense   550
              Accounts Receivable - D. Shore   550

(2)
Oct. 8   Accounts Receivable - D. Shore   550
              Uncollectible Accounts Expense   550

    8   Cash   550
              Accounts Receivable - D. Shore   550

EXERCISE 8-3

1. $80	5. $75
2. $35	6. $270
3. $60	7. $210
4. $60	

EXERCISE 8-4

	(1)	(2)
Face value	$12,000.00	$15,000.00
Interest on face value	360.00	400.00
Maturity value	12,360.00	15,400.00
Discount on maturity value	288.40	299.44
Proceeds	12,071.60	15,100.56

EXERCISE 8-5

Temporary investments in marketable equity securities (cost)..............	$68,000	
Add unrealized holding gain.........	10,200	78,200

EXERCISE 8-6

Walton Company
Balance Sheet
December 31, 19--

Assets

Current assets:

Cash		$ 37,500
Temporary investments in marketable equity securities	$55,000	
Less unrealized loss	2,000	53,000
Notes receivable		20,000
Accounts receivable	$35,000	
Less allowance for doubtful accounts	1,200	33,800
Interest receivable		9,900
Total current assets		$154,200

PROBLEM 8-1

(1)	Uncollectible Accounts Expense	24,000	
	Allowance for Doubtful Accounts		24,000
(2)	Uncollectible Accounts Expense	5,955	
	Allowance for Doubtful Accounts		5,955
(3)	Allowance for Doubtful Accounts	3,500	
	Accounts Receivable - Bentley Co.		3,500
(4)	Accounts Receivable - Apple Co.	1,235	
	Allowance for Doubtful Accounts		1,235
	Cash	1,235	
	Accounts Receivable - Apple Co.		1,235

PROBLEM 8-2

| (1) | Notes Receivable | 8,000.00 | |
| | Accounts Receivable - Dave Davidson | | 8,000.00 |

(2)	Cash	8,092.00*	
	Interest Income		92.00
	Notes Receivable		8,000.00

| (3) | Accounts Receivable - Dave Davidson | 8,160.00 | |
| | Cash | | 8,160.00 |

(4)	Cash	8,184.93	
	Interest Income		24.93**
	Accounts Receivable - Dave Davidson		8,160.00

| (5) | Notes Receivable | 3,000.00 | |
| | Accounts Receivable - Sue Smith | | 3,000.00 |

(6)	Accounts Receivable - Sue Smith	3,075.00	
	Interest Income		75.00
	Notes Receivable		3,000.00

*$8,000.00 x 60/360 x 12% = $160.00; $8,160 x 30/360 x 10% = $68.00; $8,160 - $68 = $8,092.00
**$8,160 x 10/360 x 11% = $24.93

CHAPTER 9

MATCHING		TRUE/FALSE		MULTIPLE CHOICE	
1. G	6. A	1. F	6. T	1. c	6. d
2. I	7. F	2. F	7. T	2. a	7. c
3. B	8. H	3. T	8. F	3. a	8. b
4. C	9. J	4. F	9. F	4. d	9. d
5. E	10. D	5. F	10. T	5. a	10. c

EXERCISE 9-1

		Net Income		Total Assets		Owner's Equity
19XA	(1)	under	(1)	under	(1)	under
	(2)	$5,000	(2)	$5,000	(2)	$5,000
19XB	(1)	over	(1)	correct	(1)	correct
	(2)	$5,000	(2)	-0-	(2)	-0-

EXERCISE 9-2

	Total	
	Cost	Lower of Cost or Market
Commodity A	$3,750	$3,600
Commodity B	2,760	2,760
Commodity C	1,450	1,200
Commodity D	1,440	1,290
Total	$9,400	$8,850

PROBLEM 9-1

(1)	Date Purchased	Units	Price	Total Cost
	November 1	12	$58	$696
	Total	12		$696

(2)	Date Purchased	Units	Price	Total Cost
	January 10	2	$48	$ 96
	February 15	5	54	270
	November 1	5	58	290
	Total	12		$656

(3)   Date Purchased   Units   Price   Total Cost
       November 1   12 $58 $696
          Total   12 $696

(4)   Date Purchased   Units   Price   Total Cost
       January 10   10 $48 $480
       February 15   2   54   108
          Total   12 $588

(5)   Average unit cost: $11,485
                             ------- = $54.69
                               210

       12 units in inventory @ $54.69 = $656.28

PROBLEM 9-2

	(1) Fifo	(2) Lifo	(3) Average Cost
Sales	$2,240,000	$2,240,000	$2,240,000
Ending Inventory	145,600	100,000	118,920
Cost of Merchandise Sold	1,638,300	1,683,900	1,664,980
Gross Profit	601,700	556,100	575,020

COMPUTATION OF ENDING INVENTORY

FIFO:	Date Purchased	Units	Price	Total Cost
	November 1	100	$69	$ 6,900
	December 1	1,900	73	138,700
	Total	2,000		$145,600
LIFO:	January 1	2,000	50	$100,000

AVERAGE COST: $1,783,900
                 ----------- = $59.46
                   30,000

                 $59.46 x 2,000 = $118,920

PROBLEM 9-3

(1)	Cost	Retail
Merchandise inventory, August 1	$118,500	$170,000
Purchases in August (net)	299,125	472,500
Merchandise available for sale	$417,625	$642,500

Ratio of cost to retail
    $417,625
    -------- =   65%
    $642,500

Sales in August (net)		479,000
Merchandise inventory, August 31, at retail		$163,500
Merchandise inventory, August 31, at estimated cost ($163,500 X 65%)		$106,275

(2)		
Merchandise inventory, August 1		$118,500
Purchases in August (net)		299,125
Merchandise available for sale		$417,625
Sales in August (net)	$479,000	
Less estimated gross grofit ($479,000 x 30%)	143,700	
Estimated cost of Merchandise sold		335,300
Estimated merchandise inventory, August 31		$ 82,325

CHAPTER 10

MATCHING			TRUE/FALSE		MULTIPLE CHOICE	

<table>
<tr><td>1. H</td><td>6. M</td><td>11. O</td><td>1. T</td><td>6. T</td><td>1. c</td><td>6. b</td></tr>
<tr><td>2. L</td><td>7. D</td><td>12. F</td><td>2. T</td><td>7. F</td><td>2. a</td><td>7. c</td></tr>
<tr><td>3. N</td><td>8. A</td><td>13. C</td><td>3. F</td><td>8. F</td><td>3. a</td><td>8. b</td></tr>
<tr><td>4. J</td><td>9. G</td><td>14. I</td><td>4. T</td><td>9. T</td><td>4. d</td><td>9. d</td></tr>
<tr><td>5. E</td><td>10. B</td><td>15. K</td><td>5. T</td><td>10. F</td><td>5. b</td><td>10. a</td></tr>
</table>

EXERCISE 10-1

(a) Straight-line method   Depreciation
        Year 1 $50,000
        Year 2 $50,000

(b) Declining-balance method   Depreciation
        Year 1 $105,000
        Year 2 $78,750

EXERCISE 10-2

Dec. 31   Depreciation Expense--Equipment   20,800
              Accumulated Depreciation--Equipment   20,800

EXERCISE 10-3

Mar. 8   Accumulated Depreciation--Fixtures   2,500
          Cash   2,000
              Fixtures   4,000
              Gain on Disposal of Assets   500

EXERCISE 10-4

Dec. 31   Depletion Expense   240,000
              Accumulated Depletion--Mineral Rights   240,000

EXERCISE 10-5

Dec. 31   Amortization Expense--Patents   20,000
              Patents   20,000

PROBLEM 10-1

                          Depreciation Expense

Year	Straight-Line	Declining-Balance	Units-of-Production
19xA	$18,750	$40,000	$17,000
19xB	18,750	20,000	20,000
19xC	18,750	10,000	30,000
19xD	18,750	5,000	8,000
Total	$75,000	$75,000	$75,000
	=======	=======	=======

PROBLEM 10-2

(1)

Dec. 31   Depreciation Expense--Automobile   5,000
              Accumulated Depreciation--Automobile   5,000

Dec. 31   Depreciation Expense--Automobile   5,000
              Accumulated Depreciation--Automobile   5,000

(2)

| Dec. 31 | Depreciation Expense--Automobile | 10,000 | |
| | Accumulated Depreciation--Automobile | | 10,000 |

| Dec. 31 | Depreciation Expense--Automobile | 2,500 | |
| | Accumulated Depreciation--Automobile | | 2,500 |

(3)

| Dec. 31 | Depreciation Expense--Automobile | 7,000 | |
| | Accumulated Depreciation--Automobile | | 7,000 |

| Dec. 31 | Depreciation Expense--Automobile | 5,600 | |
| | Accumulated Depreciation--Automobile | | 5,600 |

PROBLEM 10-3

(a)

Apr. 30	Accumulated Depreciation--Truck	12,000	
	Truck	20,200	
	Truck		15,000
	Cash		17,200

(b) (1)

Apr. 30	Accumulated Depreciation--Truck	12,000	
	Truck	20,700	
	Loss on Disposal of Plant Assets	2,000	
	Truck		15,000
	Cash		19,700

(b) (2)

Apr. 30	Accumulated Depreciation--Truck	12,000	
	Truck	22,700	
	Truck		15,000
	Cash		19,700

CHAPTER 11

MATCHING   TRUE/FALSE   MULTIPLE CHOICE

1. L   6. D   1. T   6. T   11. T   1. c
2. K   7. B   2. F   7. F   12. T   2. a
3. G   8. A   3. F   8. T   13. F   3. d
4. E   9. H   4. F   9. T   14. T   4. a
5. I   10. J   5. F   10. F   15. F   5. c

EXERCISE 11-1

1. $770
2. $60
3. $45
4. $727.50

EXERCISE 11-2

| Dec. 31 | Vacation Pay Expense | 3,225 | |
| | Vacation Pay Payable | | 3,225 |

| Dec. 31 | Product Warranty Expense | 4,500 | |
| | Product Warranty Payable | | 4,500 |

Dec. 31	Pension Expense	40,000	
	Cash		27,500
	Unfunded Accrued Pension Cost		12,500

PROBLEM 11-1

(1)
```
Dec. 7    Sales Salaries Expense                        34,000
          Office Salaries Expense                       16,000
             FICA Tax Payable                                        3,750
             Employees Income Tax Payable                            7,500
             Union Dues Payable                                        900
             United Way Payable                                        450
             Salaries Payable                                       37,400
```

(2)
```
Dec. 7    Salaries Payable                              37,400
             Cash                                                  37,400
```

(3)
```
Dec. 7    Payroll Taxes Expense                          6,850
             FICA Tax Payable                                      3,750
             State Unemployment Tax Payable                        2,700
             Federal Unemployment Tax Payable                        400
```

(4)
```
Dec. 7    Payroll Taxes Expense                          3,150
             FICA Tax Payable                                      3,150
```

PROBLEM 11-2

			Employer's Taxes			
Employee	Annual Earnings	Employee's FICA Tax	FICA	State Unemployment	Federal Unemployment	Total
Avery	$ 12,000	$ 900	$ 900	$ 378	$ 56	$ 1,334
Johnson	5,000	375	375	270	40	685
Jones	59,000	4,425	4,425	378	56	4,859
Smith	73,000	5,295	5,295	378	56	5,729
Wilson	141,000	6,315	6,315	378	56	6,749
	$290,000	$17,310	$17,310	$1,782	$264	$19,356

PROBLEM 11-3

(1)
```
          Accounts Payable--Mayday Co.                   2,000
             Notes Payable                                         2,000
```

(2)
```
          Notes Payable                                  2,000
          Interest Expense                                  60
             Cash                                                  2,060
```

(3)
```
          Cash                                           8,000
             Notes Payable                                         8,000
```

(4)
```
          Notes Payable                                  8,000
          Interest Expense                                 220
             Notes Payable                                         8,220
```

(5)
```
          Cash                                           5,910
          Interest Expense                                  90
             Notes Payable                                         6,000
```

(6)
```
          Notes Payable                                  6,000
             Cash                                                  6,000
```

CHAPTER 12

MATCHING		TRUE/FALSE				MULTIPLE CHOICE	
1. B	9. L	1. F	11. F	21. T		1. b	7. b
2. I	10. D	2. F	12. T	22. F		2. c	8. d
3. F	11. A	3. T	13. T	23. F		3. a	9. a
4. H	12. C	4. F	14. F	24. T		4. c	10. c
5. N	13. G	5. F	15. T	25. T		5. a	11. d
6. J	14. K	6. T	16. F	26. T		6. d	12. b
7. M	15. O	7. F	17. T	27. F			
8. E		8. F	18. T	28. F			
		9. F	19. T	29. F			
		10. T	20. F	30. T			

EXERCISE 12-1

(1) $5,000,000
(2) $4,100,000
(3) $900,000

EXERCISE 12-2

    $76,350
(1) (2,000)
(2) (5,200)
(3) $69,150
  =======

EXERCISE 12-3

(1) a. 37,600
    b.   13
    c.   (15)
    d.   (6)
    e.   (20)
    f. $37,572
    =======

(2) Materiality

PROBLEM 12-1

(1) $250,000
(2) $4,450
(3) $470,400
(4) $735,000
(5) $6,750

CHAPTER 13

MATCHING		TRUE/FALSE				MULTIPLE CHOICE
1. C	6. D	1. F	8. T	15. T		1. b
2. F	7. I	2. T	9. T	16. T		2. d
3. H	8. G	3. T	10. F	17. T		3. d
4. A	9. J	4. F	11. T	18. F		4. a
5. E	10. B	5. F	12. F	19. T		5. c
		6. F	13. F	20. T		
		7. T	14. F			

EXERCISE 13-1

Cash	100,000	
Merchandise Inventory	80,000	
Cutco, Capital		180,000

Cash	10,000	
Land	115,000	
Equipment	45,000	
Merchandise Inventory	5,000	
Robbs, Capital		175,000

EXERCISE 13-2

(1)

June 30	Hartly, Capital	20,000	
	Smetz, Capital	11,000	
	Grasso, Capital	7,000	
	Schafer, Capital		38,000

(2)

July 1	Cash	50,000	
	Hartly, Capital	7,000	
	Smetz, Capital	7,000	
	Grasso, Capital	7,000	
	Masko, Capital		71,000

EXERCISE 13-3

(1)	Inventory		12,750	
	Arway, Capital			4,250
	Batts, Capital			4,250
	Carlone, Capital			4,250
	Carlone, Capital		44,250	
	Arway, Capital			44,250
(2)	Inventory		6,000	
	Arway, Capital			2,000
	Batts, Capital			2,000
	Carlone, Capital			2,000
	Carlone, Capital		42,000	
	Cash			42,000

PROBLEM 13-1

(1)	Bulley's share			$100,000
	Scram's share			100,000
	Total			$200,000
				========
(2)	Bulley's share			$ 80,000
	Scram's share			120,000
	Total			$200,000
				========
(3)	Bulley's share			$ 60,000
	Scram's share			140,000
	Total			$200,000
				========

(4)		Bulley	Scram	Total
	Salary allowance	$30,000	$ 50,000	$ 80,000
	Remaining income	60,000	60,000	120,000
	Net income	$90,000	$110,000	$200,000
		=======	========	========
(5)	Interest allowance	$15,000	$ 35,000	$ 50,000
	Remaining income	75,000	75,000	150,000
	Net income	$90,000	$110,000	$200,000
		=======	========	========
(6)	Salary allowance	$15,000	$ 25,000	$ 40,000
	Interest allowance	15,000	35,000	50,000
	Remaining income	55,000	55,000	110,000
	Net income	$85,000	$115,000	$200,000
		=======	========	========
(7)	Salary allowance	$80,000	$ 78,000	$158,000
	Interest allowance	15,000	35,000	50,000
	Total	$95,000	$113,000	$208,000
	Excess of allowances over income	4,000	4,000	8,000
	Net income	$91,000	$109,000	$200,000
		=======	========	========

PROBLEM 13-2

		Cash +	Noncash Assets =	Liabilities +	Capital		
					Triste +	Sandpipe +	Hinkle
(1)	Balances before realization	$100,000	$300,000	$120,000	$ 90,000	$ 60,000	$130,000
	Sale of noncash assets and division of gain	+400,000	-300,000		+ 30,000	+ 50,000	+ 20,000
	Balances after realization	$500,000	-0-	$120,000	$120,000	$110,000	$150,000
	Payment of liabilities	-120,000		-120,000			
	Balances after payment of liabilities	$380,000	-0-	-0-	$120,000	$110,000	$150,000
	Distribution of cash to partners	-380,000			-120,000	-110,000	-150,000
	Final balances	-0-	-0-	-0-	-0-	-0-	-0-
		========	========	========	========	========	========
(2)	Balances before realization	$100,000	$300,000	$120,000	$ 90,000	$ 60,000	$130,000
	Sale of noncash assets and division of loss	+130,000	-300,000		-51,000	-85,000	- 34,000
	Balances after realization	$230,000	-0-	$120,000	$39,000	$25,000 Dr.	$ 96,000
	Payment of liabilities	-120,000		-120,000			
	Balances after payment of liabilities	$110,000	-0-	-0-	$39,000	$25,000 Dr.	$ 96,000
	Receipt of deficiency	+ 25,000				+25,000	
	Balances	$135,000	-0-	-0-	$39,000	-0-	$ 96,000
	Distribution of cash to partners	-135,000			-39,000		- 96,000
	Final balances	-0-	-0-	-0-	-0-	-0-	-0-
		========	=========	=========	=======	=======	========

(3)			
	Cash	130,000	
	Loss and Gain on Realization	170,000	
	Noncash Assets		300,000
	Triste, Capital	51,000	
	Sandpipe, Capital	85,000	
	Hinkle, Capital	34,000	
	Loss and Gain on Realization		170,000
	Liabilities	120,000	
	Cash		120,000
	Cash	25,000	
	Sandpipe, Capital		25,000
	Triste, Capital	39,000	
	Hinkle, Capital	96,000	
	Cash		135,000